Leer.

MONITORING HUMAN RIGHTS IN EUROPE

Comparing International Procedures and Mechanisms

International Studies in Human Rights

VOLUME 30

The titles published in this series are listed at the end of this volume.

MONITORING HUMAN RIGHTS IN EUROPE

Comparing International Procedures and Mechanisms

Edited by

ARIE BLOED
Associate Professor of Law, University of Utrecht

LISELOTTE LEICHT
Programme Director, International Helsinki Federation for Human Rights, Vienna

MANFRED NOWAK
Director, Ludwig Boltzmann Institute of Human Rights, Vienna

and

ALLAN ROSAS
Director, Åbo Akademi Institute for Human Rights, Finland

MARTINUS NIJHOFF PUBLISHERS
DORDRECHT / BOSTON / LONDON

in co-operation with

THE INTERNATIONAL HELSINKI FEDERATION FOR HUMAN RIGHTS

A C.I.P. Catalogue record for this book is available from the Library of Congress.

ISBN 0-7923-2383-1 (HB)

Published by Martinus Nijhoff Publishers,
P.O. Box 163, 3300 AD Dordrecht, The Netherlands.

Sold and distributed in the U.S.A. and Canada
by Kluwer Academic Publishers,
101 Philip Drive, Norwell, MA 02061, U.S.A.

In all other countries, sold and distributed
by Kluwer Academic Publishers Group,
P.O. Box 322, 3300 AH Dordrecht, The Netherlands.

Printed on acid-free paper

Kluwer Academic Publishers incorporates the publishing programmes of
Martinus Nijhoff Publishers.

Printed in the Netherlands

THE INTERNATIONAL HELSINKI FEDERATION FOR HUMAN RIGHTS

The International Helsinki Federation for Human Rights (IHF) is a non-governmental organization that monitors compliance with the human rights provisions of the Helsinki Final Act and its Follow-up Documents with their reference to international law. It co-ordinates the work of national Helsinki committees in 27 countries and has direct links with human rights activists in countries where no Helsinki committees exist. It criticizes human rights abuses regardless of the political system of the state in which these abuses occur.

International Helsinki Federation for Human Rights
Rummelhardtg. 2/18, A-1090 Vienna, Austria; Tel. +43 1-402 73 87, 408 88 22; Fax. +43 1-408 74 44

LUDWIG BOLTZMANN INSTITUTE OF HUMAN RIGHTS

The Ludwig Boltzmann Institute of Human Rights (BIM) is a centre for documentation, research and information services on human rights. It was established in 1992 in Vienna within the framework of an Association of Research Institutes named after the Austrian physicist and philosopher Ludwig Boltzmann (1844-1906). Among other things it prepares human rights reports on the most important countries of origin of asylum seekers in Austria and on the priority countries of Austrian development co-operation. On the occasion of the United Nations World Conference on Human Rights in Vienna in June 1993 BIM will co-ordinate the various NGO parallel activities.

Ludwig Boltzmann Institute of Human Rights
Möllwaldplatz 4, A-1040 Vienna, Austria, Tel. +43 1-504 46 77; Fax. +43 1-504 46 79

INSTITUTE FOR HUMAN RIGHTS IN FINLAND

The Institute for Human Rights in Finland started its activities in 1985. It operates within the Abo Akademi University, the Swedish-speaking university of Finland, and its Department of Law. The Institute's purpose is to promote research, education and dissemination of material relevant for the protection of human rights.

Institute for Human Rights, Turku/Abo Akademi University
Gezeliusgatan 2, SF-20500 Turku/Abo, Finland; Tel. +358 21-65 43 25; Fax. +358 21-65 46 99

TABLE OF CONTENTS

ABBREVIATIONS

ACT	Austrian Committee against Torture
AI	Amnesty International
BIM	Ludwig Boltzmann Institute of Human Rights
CAT	United Nations Convention against Torture and Other Cruel, Inhuman or Degrading Treatment
CBSS	Council of the Baltic Sea States
CCPR	International Covenant on Civil and Political Rights
CEDAW	Convention on the Elimination of All Forms of Discrimination against Women
CEPTA	Committee of Experts for the Prevention of Torture in the Americas
CERD	International Convention on the Elimination of All Forms of Racial Discrimination
CESCR	International Covenant on Economic, Social and Cultural Rights
CHD	CSCE Conference on the Human Dimension
CPC	CSCE Conflict Prevention Centre
CPCJB	United Nations Crime Prevention and Criminal Justice Branch
CPT	European Committee for the Prevention of Torture
CRC	Convention on the Rights of the Child
CSCE	Conference on Security and Co-operation in Europe
CSO	CSCE Committee of Senior Officials
EC	European Community/European Communities
ECHR	European Convention for the Protection of Human Rights and Fundamental Freedoms
ECJ	European Court of Justice
ECMM	EC Monitoring Mission

ECPT	European Convention for the Prevention of Torture and Inhuman or Degrading Treatment or Punishment
ECOSOC	UN Economic and Social Council
EPC	European Political Co-operation
ESC	European Social Charter
FAO	Food and Agricultural Organization
HCNM	CSCE High Commissioner on National Minorities
HRC	United Nations Human Rights Committee
ICJ	International Commission of Jurists
ICRC	International Committee of the Red Cross
IGO	Inter-governmental organization
IHF	International Helsinki Federation for Human Rights
ILO	International Labour Organization
NGO	Non-governmental organization
OAS	Organization of American States
OAU	Organization of African Unity
ODIHR	CSCE Office for Democratic Institutions and Human Rights
OIC	Organization of Islamic Conference
ONUSAL	United Nations Observer Mission in El Salvador
SAM	CSCE sanctions assistance mission
SCAT	Swiss Committee against Torture
UN	United Nations
UNGA	UN General Assembly
UNESCO	United Nations Educational, Scientific and Cultural Organization
UNHCR	United Nations High Commissioner for Refugees

UNICEF	United Nations Children's Fund
UNITAR	United Nations Institute for Training and Research
UNPAs	United Nations Protected Areas
UNPROFOR	United Nations Protection Force
UNTAC	United Nations Transitional Authority in Cambodia
WFP	World Food Programme
WHO	World Health Organization

ACKNOWLEDGEMENTS

The International Helsinki Federation for Human Rights (IHF), the Ludwig Boltzmann Institute of Human Rights (BIM) and the Institute for Human Rights in Finland wish to thank all the contributors who accepted our invitation to participate in the project on international mechanisms and who, with their great wisdom, dedication and time, made this volume a reality.

We gratefully acknowledge the financial support of the Austrian Ministry of Foreign Affairs, the Austrian Ministry of Science and Research, the Finnish Red Cross and the Dr. Karl Renner Institute in Vienna.

We wish to express our appreciation to Sylvia Hordosch and Kristiina Kumpula, thanks to whom the two meetings of the contributors in Helsinki and Vienna ran smoothly.

We thank Peter Morris for additional editorial assistance and Margit Fritz for helping in the publication process.

We are grateful to them all.

Vienna, May 1993

INTRODUCTION

In 1993, more than 40 years after the adoption of the Universal Declaration of Human Rights, after the end of the ideological confrontation between East and West and in the year of the United Nations World Conference on Human Rights, Europe faces massive violations of human rights. For millions of people the human rights guarantees as laid down in the myriad of international treaties and politically binding documents remain unrealized.

The years which have followed the demise of communism have been most turbulent and have reshaped the map of Europe, adding to it new and independent states.

Traditional human rights violations such as oppression of freedom of expression and opinion, lack of due process in courts, intimidation of the free press and political opponents, continue on a wide scale. Severe discrimination against ethnic, national, religious and linguistic minorities has increased. Racism and nationalism have made minorities and other vulnerable groups targets of attacks which are often welcome and appreciated by large portions of the general public and authorities.

Armed conflicts over territory, triggered by nationalist governments and extremist rulers, have become exacerbated in the former Yugoslavia and parts of the former Soviet Union, resulting in millions of refugees and displaced persons. Grave breaches of human rights and humanitarian law including torture, extra-judicial killings, rapes and the horrifying practice of "ethnic cleansing" are violations currently occurring in Europe.

The weaknesses of the international machinery for the implementation of human rights and the prevention of their abuses, be it within the framework of the United Nations (UN), the Conference on Security and Co-operation in Europe (CSCE), the Council of Europe, or the European Community (EC), can be measured by the extent to which it has been able to anticipate and prevent human rights violations or taken prompt action when they occur.

As regards the effectiveness of the international machinery the question of objectivity, impartiality and determination comes readily to mind. That there is often a big gap between the international commitments and the political reality and will to combat and prevent human rights violations is an obvious phenomenon. The international community has not persistently viewed the respect for human rights and humanitarian law as a value in itself without subordinating it to political considerations.

In Bosnia-Herzegovina we are experiencing the extermination of a people in whole or in part because of their race, religion or nationality, in other words attempted genocide. The states parties to the 1948 Convention on the Prevention and the Punishment of the Crime of Genocide have failed to meet their treaty obligations to take appropriate measures to "prevent and suppress" genocide. Serious concerns ought to be raised in that the international community has been neglecting the human rights of the people of Bosnia-Herzegovina in the interest of signing a peace accord.

The sophisticated human rights machinery has not been able to tackle the continuing pattern of severe human rights violations, including the systematic practice of torture in police and gendarmerie detention centres, disappearances and extrajudicial killings, in Turkey, a country which is a member of the Council of Europe and which is also a state party to international conventions such as the International Convention against Torture and Other Cruel, Inhuman or Degrading Treatment or Punishment.

One of the key questions for the United Nations World Conference on Human Rights is to analyse the achievements and shortcomings of the international human rights machinery and to find ways to deal with the apparent inadequacies of existing mechanisms and frameworks.

The obstacles to a more efficient implementation of human rights are many and still several states have not ratified or acceded to international treaties or have made far-reaching reservations. The allocation of a mere 0.7 percent of the United Nations regular budget to human rights issues is in critical contrast to the increase in human rights violations and the activities and programmes rapidly required to prevent and respond to such violations. One of the main points of departure is that if, the human rights mechanisms and initiatives are to be efficient and serve properly, adequate financing, including staff and equipment, is needed. In view of the limited resources and for the sake of a more efficient implementation of human rights better co-ordination and cooperation of activities and information between the United Nations, its specialized bodies and regional inter-governmental organizations engaged in human rights, are greatly needed when setting priorities and assessing projects and their impact, including the best suitable bodies to realize them.

The Working Group on International Mechanisms

Given the massive human rights violations in today's Europe and the apparent failure of the international machinery to combat and prevent abuses even in situations of grave breaches of human rights and humanitarian law, the International Helsinki Federation for Human Rights (IHF) decided to convene a working group of international experts.

The project on international mechanisms for the monitoring and protection of human rights and the prevention of human rights violations in Europe was carried out by the IHF in collaboration with the Ludwig Boltzmann Institute of Human Rights (BIM) and the Institute for Human Rights in Finland.

The working group of experts met twice in early 1993 in Helsinki and in Vienna in order to prepare thorough analyses of a number of the established human rights mechanisms under the UN, the CSCE, the Council of Europe and the EC. The studies focus on the effectiveness of the various mechanisms and frameworks, their different legal and political characters and contexts, including a discussion of their interrelationship, the various procedures and institutions, their advantages and disadvantages.

The individual contributions and recommendations of the participants were subjected to in-depth discussions during the two sessions of the working group. The working group generally agreed that the available machinery for the protection of human rights and the prevention of their abuses should be considered in a complementary rather than a competitive fashion. The working group, however, also found that better co-ordination and cooperation of activities as well as sharing of information between the international and regional machinery is crucial. In this context, agreement was reached on a set of general recommendations included in this volume.

This book does not offer a complete overview of all the available mechanisms which impact human rights in Europe. The contributions, however, provide a broad picture of the complexity of this machinery.

More and substantial research and new thinking is needed for the evaluation of the international human rights machinery in order to secure the realization of civil, cultural, economic, political and social rights. This book does not attempt to present a coherent programme for these complex issues but rather to stimulate discussion and to suggest some further steps which could be taken.

THE MONITORING OF HUMAN RIGHTS AND THE PREVENTION OF HUMAN RIGHTS VIOLATIONS THROUGH REPORTING PROCEDURES

by Vojin Dimitrijević

1. THE LEGAL NATURE OF A HUMAN RIGHTS TREATY

The purpose of so-called human rights treaties is that the rights guaranteed should be enjoyed by individual human beings and groups. At present such treaties owe their legal nature and structure to the modern humanistic and individualistic trends positing the human being as the prime subject of international concern and its well-being as a fundamental value of the international society, on the one side, and to the traditional "Westphalian" concept of that society as composed of sovereign states, on the other. A typical human rights treaty is therefore a multilateral international treaty concluded among states, from which, unlike from most other international treaties, the principal rights and entitlements are derived by non-state beneficiaries, i.e., a wide range of individuals, who need not necessarily be the nationals of the states parties.[1] However - and this is the influence of classic international law - the entitlements of individuals are formally not international: technically a signatory state fulfils, by promoting and securing individual human rights of the beneficiaries, its international obligations toward other signatory states. If it denies a right, it "violates" a provision of the relevant treaty; however, it is not internationally responsible to the victim of the violation, but to other states parties. In many cases, at least in dualist systems where an international norm becomes internally valid only if incorporated and transformed into municipal law, the individual does not even derive his/her rights from the treaty itself, but from the provision of internal law that conforms in its content to the international norm.

[1]The beneficiaries of a modern human rights treaty are all individuals within the territory of the contracting party and subject to its jurisdiction - see, e.g., Art. 2.1 of the International Covenant on Civil and Political Rights.

A. Bloed et al. (eds.), Monitoring Human Rights in Europe, 1–24.

2. THE EXISTING METHODS OF SUPERVISING THE IMPLEMENTATION OF A HUMAN RIGHTS TREATY AND THEIR INADEQUACIES

2.1 International responsibility vis-à-vis other states

If the true enjoyment of human rights is taken as the prime concern, the arrangement described above appears highly artificial. Namely, it is expected that the protector of human beings in another country is a state that has no particular link with them. We know from experience that other contracting states will not "automatically" move to protest against violations of the provisions of a human rights treaty. More precisely, as a rule they will do so only if the stimulus is very strong and if action against another state party appears to coincide with other interests or does not run counter to any of them. This is why they will normally not make frequent use of the rights *they* (and not the individuals) directly have under international law, especially if such rights are not refined and are derived only from the general rules regarding international responsibility, where the questions about the existence of the delict, the nature of the damage, the means of settlement of the dispute, and the nature of the remedy and restitution, etc., remain ill-defined.[2]

Even where these matters are better regulated by the treaty itself, there has been little inclination to use such procedures. Thus, for example, the International Covenant on Civil and Political Rights (CCPR), in its Article 41, envisages a procedure enabling the UN Human Rights Committee (HRC) "to receive and consider communications to the effect that a State Party claims that another State Party is not fulfilling its obligations under the ... Covenant". So far, no contracting party has made use of this procedure, although the HRC, employing other procedures, has been able to conclude that there have been serious violations of the CCPR in a number of signatory states and has been supported in that conclusion by international organizations and international public opinion.

---

[2]Cf., the contribution of L. Boisson de Chazournes in the present volume.

2.2 Complaints by individuals[3]

This leaves two other alleys to secure the implementation of human rights treaties. One of them has been to elevate the individual beneficiary to a party to the proceedings, to give him/her the initiative to protest against violations which concern him/her and to seek redress, which results in his/her *locus standi* before an international organ. As could have been expected, this was highly objectionable in terms of classic international law, because it could lead, and has led, to situations where a state (an international legal person) and its national (having normally no international standing) are treated on equal terms. Control through individual complaints has, for reasons of this nature, been successful on the regional plane, most notably in Europe, but it is only an exception at the universal level. The competence of relevant universal organs to receive individual complaints is optional and the examination results in non-binding decisions, such as "suggestions and recommendations" (Art. 14.7 b of the International Convention on the Elimination of All Forms of Racial Discrimination - CERD) or "views" (Art. 5.4 of the Optional Protocol to the CCPR).

For our topic, it is important to determine whether the procedures based on individual complaints, even if they are all-encompassing, widely used and effective in terms of offering remedy to the individual concerned, are sufficient to secure the implementation of a human rights treaty and to prevent future violations.

Three limitations are obvious, and the existing human rights treaties seem to have been adapted to them.

a) Individual complaints are pointless if the right provided is not justiciable. Traditionally, economic, social and cultural rights were believed to belong to this category and this explains why there is no complaint mechanism provided for in the International Covenant on Economic, Social and Cultural Rights (CESCR). With the realization that at least some rights generally believed

---

[3]Cf., the contribution by R. Müllerson in the present volume.

to be of this kind are in fact justiciable, suggestions have been made that an optional protocol should also be attached to CESCR.[4]

b) Complaints cannot meaningfully be lodged if the relevant treaty provides for its gradual implementation, where it is left to the discretion of the state party to determine at what pace the scope of the right and the circle of its beneficiaries will be expanded until the optimum is eventually reached. Gradual implementation can be envisaged for rights that are otherwise justiciable but seem to require long-term legislative action and social adaptation. For instance, according to Article 23.4 of the CCPR, states parties "shall take appropriate steps to ensure equality of rights and responsibilities of spouses as to marriage, during marriage and at its dissolution". It could be argued that the enjoyment of such temporarily reserved rights cannot be postponed indefinitely and this is true. But can it be expected that an international organ should determine when the time is ripe in quasi-judicial proceedings?

c) Many states are still reluctant to accept complaint mechanisms, with the result that concerned individuals have no means of raising the issue of respecting a relevant human rights treaty.

It appears, however, that the main reason why mechanisms based on individual complaints cannot cover the whole gamut of the rights provided and gauge the general compliance with a given human rights treaty lies elsewhere. A modern human rights treaty aims at a generally favourable human rights situation, which includes creating the necessary conditions for the enjoyment of human rights and the elimination of factors that lead to violations. If a state is remiss, this very often cannot be related to an individual "victim" such as, for instance, when the cost of human life becomes low due to disease, uncontrolled and unrestricted use of dangerous installations and noxious substances, terrorism, poor police protection and other circumstances and the right to life is thus threatened and violated. It is hard to

[4]See the contribution of A. Eide in the present volume.

imagine a case where an individual could claim that his/her life or the life of his/her next of kin has been lost through culpable negligence on the part of the state and could thus establish a viable case before international jurisdiction.

Another example is contained in Article 10.3 of the CCPR, which provides that "the penitentiary system shall comprise treatment of prisoners the essential aim of which shall be their reformation and social rehabilitation". Now, it is notorious that in many states the appropriate funds are missing and that as a result of this the prisons are bleak, overcrowded and the prison personnel are insufficient, underpaid and incompetent. It is, however, hard to imagine a recidivist establishing a case that a state has violated its international obligation by failing to rehabilitate him and thus returning him to the path of crime.

Or, how can an individual lodge a complaint because he/she has been a victim of incitement to national, racial or religious hatred, which states parties of the CCPR are, under its Article 20.2, obligated to prohibit by law, if the state has failed to enact appropriate laws or if they have been ineffective? To go on, how can the obligation of the society and the state to protect the family (Art. 23.1 of the CCPR) be controlled through individual petitions of its members? It will be observed here that the bearer of the obligation is not only the state, but also the society. If we proceed to the right of the child, covered in Article 24 of CCPR, we notice that "measures of protection required by his status as a minor" are expected from "his family, society and the State". Can a minor, even if residing in a country that has ratified the Optional Protocol to the CCPR, submit an application to the HRC complaining that the family, society or the state has not provided adequate measures of protection?

The inadequacy of individual complaints becomes even more evident if it is borne in mind that it is not always the state agencies that are prime violators of human rights. In many cases human suffering and grand-scale violations of human rights are caused by non-state actors, sometimes facing indifferent or well-meaning but powerless governments. In this respect, the problematic of the rights of women comes readily to mind. In most countries, legislation condoning discrimination based on sex has been gradually abolished; even if it remains, the victim of discrimination can submit a complaint referring to the discriminatory law or act. However, most painful and degrading practices against women are still imposed by religious and social groups, frequently, as in the case of *sati* and dowry deaths in India, when faced with strong opposition and criminalization by the state.[5] It is no wonder then that the Convention on the Elimination of All Forms of Discrimination against Women (CEDAW) does not provide for a mechanism based on individual complaints.

3. EXAMINATION OF REPORTS BY IMPARTIAL BODIES

3.1 Reporting systems under human rights treaties concluded under the auspices of the United Nations

In order to fully supervise and control the implementation of a human rights treaty and to avoid the deficiencies caused by indifference or laxity of the contracting parties or the impossibility of raising all points through a complaint procedure, states parties can delegate the supervisory powers to an independent body created jointly by them, or to an international organization. It has so far been normal to base this supervision on the obligation of states parties to submit periodic reports on the measures they have undertaken to implement the treaty.

The International Labour Organization was the first to establish a reporting system in respect of rights falling within its mandate and based on international instruments adopted under its auspices. This was followed by the United Nations (UN) as regards the recommendations of its organs. However, the relevant Article 64 of the UN Charter has never been put to proper use and the human rights treaties, drafted and adopted under the auspices of the United Nations, have envisaged supervisory bodies that are entirely based on

---

[5]The characteristic Indian legislative acts are The Immoral Traffic (Prevention) Act, 1956; The Dowry Prohibition Act, 1961; The Muslim Women (Protection of Rights on Divorce) Act, 1986; The Commission of Sati (Prevention) Act, 1987.

the relevant treaty and elected only by its signatories[6]. Although not organs of the United Nations, these bodies are nevertheless in many respects linked to this Organization and serviced by its Secretary-General. They are composed of independent experts, acting in their personal capacity. In UN parlance, they are referred to as "treaty bodies".

States parties have to report to treaty bodies according to Article 40 of CCPR, Article 16 of the CESCR[7], Article 9 of CERD, Article 18 of CEDAW, Article 19 of the Convention against Torture and Other Cruel, Inhuman or Degrading Treatment or Punishment (CAT), Article VII of the International Convention on the Suppression and Punishment of the Crime of Apartheid and Article 44 of the Convention on the Rights of the Child (CRC). Similar obligations also exist in the UNESCO[8] Convention against Discrimination in the Field of Education (Art. 17).

3.2 Rudimentary reporting obligations under the European system[9]

As a contrast to the developed system of reporting obligations on the universal plane, European human rights treaties seem to rely on other methods of monitoring. In fact, the logic of the European arrangement is related to the nature of human rights guaranteed and protected by the treaty. The European Convention for the Protection of Human Rights and Fundamental Freedoms (ECHR) deals mainly with the cluster of human rights generally referred to as civil and political and starts from the presumption that all of them are

---

[6]The only exception is the Committee on Economic, Social and Cultural Rights, which receives the reports on the implementation of ICESCR. According to Art. 16 of the Covenant, reports were to be submitted to the Economic and Social Council (ECOSOC). Until 1987 this UN organ examined the reports with the assistance of its Sessional Working Group of Governmental Experts. The Committee is elected by the ECOSOC and not, as other treaty bodies, by the contracting parties.

[7]See the preceding footnote.

[8]United Nations Educational, Scientific and Cultural Organization

[9]Cf., the contribution of M. Pentikäinen and M. Scheinin in the present volume.

enforceable before courts. It is then held that, in this respect, the ratification of the ECHR should have immediate internal effects and that there is no excuse whatsoever for a right contained therein not to be enjoyed in its full scope and as such judicially enforceable. Non-compliance can therefore be detected through individual complaints directed to the organs of the Council of Europe or action by states parties to establish that another state party does not fulfil its international obligations. Following this line of thinking, it is natural that the only reporting obligation of the signatories of the ECHR, contained in Article 57, refers in fact to information as to how their "internal law ensures the effective implementation of any of the provisions of the Convention". These explanations can be requested by the Secretary-General of the Council of Europe, who cannot pronounce any judgment as to whether the internal arrangements described by the state party do in fact ensure effective implementation; for that matter, under the Convention there is no organ competent to judge compliance with the Convention *in abstracto*, unless a case is referred to the European Commission of Human Rights by a contracting party under Article 24, referring to an alleged breach of the provisions of the Convention by another state party.

A confirmation of the reasoning described above can be found in the European Social Charter and its Additional Protocol, which deal at the European level with that cluster of human rights called economic and social. These rights are not judicially enforceable and the states parties undertake only to treat them as goals to be attained by various means, with a minimum (to be determined by each state party) which they consider to be valid immediately (Art. 20). It then naturally follows that there is a need for the signatory states to report on their decisions as to which obligations they accept or do not accept and to record progress made toward the goals determined in the Charter. These reports are examined by a series of bodies and organs of the Council of Europe, who can issue relevant views and recommendations (Arts. 21-29 of the Social Charter and Art. 6 of the Protocol). In this case the nature of the international obligation, which heavily depends on the particular circumstances, dictated the nature of the supervision. The Charter and the Additional Protocol do not even envisage the possibility of violation and consequently do not contain provisions on the settlement of disputes between states parties.

3.3 Reporting and the nature of the rights protected

The Western European idea of social and related human rights seems to be that international norms pertaining thereto are "soft law" and that reporting procedures are adequate only where information, consultation and advice is needed on how the states will gradually, reasonably and *bona fide* fulfil their "soft" obligations. On the other hand, "hard" obligations relating to civil and political rights are viewed as immediate and unconditional so that their fulfilment can only be tested in judicial or quasi-judicial proceedings, there being no need to report on any "progress", which is logically unthinkable for absolute and present obligations.

Apart from the objection, proffered by "socialist" states, that the reporting obligation violates state sovereignty - which has by now become obsolete - one of the principal reasons for the initial opposition to the introduction of this obligation in the CCPR was the principle of immediate applicability described above.[10] The obligation was eventually included in this and other instruments and it has proved to be one of the most important means of monitoring compliance with universal human rights treaties.

It can be argued that the wording of the CCPR, and in particular, other human rights treaties concluded under the auspices of the United Nations is broader and less legally spartan than that of the ECHR and that the examples given above of violations not cognizable under contentious proceedings are not to be found in the European system. This is true only to a certain measure.

Certainly the right to life in Article 6,1 of CCPR ("Every human being has the inherent right to life"), for example, appears much broader than the right to life in Article 2,1 of the ECHR ("Everyone's right to life shall be protected by law"), but the question remains whether the legal protection is adequate. However, in the Protocols to the ECHR the trend toward broader definitions has been discernible. For

---

[10]See M. Nowak, "UNO-Pakt über bürgerliche und politische Rechte und Fakultativprotokoll", *CCPR-Kommentar* (1989), pp. 586, 590 et seq. and references therein.

instance, can the violation of the right to education (Art. 2 of the First Protocol) be determined only on the basis of an individual complaint by a person denied this right in a particular case, if the state policies can be shown to lead to the massive exclusion of large underprivileged groups from education? Turning to the next article of the same Protocol, can we expect that the European Commission and the Court can determine whether elections in a state are "free", "at reasonable intervals", and "under conditions which will ensure the free expression of the opinion of the people" solely on the basis of the complaint by a voter or a candidate that his/her rights have been violated?

That questions of this nature have not occurred more frequently in the jurisprudence of the Commission and the Court can be explained by the fact that most signatories of the ECHR have been remarkably similar in their understandings and circumstances. Taking into account the very different backgrounds of the countries of former "really existing socialism", which are now joining them, some of the matters highlighted above may prove to be more difficult to assess.[11]

3.4 The need to introduce monitoring through reports in the European system

Thus, for inherent reasons of adequate monitoring of human rights treaties and in order to complete the nascent new system of the promotion and protection of human rights in Europe, it appears necessary to introduce at the regional level the possibility of appraising the human rights situation through the study, by competent bodies, of reports provided by states on the progress made in implementing their obligations concerning human rights.

---

[11]See V. Dimitrijević, "The Human Dimension of Post-Totalitarianism", in A. Eide and J. Helgesen (eds.), *The Future of Human Rights Protection in a Changing World* (Oslo 1991) p. 29 et seq.; "Political Pluralism in the Aftermath of the Eastern European Upheavals", in A. Rosas and J. Helgesen, *The Strength of Diversity* (Dordrecht 1992) p. 5 et seq.

It is true that most European states are parties to most universal human rights treaties and that their reports are studied by relevant "treaty bodies". This does not appear sufficient for a number of reasons. They mostly relate to higher or different European standards in some areas of human rights, not only as regards the rights themselves (e.g., the right to the peaceful enjoyment of one's possessions) but also in terms of the conditions of their enjoyment (e.g., the "necessary in a democratic society" standard). The dialogue that is contingent to the examination of reports can be deeper and more useful if it benefits fully from the advantages of cultural propinquity among European countries. On the universal plane, where the reports are currently being discussed, the common denominator is of necessity lower.

4. EXPERIENCES WITH REPORTING ON THE UNIVERSAL PLANE AND THEIR APPLICABILITY TO EUROPE

In order to make proper use of the reporting procedures, the merits and demerits of the universal (United Nations) system have to be carefully studied and identified. In fact, this may be a welcome opportunity for a reassessment, which can then, in turn, help reform or streamline the universal system. The following remarks are made with this aim in mind and are based on experience recorded by the treaty bodies themselves and by informed observers.[12]

---

[12]There has been a series of meetings of chairpersons of human rights treaty bodies convened pursuant to various General Assembly resolutions since 1984 - see UN Doc. A/39/484, A/44/98, A/45/636, A/47/628. See also United Nations Centre for Human Rights - United Nations Institute for Training and Research (UNITAR), *Manual on Human Rights Reporting* (New York 1991) and the bibliography on p. 195 et seq.; Norwegian Institute of Human Rights, *Making the Reporting Procedure under the International Covenant on Civil and Political Rights More Effective* (Oslo 1991) and the bibliography on p. 42 et seq.

4.1 The content of the report

There are significant differences in the wording of various human rights treaties. The basic duty is expressed in CERD: "States Parties undertake to submit ... a report on the legislative, judicial, administrative or other measures which they have adopted and which give effect to the provisions of this Convention (Art. 9.1). To the same wording CEDAW adds: "Reports *may* indicate factors and difficulties affecting the degree of fulfilment of obligations ..." (Art. 18.2 - emphasis added). The wording of Article 40 of CCPR is wider and more general: "States Parties ... undertake to submit reports on the measures they have adopted which give effect to the rights recognized herein and on the progress made in the enjoyment of those rights [para. 1]. Reports *shall* indicate the factors and difficulties, if any, affecting the implementation of the present Covenant [para. 2 - emphasis added]. Following closely the pattern set by CCPR, the CRC, chronologically the latest universal human rights treaty, contains an important additional provision: "Reports shall also contain sufficient information to provide the Committee with a comprehensive understanding of the implementation of the Convention in the country concerned" (Art. 44.2).

These differences can partly be explained by the nature of the rights concerned and thus reflect the debate on the sense of reporting on progress and partial fulfilment where the obligations are immediate and unconditional. Simultaneously, they are due to experiences gathered in the course of the examination of reports by treaty bodies, which indicated that a meaningful study and evaluation of reports necessitated not only information about measures that have the nature of legal acts (acts of state), but a deeper understanding of the wider conditions in the whole society ("factors and difficulties", "comprehensive understanding of the situation").

The general impression of all reports submitted to treaty bodies is that they have been closer to the minimal standards of CERD. The reports - with very few exceptions - have paraphrased the relevant constitutional and legislative provisions in an attempt to prove that the latter have been in accordance with the provisions of the relevant human rights treaty. Difficulties have been addressed more frankly in oral exchanges between the members of the treaty body and the representatives of governments "defending" the report, provided that they had sufficient knowledge. Even then, the assumption was that the government was on the side of human rights, that allegations against it were false, that there was external involvement, etc. The only concessions willingly made related to financial shortages.

Constant prodding by members of treaty bodies has been possible only when the body has been in a position to allocate sufficient time for oral dialogue. After a while, even if the reports themselves remained elementary and "legalistic", governments started reacting by letting their representatives precede the dialogue by an introduction, which came closer to the non-legal factors. A good example of this were recent considerations of some reports before the HRC that supervises the implementation of CCPR, resulting in in-depth consideration of factors and difficulties in a number of countries, such as, e.g., Algeria (potential abuse of democracy by anti-democratic forces), Peru (widespread terrorism by groups determined to abolish human rights altogether) and Colombia (the menace of powerful drug cartels).[13]

It seems clear by now that only a comprehensive consideration of the situation in a country can be profitable, both for the international community, for the reporting state and, for that matter, the general cause of human rights. Initial hesitations as to the scope of information to be provided seem to have dissipated. However, a "good" report is only a part of the whole endeavour - the rest is achieved through interaction with others, first of all experts in the treaty body, who cannot rely only on the report. It is very important to note that a government, that is the executive branch, is inherently limited when it attempts to indicate "factors and difficulties" in the country it represents. The legislature, public opinion, parties not represented in the government, scholars, etc., may have different opinions and select their facts in another fashion. To be sure, government representatives have on occasion attempted to present a neutral account of current

---

[13]See *Report of the Human Rights Committee*, GAOR, 47th Sess., Suppl. No. 40 (1992) paras. 264-395.

debates regarding human rights matters in their countries, but this necessarily remains lifeless and too detached. It is therefore necessary not only to secure that reports are satisfactory to the extent that they can be so, but also to give attention to other elements of the reporting procedure.

4.2 Compliance with the reporting obligation

There are several criteria to judge whether the state has fulfilled its reporting obligations under the human rights treaty.

An obvious case of non-compliance exists when the state party *fails to submit the report*. Human rights treaties usually envisage a duty to submit the initial report within a relatively short period of time after ratification or adherence, whereas later (periodic) reports are to be submitted at intervals determined by the treaty body or by the treaty itself. The multitude of human rights treaties and the relatively short reporting intervals in some cases have put a serious strain on administrations of some states, especially the developing ones. Practically speaking, serious problems arise when the delays become enormous and states do not respond to numerous reminders.[14]

Until very recently, the obligation to submit a report was only related to the expiry of time, and not to other stimuli. Although in some treaties the submission of reports, after the initial obligatory one, is subject exclusively or alternatively to the free decision of the treaty body, this has as a rule been reduced to some kind of periodicity. For instance, the provision in Article 40.1.b of the CCPR that reports, after the initial one, are to be submitted "whenever the Committee so requests" was translated by the HRC in its "Decision on Periodicity" as a duty to submit periodic reports every five years.[15]

---

[14]Some states parties of ICCPR are in arrears amounting to nine years and have allowed themselves to be reminded in written form up to 18 times! *Report of the Human Rights Committee*, GAOR, 47th Sess., Suppl. No. 40 (1992), Annex IV.

[15]Decision of the Human Rights Committee of 22 July, 1981, CCPR/C/19.

The fact that each contracting party has to appear before the treaty body at regular intervals has the advantage of impartiality: unlike some other procedures, the government is not summoned before an international organ as a potential violator. This thesis is supported by the fact that some governments, such as the Pinochet regime in Chile, while consistently refusing to appear before the United Nations organs to account for their human rights record, agreed to have their reports discussed by treaty bodies. On the other hand, this attitude has been regarded as unduly passive: it has compelled treaty bodies to behave, in situations where allegations of massive human violations were made, as if nothing had happened and to wait for years until the time for the submission of the report was due. Even when a government declared a state of emergency and then derogated some rights under the human rights treaty and duly notified the United Nations, the treaty body was supposed to remain inactive, not to speak of the more frequent *de facto* states of emergency.

Under such pressures, the HRC has lately made a breakthrough. In the case of Iraq, it used the opportunity offered by the fact that allegations of human rights abuses regarding this country came when its periodic report was due to urge the government to submit, as a matter of urgency, a report that was to centre on a number of most important issues. The Iraqi government complied and the report was considered at the 42nd and 43rd session of the Committee, in July and October 1991.[16] The third periodic report by Yugoslavia was also overdue so that the same method was applied with the result that the Yugoslav report was examined at the 44th session in April 1992.[17]

Regarding the situation in the former Yugoslavia, the Committee, in the summer of 1992, went a step further. After consultation with its members its chairman addressed the governments of Bosnia-Herzegovina, Croatia and Yugoslavia with an urgent request to submit specific reports on the implementation of those Articles of CCPR

---

[16]*Report of the Human Rights Committee*, GAOR, 46th Sess., Suppl. No. 40, paras. 618-656.

[17]Ibid. paras. 431-469. The decision of the Committee to request the report is reproduced in Annex VII.

(6,7,9,10,12 and 20) which appeared to have been massively violated in the territory of Bosnia-Herzegovina.[18] This came before the deadline for the initial reports of Bosnia-Herzegovina and Croatia had expired, and only seven months after the third periodic report of Yugoslavia had been considered.[19] All three governments complied and their reports were considered at the 46th session, in November 1992. This compliance is even more important than that of Iraq, since no government objected to the departure from periodicity.[20] It remains to be seen whether other treaty bodies will follow suit and thus introduce a new phase of active involvement in pursuit of critical information and debate.[21] In any case, the absence of the report has the same legal consequences in cases of "normal" periodicity and upon a special request of the treaty body.

The failure to submit the report is clearly a violation of a treaty obligation vis-à-vis other states parties. So far, parties to human rights treaties have not raised this problem at their meetings or before treaty bodies (when the latter are competent to determine violations),

---

[18]See CCPR/C/SR.1178/Add.1, para. 5.

[19]It is disputed whether the Socialist Federal Republic of Yugoslavia, which had submitted its report in April 1992, is identical to the Federal Republic of Yugoslavia (Serbia and Montenegro), which submitted the report in November 1992, or whether it should be treated as a new state. In any case, its report was not due under normal rules of periodicity.

[20]Bosnia-Herzegovina and Croatia even agreed to submit a report before the expiry of the time for the initial report, which appears to go further than their obligation under Art. 40.1, according to which the first report is due within one year after the entry into force of the Covenant and the Committee is empowered to request a report only "thereafter". This case raises other interesting points, such as the assumption of the Committee that successor states are bound by the ICCPR even if they are not recognized (Yugoslavia) or have not made a declaration to that effect (Bosnia-Herzegovina), but they cannot be dealt with here. The Committee explicitly referred to the entitlement of the people in the territories of the former Yugoslavia to the guarantees of ICCPR.

[21]The Human Rights Committee amended its Rules of Procedure to empower its chairman, acting in consultation with other members, to request a report in the case of an exceptional situation and when the Committee is not in session (new Rule 66.2). For a similar decision of the Committee on the Rights of the Child see CRC/C/10, paras. 58-58. For proposals in the same vein by the Committee on Economic, Social and Cultural Rights see E/C.12/1992/CRP.1/Add 11, paras 18-20. For the Committee on the Elimination of Racial Discrimination see CERD/C/1993/ Misc.1/Rev.2, para. 10(h).

but have been content with exhortations at the UN General Assembly. The treaty bodies themselves do not appear to have the right to pronounce judgement on this type of violation without the initiative of a state party. Action so far has been to try to assist developing countries in preparing their reports and to streamline them in order to avoid repetition in reports to various treaty bodies.[22]

Another easy way to determine a defect is when *the report is obviously incomplete and superficial*. If it does not provide a modicum of information, it does not even deserve to be called a report. The practice of the treaty bodies has been to request additional information. Only when this is present, can consideration be said to have started and the reporting obligation to have been fulfilled.[23]

4.3 The quality of the report

Minimal information may be sufficient to determine that the report has been prepared, but not for it to be satisfactory. Two aspects of the quality of the report are of importance.

One relates to the completeness of information, which depends on the specific nature of the report described in the relevant human rights treaty. For instance, if the report does not refer to "progress" or "factors and difficulties", and this is clearly required by the treaty, it cannot be considered to be complete. This has been largely remedied by the presence of government representatives who furnish additional information and by additional reports.

Much more difficult and delicate problems are those relating to the *veracity* of the report. Although the tendency of practically every government is to present the human rights situation in its own country in a favourable light, this sometimes exceeds the bounds of what is

---

[22]See *Effective Implementation of International Instruments on Human Rights, Including Reporting Obligations under International Instruments on Human Rights*, UN Doc. A/44/668. In the Annex: report by Philip Alston.

[23]Cf., Rules 66 and 70 of the *Rules of Procedure of the Human Rights Committee*, CCPR/C/3/Rev. 2.

excusable and results in a false and distorted picture of the reality and further deprives the report of its true meaning.

In order to determine that what the report says is untrue or irrelevant, members of the treaty bodies have to base their assessment on some other sources of information. They have been known to refer to media reports, scholarly works and, above all, reports of international governmental and non-governmental organizations (NGOs), but this has been met with resolute objections from government representatives and some members of the treaty bodies, including admonitions by the chair declaring the official use of non-governmental material to be out of order.[24] Opposition to "unorthodox" sources has now weakened, partly due to the habit of members of treaty bodies phrasing their observations in the form of polite questions as to whether a statement contained in a source is true or not. It must be said, however, that experts in treaty bodies collect their information entirely on their own: they still receive NGO publications addressed to them personally and not as officially distributed documents and treaty bodies are not equipped with documentation facilities, libraries, or databases, let alone personnel who could systematically prepare background information.

The role of NGOs can and should be greatly enhanced, not only in respect of written contributions, but also as regards their participation in oral proceedings, from which they have been completely excluded. In the most recent past, some advances have been made in bodies which monitor the implementation of treaties on rights that are not immediately enforceable and allow for the dimension of gradual progress, such as CESCR and CRC. The really significant breakthrough

---

[24]See Nowak, loc.cit. n. 9, p. 606 et seq. and references contained therein.

was recorded in the Committee against Torture (CAT), which can invite formal submissions from NGOs.[25]

Another possibility would consist of on-the-spot inspection by members of the treaty body. Although the Commission on Human Rights, which is an organ of the United Nations composed of state representatives, has resorted to special rapporteurs for that purpose, treaty bodies have so far refrained from sending missions to signatory states. However, the Economic and Social Council has followed a proposal of the Committee on Social, Economic and Cultural Rights and in July 1992 offered the Dominican Republic the possibility of accepting "one or two ... members" of the Committee to advise the government of that country.[26] It should be noted that under such an arrangement members of the treaty body act as advisers and not as fact-finders.[27]

4.4 Evaluation of the human rights situation

The obvious purpose of the examination of the report is to determine whether the human rights treaty is implemented in a given country. This simple truth has been obfuscated by the argument that the reports come from sovereign states unwilling to be submitted to any kind of investigation, and that the words "study", "examine" or "consider" used in various human rights treaties to describe the action of the treaty bodies implied only a respectful and friendly exchange

---

[25]For this and proposals for other improvements see Amnesty International, *World Conference on Human Rights. Facing up the Failures: Proposals for Improving the Protection of Human Rights by the United Nations*, London 1992 (AI Index IOR 41/16/92) p. 36. Proposals have been advanced to involve national NGOs in the preparation of state reports: in fact this has been practiced by some governments (e.g., Norway). Opinions as to the advisability of this are divided. It is feared that NGOs would lose their full independence and enter into some kind of complicity with the government.

[26]See E/1992/23, Ch. I, draft decision III.

[27]For a similar suggestion in the Committee on the Elimination of Racial Discrimination see CERD/C/1993/Misc.1/Rev.2, para. 10(b).

of information and views.[28] In most treaty bodies, and in particular in those which have been able to allot more time to the consideration of reports, this has been denied by the practice of members who not only try to determine the real facts but also to express their views as to compliance with the provisions of the treaty. Any careful reader of the reports of the treaty bodies, and especially of the summary records of their meetings, is able to determine the prevalent opinion.

Impressions gained by the perusal of such documents cannot, however, be attributed to the treaty body itself, so the difficult question remained as to what was to be the formal outcome of the consideration of a report. The wording of some human rights treaties being inconclusive, the most important debate has taken place in the HRC, which, according to Article 40.4, after having studied the report, "shall transmit its reports, and such general comments as it may consider appropriate, to the States Parties". Some members of the Committee, mostly from "socialist" states, who denied the competence to investigate the human rights situation, argued that "reports" were the reports of the Committee on its activity and that "general comments" were to be really general, that is, referring to all reports. Other members held that both the reports and comments had to reflect the purpose of the study of the country report, which is "to ascertain whether the State party had reported as it should and, on that basis, whether it had implemented or was implementing the Covenant as it had undertaken to do".[29]

As a result of this impasse the Committee has until very recently refrained from adopting its own reports on state reports and thus has possibly not fulfilled its obligations under the Covenant.[30] General Comments, issued occasionally by the Committee, have gradually

---

[28]See, e.g., B. Graefrath, *Menschenrechte und internationale Kooperation* (Berlin 1988) p. 166 et seq.

[29]*Report of the Human Rights Committee*, GAOR, 35th Sess., Suppl. No. 40, para. 378. For a summary of the debate, see para. 370 et seq.

[30]For a forceful argument in that direction see Nowak, loc.cit. n. 9, p. 611 et seq. In support of this it should be noted that the reports on the activities of the Human Rights Committee are a separate obligation of this body, stipulated in Art. 45 of ICCPR.

become a combination of comments on all reports previously examined and commentaries on specific articles or themes in CCPR. This changed in 1992, when the Committee decided to adopt specific comments after the study of each report, which carry the weight of consensual opinion of the Committee as a whole.[31] They are simply called "comments", which means that the Committee has not followed the suggestions of those who believed that, general comments being optional and reports obligatory, the proper designation would be "reports of the Committee". In defence of the Committee, it must be noted that their attitude has corresponded to the general trend, exemplified in the wording of 19.3 of CAT, which was adopted on 10 December 1984, in full cognizance of the dilemma: "Each report shall be considered by the Committee which may make such *general comments on the report* as it may consider appropriate ..." (emphasis added).

As a result of these developments the general statement seems to be that treaty bodies when studying reports can examine the human rights situation in the contracting state, on the basis of information derived from the report, from the oral presentation of the representatives of the government and from other sources and are entitled to express their views on the implementation of the relevant human rights treaty in that country.

4.5 The preventive function of reporting

If the true interests of the international community are to be taken into account, the real purpose of the reporting exercise must be deeper than *ex post facto* determination of compliance with the human rights treaty. Human rights violations should not only be condemned and repaired, but prevented. Recently, more attention has been given to this preventive function of the treaty bodies, in response to the general "early warning" policies advocated by the UN

[31]The first comments were adopted at the 44th session after the examination of the report of Algeria. *Report of the Human Rights Committee*, GAOR, 47th Sess., Suppl. No. 40, paras. 292-299.

Secretary-General.[32] Some procedural innovations described above, such as the requests for urgent reports and the sending of members of human rights bodies to the territories of states parties have to be seen in this light. The question remains as to how the treaty bodies, if their own assistance in preventing massive violations is inadequate, will alert the political organs of the United Nations. The regular annual reports of the treaty bodies are certainly not sufficient.

In this context the experience of those bodies which have the sole responsibility to help prevent violations by examining the circumstances conducive to violations is of great interest.[33] In any case, a deeper study of the "difficulties" should serve this purpose as well.

4.6 "Constructive dialogue"

The outcome of the reporting exercise has proved to be more than the rigid determination of the facts and the degree of fulfilment of the obligations under the human rights treaty. To their credit, most treaty bodies have endeavoured to understand the legal, political, societal, economic and cultural factors influencing the implementation of the treaty and, after initial hesitation and defensiveness, reporting governments have followed suit. Both the members of the treaty bodies and government representatives, at the conclusion of the examination of reports, have referred to it as "constructive and fruitful dialogue".[34] The dialogue, however, has been between the members of the treaty body and government representatives: the third party that would represent the society (and human rights NGOs, national and international, come closest to exercising this function) has unfortunately been absent from the oral exchanges. Apart from this, in some cases the exercise has approached an ideal learning experience: the members of the treaty body have come to better

---

[32]See the recommendations of the fourth meeting of the chairpersons of human rights treaty bodies in A/47/628, para. 37 et seq.

[33]See the contribution of M. Nowak and W. Suntinger in the present volume.

[34]See, e.g., *Report of the Human Rights Committee*, GAOR, 47th Sess., Suppl. No. 40, para. 420.

understand the situation in the country and the governments to realize that their problems are not unique and that they stand to gain from the experience of the experts. The treaty body can then meaningfully proceed to offer specific recommendations to the particular state in its comments on the report and to transmit its experiences, insights and conclusions on the best ways to interpret and implement the treaty in its general comments. This will become increasingly important in the new international context, where governments as a rule do not harbour doubts as to the idea of human rights and are really concerned with their promotion, protection and enjoyment.

5. CONCLUSIONS AND RECOMMENDATIONS

The understanding and the treatment of the reporting procedures described above have been the result of adaptation, interpretation and reinterpretation. If the monitoring of the human rights situation is to be introduced at the European level, the drafting of the relevant future instruments can profit therefrom and advance in terms of clarity and refinement. There is room for improvement due to the advantages of political and cultural proximity of the European countries.

Reporting shall involve all the aspects of the implementation of human rights treaties which cannot be covered by other procedures. It shall not only encompass a review of the compatibility of the legislation with the human rights treaty but attempt to understand the human rights situation in its complexity, so as to allow the treaty body and other international organs to advise and assist the governments. In doing this, the treaty body can act in a preventive fashion: if it determines that there are signs that the situation will worsen, it should be empowered not only to react itself, but also to initiate proceedings with organs competent to make political decisions.

Experience has shown that hasty and summary consideration tends to degenerate into mere formality. It is therefore important to allow for sufficient time for oral dialogue. In this connection the visits of treaty bodies or their representatives to the country under review should be institutionalized.

Treaty bodies should be invited and encouraged to offer extensive reports and comments after the examination of each state report. Their statements and opinions should not only be considered by international organizations, but given wide publicity.

In order to perform their functions treaty bodies have to be properly equipped. They must be supported by adequate secretarial support, which does not only include administrative assistance but help in extensive data gathering.

State reports have to provide a good basis for understanding the situation in the country. States shall be encouraged not to treat them as an administrative exercise, but as a joint effort that would involve at least all the relevant government branches. To achieve this, states should not be burdened with a duty to report to too many bodies too frequently.

The abundance and sophistication of NGOs in Europe and their general acceptance make their orderly introduction in the reporting procedure a matter of highest priority. Their reports and "counter-reports", as well as the participation of their representatives in the oral debate, would greatly increase the benefits of the regular examination of the human rights situation in European countries.

THE EFFICIENCY OF THE INDIVIDUAL COMPLAINT PROCEDURES: THE EXPERIENCE OF CCPR, CERD, CAT AND ECHR[1]

by Rein Müllerson

1. INDIVIDUAL COMPLAINT PROCEDURES AS A METHOD OF MONITORING COMPLIANCE WITH INTERNATIONAL HUMAN RIGHTS STANDARDS

There are different methods by which to monitor the implementation of international human rights instruments by states parties. Three of them: reports by states parties, inter-state complaints and individual complaints (communication, petitions, applications, etc.) are provided for in many instruments. At the universal level, the consideration of state reports on their implementation of respective instruments by so-called treaty bodies is certainly the most important procedure for monitoring the compliance of domestic laws and practices with international human rights standards. Under some instruments this is the only available procedure.

An inter-state complaint procedure, which was deemed to be the main monitoring procedure under the European Convention for the Protection of Human Rights and Fundamental Freedoms [ECHR (Art.24)], but which was eventually superseded by the procedure of individual complaints (Art.25), initially meant to be an optional one, has not been used under the Covenant on Civil and Political Rights (CCPR) at all.

Even under the ECHR, as P. van Dijk and G.J.H. van Hoof write, "it is evident that the right of complaint of States has not proved to be

[1]International Covenant on Civil and Political Rights (CCPR), International Convention on the Elimination of All Forms of Racial Discrimination (CERD), United Nations Convention against Torture and Other Cruel, Inhuman or Degrading Treatment (CAT), European Convention for the Protection of Human Rights and Fundamental Freedoms (ECHR)

A. Bloed et al. (eds.), Monitoring Human Rights in Europe, 25–43.

very effective".[2] There are several reasons for this, but here is not the place to analyse them. This leaves only two really operative procedures[3] - state reports and individual complaints - to monitor compliance with international human rights instruments.

Within the framework of the Council of Europe it may be the case that the system of state reports is not really a necessary procedure, especially when taking into account that states parties to the ECHR in any case report to the universal treaty bodies as states parties to respective instruments.[4] But at the universal level both (the reports system and the individual complaint system) mutually complement each other. Usually a consideration of states' reports gives an overall picture of the situation with regard to human rights in a given country. This panorama is indispensable in order to evaluate a state's compliance with international human rights standards. But frequently during any consideration of reports details become lost (I would like to emphasize that in the protection of human rights there are no details which are unimportant). Very often, it is only with the consideration of individual complaints that the complete conformity of national legislation and practice with the requirements of international law can be assessed. For example, the Human Rights Committee (HRC), supervising the implementation of the CCPR, could only discover certain inconsistencies in the internal legislation and practice of Finland and France with the Covenant [case No. 265/1987 (*Vuolanne* v. *Finland*)[5] and case No. 196/1985 (*J.*

---

[2]P. van Dijk and G.J.H. van Hoof, *Theory and Practice of the European Convention on Human Rights* 2nd ed. (Dordrecht 1990) p. 36.

[3]Under the ECHR (Art. 57), a procedure whereby the Secretary-General of the Council of Europe can request "any High Contracting Party to furnish explanation of the manner in which its internal laws ensure the effective implementation of any of the provisions of the Convention". The Secretary-General has used this procedure, which in some aspects is analogous to the system of reports under universal human rights instruments.

[4]At the moment, only three members of the Council of Europe (Greece, Liechtenstein and Turkey) do not participate, for example, in the CCPR.

[5]Report of the Human Rights Committee, UN GAOR, 44th Sess.,Suppl. No. 40, para. 10, p. 249 at p. 257, UN Doc. A/44/40 (1989).

Gueye et al. v. *France*)[6]] by considering individual communications. Consideration of state reports did not reveal anything amiss in these domains.

Individual complaints to international bodies may fulfil, in principle, three functions: first, as a result of considering such a complaint an individual, whose rights have been violated, may have a remedy against the wrong suffered by him, and the violation could be stopped and/or compensation paid, etc.; second, considering a complaint may result not only in a remedy for the victim of the violation, whose complaint has been considered, but also in changes to internal legislation and practice; and third, an individual complaint (or more often, a series of complaints) may serve as evidence of systematic and/or massive violations of certain rights in a given country.

One and the same complaint may, in principle, serve all three functions, but more often than not this is not the case. In the case of massive and gross violations of human rights in a particular country it is difficult to expect that much would change simply as a result of the consideration of individual communications. The 1503 procedure in the United Nations (UN) Commission on Human Rights, which is intended for gross and massive violations of human rights, and the Optional Protocol to the CCPR clearly envisage different situations.

Systematic human rights violations do not occur as a result of some specific shortcomings in the functioning of a legal system of a country or as a result of certain failures of that system, which can be corrected by international bodies via the consideration of complaints from particular victims. Such violations are either a result of deliberate state policy or a breakdown of law and order in a country.

Generally speaking, individual complaint procedures under universal human rights instruments, especially under the CCPR, can, from my point of view, realistically and effectively serve only the second function, to wit, to monitor the compliance of laws and practices of

---

[6]Ibid.

states with international human rights standards and thereby to contribute to positive changes in internal law and practices.

By the end of 1992, out of 112 states parties to the CCPR, 66 had accepted the HRC's competence to deal with individual communications by becoming parties to the Optional Protocol.[7] The International Convention on the Elimination of All Forms of Racial Discrimination, having been ratified or acceded to by 132 states, only received 16 declarations from states parties under Article 14 recognizing the competence of the Committee on the Elimination of Racial Discrimination to receive individual communications and, by the end of 1992, only two communications had been considered on their merits.[8] 28 out of 66 states parties to the Convention against Torture and Other Cruel, Inhuman and Degrading Treatment (CAT) have made a declaration under Article 22, enabling the Committee against Torture to receive individual communications. By the end of 1992, one communication had been declared admissible and the Committee at that time had four communications before it.[9]

The scarce jurisprudence of the CAT under Article 22 may be partly due to the fact that the Convention entered into force only in June 1987. But in any case it is only possible to speak realistically of the effectiveness of individual complaint procedures at the universal level under the Optional Protocol to the CCPR.

---

[7]GA Report of the Human Rights Committee, 1992, A/47/40, 47th Sess., p. 153.

[8]GA Report of the Committee on the Elimination of Racial Discrimination, 1992, A/47/18, 47th Sess., p. 73.

[9]GA Report of the Committee against Torture, 1992, 47th Sess., Suppl. No. 44/47/44, pp. 69-70.

2. CONSIDERING INDIVIDUAL COMPLAINTS UNDER THE CCPR AND ECHR

Under the CCPR the HRC is the only body which deals with communications from the very beginning to the very end.[10] The mechanism under the ECHR is more complicated. All petitions are first considered by the European Commission of Human Rights (the Commission), which shall, if an amicable settlement of the matter between the parties on the basis of respect for human rights as defined by the Convention is not reached, draw up a report on the facts and also state its opinion as to whether these facts disclose a breach by the state concerned of its obligations under the Convention. This report is transmitted to the Committee of Ministers of the Council of Europe, which decides whether the Convention has been violated or not. The Commission may also refer any case to the European Court of Human Rights (the Court), whose judgments are obligatory for the parties concerned just like the decisions of the Committee of Ministers. States parties may also refer cases to the Court.

Currently, more cases are referred to the Court by the Commission than to the Council of Ministers and after the entry into force of Protocol no. 9, under which individuals may also refer cases to the Court, the workload of the latter will increase sharply.

All individuals under the jurisdiction of states parties to the Optional Protocol to the CCPR or states which have made a declaration under Article 25 of the ECHR (in practice this means all states parties to the ECHR) can send complaints to these bodies if their rights and freedoms under the respective instruments have been violated and they have exhausted all available domestic remedies. Consideration of complaints consists of two separate stages: on the admissibility and on the merits. Both stages are confidential, although all decisions are published.

---

[10]One should not forget, of course, the valuable work done by the various Secretariats, which is even more important as neither the HRC, nor the European Commission and Court function permanently.

The conditions of admissibility under the Optional Protocol and the ECHR are rather similar, though there are some important differences.

Non-exhaustion of local (or domestic) remedies is one ground on which complaints are often declared inadmissible. While individuals have to exhaust all available domestic remedies before appealing to international bodies, states, when arguing that individuals have not exhausted these remedies (which they often do), have to show in concrete terms which remedies are still available for the alleged victim. These remedies have to be not only formally available but they also have to be effective.[11] Under the ECHR individuals can send a petition only within a period of six months from the date on which the final decision was taken. The Covenant does not have any such limitations.

Under the Optional Protocol only individuals, which means the victims themselves as well as their representatives (counsel) or relatives, can send communications to the HRC. Under Article 25 of the ECHR groups of individuals and non-governmental organizations also have the right to send petitions to the Commission. In practice, of course, the HRC considers communications sent by groups of persons if they all claim to be the victims of the same violation of the Covenant. The Committee sometimes even joins communications which have been sent separately by different individuals but relate to the same facts. But non-governmental organizations, unfortunately, do not have any standing before the Committee.

Both the HRC and the Commission do not deal with anonymous complaints. The HRC does not consider communications which are currently being examined under another procedure of international investigation or settlement (this does not include political bodies where the same case may be considered, for example, as one of the examples of massive violations of human rights or by non-governmental organizations). This means that after consideration by

[11]See, for example, Ramirez *v.* Uruguay, Human Rights Committee. Selected Decisions under the Optional Protocol, Vol. I, p. 49.

another international body (e.g., by the European Commission or Court or Inter-American bodies) the Committee may consider the case. To avoid such a situation all states parties to the ECHR, except, e.g., the Netherlands and Finland, have made reservations to the Optional Protocol whereby they exclude communications which have been considered under the ECHR.

The European Commission does not consider petitions which are incompatible with the provisions of the Convention, are manifestly ill-founded, or amount to an abuse of the right of petition. The same is true under the Optional Protocol. Although the Optional Protocol does not expressly mention communications which are manifestly ill-founded, the practice of the Committee has created the rule (now enshrined in Rule 90(b) of the Rules of Procedure of the Human Rights Committee) that a claim, in order to be declared admissible, has to be "sufficiently substantiated".

No complaint is declared admissible before a state party, which has allegedly violated human rights, has been given an opportunity to comment on the complaint. The second stage of consideration is consideration on the merits.

The HRC, during the last 15 years, has received 514 registered cases, 138 of which were concluded amicably. 155 were declared inadmissible, and 80 were discontinued or withdrawn. 49 were declared admissible, but have not been concluded and 92 were pending at the pre-admissibility stage.[12] Though the workload of the Committee under the Optional Protocol is increasing every year and in the 1990s there has been a drastic increase in the number of accessions to the Protocol, it would not be realistic to expect that the Committee could remedy the thousands of violations of the provisions of the CCPR, which occur every year in states parties to the Covenant and often remain without domestic remedies. This conclusion would be true even in the highly hypothetical case of states parties' perfect compliance with the views adopted by the Committee. Therefore, the individual complaint procedure in this supervisory body, which deals

---

[12]GA Report of the Human Rights Committee (1992) p. 153.

most successfully with individual complaints at the universal level, should not be seen as a kind of "fourth instance" capable of dealing with every or even most cases of violation of CCPR provisions. Its real effectiveness depends on how the laws and practices of states change as a result of the consideration of cases against them. The purpose of the procedure is to affect, through the consideration of one or several cases, positively and in accordance with the requirements of the CCPR, the plight of thousands of individuals under the jurisdiction of a given state.

Certainly, individual complaints to treaty bodies can also provide evidence that grave and massive violations are taking place in a particular country. But most often such countries, even when participating in respective instruments, do not accept individual complaint procedures or, if they do, their co-operation with treaty bodies is in practice non-existent.[13] Human rights situations in such countries can and should be dealt with more effectively through consideration of state reports or in political bodies of the UN (the Commission on Human Rights, the General Assembly or even the Security Council), where the findings of treaty bodies can serve as evidence.

Individual complaint procedures can function effectively only if certain domestic conditions are met. A country has to have a minimum degree of democracy or its government should be sincerely committed to democratic reform and protection of human rights. Certain domestic remedies should also be available, not only because their exhaustion is a *conditio sine qua non* for an individual to send a complaint to any international body, but also because the views or decisions of these bodies need to be implemented through certain domestic mechanisms and procedures (courts, administrative agencies, etc.). It is also absolutely necessary that the possibilities of and

---

[13]The only exception is Uruguay under the military dictatorship. Having ratified the CCPR before the military took power, Uruguay continued to be bound by the Covenant and the Optional Protocol, and there were hundreds of communications against it during the first years of the functioning of the procedure of individual communications under the Optional Protocol. Some cases were resolved positively after the Committee had found Uruguay to be in violation of the Covenant.

conditions for applications to international bodies by individuals are known among the population at large and that a degree of legal consciousness exists in any given country. It is not realistic to expect that citizens of totalitarian or extreme authoritarian states would communicate with international bodies after the exhaustion of local remedies if such remedies are non-existent or practically ineffective, and where individuals may even be punished for communicating with international bodies.[14]

The absence of communications, at least from some countries, is not necessarily indicative of the perfect implementation of the Covenant. Often it means that the population has not been made aware of the existence of the procedure and has no experience of using judicial or quasi-judicial (especially, international) forms of protection of individual rights and freedoms.

Therefore, the rather heavy workload of the European Commission and the Court of Human Rights in comparison with universal and even other regional mechanisms does not mean that domestic remedies in European countries are less effective than those of other states. Rolv Ryssdal - the President of the European Court - stressed:

> "The States which are parties to the Convention are already committed to upholding human rights, since by virtue of their membership of the Council of Europe they have undertaken to 'accept the principles of the rule of law and of the enjoyment by all persons within [their] jurisdiction of human rights and fundamental freedoms'. The Strasbourg Court as a consequence does not in practice have to deal with allegations of serious and wide-scale violations of human rights of the kind that occurred in Europe before and during the Second World War and which even today are sadly too frequent in other parts of the world"[15].

---

[14]Such an issue arose, for example, before the HRC in the case Hammel *v.* Madagascar (Doc. A/42/40).

[15]R. Ryssdal, "The Future of the European Court of Human Rights", Public Lecture at King's College, London, 22 March 1990. Council of Europe. European Court of Human Rights, Strasbourg, 23 November, 1990.

Unfortunately, atrocities of the same scale are nowadays also committed in Europe. They are usually not dealt with by procedures for individual complaints. Political decisions and even the use of military force by the international community, as well as the establishment of international criminal jurisdiction, are necessary to cope with crimes against humanity. But neither is it excluded that the Strasbourg bodies have to consider serious and widespread violations of human rights.

While in 1955 - the year when the procedure for individual petitions under Article 25 of the ECHR entered into force - the Secretariat registered 138 petitions,[16] in 1991 1,648 petitions were registered and the Commission during the same year disposed of 1,619 applications, while 2,332 applications were pending before the Commission.[17] The Commission, during the same period, delivered 1,658 decisions concerning individual applicants, of which 1,371 were declared inadmissible, 70 were struck off the list and 217 were declared admissible. It adopted 141 reports (concerning 178 applications), of which 108 (144) were on the question of violation under Article 31 of the Convention, 31 (32) concerned friendly settlement under Article 28 of the Convention and two were struck off the list. The Commission, which held eight two week sessions, referred 94 cases to the European Court on Human Rights.[18]

The Court, which at the beginning was rather inactive, has also increased its activities considerably. It took 17 years for it to deliver its first 20 judgments. During the following 15 years (by the end of 1990) 214 judgments had been delivered.[19]

---

[16]See, T. Opsahl, "The Coexistence between Geneva and Strasbourg", *Canadian Human Rights Yearbook* (1991-1992) p. 154.

[17]See Council of Europe. European Commission of Human Rights, *Survey of Activities and Statistics* (1991) p. 2.

[18]Ibid., p. 6.

[19] See the Appendix to the Public Lecture given by Rolv Ryssdal, President of the European Court of Human Rights, at King's College, London, 22 March 1990, p. 13.

The fact that notwithstanding the rather effective functioning of the European system of human rights protection, quite a substantial portion of communications to the HRC nevertheless concerns Western European countries indicates, on the one hand, of course, that there is always room for improvement and perfection, but most importantly, that individuals in these countries know their rights and the means by which to protect them.

Taking into account the level of development of domestic remedies in most Western European countries and the number of cases considered by the European Commission and the Court of Human Rights, which significantly exceeds that considered even by the most successful UN treaty body - the Committee on Human Rights - the former can also find their *raison d'être* in serving as a body providing a remedy for applicants. But even in the European system of human rights protection in many cases, if not most, where the European bodies have found a state party to be in violation of the Convention, the consideration resulted not only in a remedy for the applicants, but most importantly in changes in domestic legislation.[20]

There are two categories of human rights violations in addition to systematic and massive ones: first, when the rights of an individual are violated notwithstanding that the laws and even practices of the country in that domain have been in conformity with international standards, and, second, when a violation takes place because the laws themselves contradict to the requirements of these standards. The first category of cases is not characteristic. Such individual violations, which occur in every country (there is no human rights paradise on this Earth!), are usually rectified by domestic remedies. But the second category of cases is proper for consideration by international bodies by way of individual complaint procedures.

Individual complaint procedures, remaining an important method for controlling human rights situations in all European countries, can and should play an especially crucial role in improving the protection of human rights in the states of Eastern Europe and the former Soviet

---

[20]See, e.g., Van Dijk and Van Hoof, op.cit. n. 2, pp. 156-157.

Union. For those who join the Council of Europe, the procedures of the European Convention will become the most important, though even for them the CCPR and the Optional Protocol are far from superfluous. There are some rights in the Covenant (e.g., non-discrimination extending to all rights and not only to those protected by other articles of the Covenant, and minority rights), which are not covered by the European Convention, and as the jurisprudence of the HRC testifies, citizens of even the most law-abiding Western European countries have benefitted from the UN system of human rights protection. For newly independent countries or countries undergoing radical changes, which have only started to create their own democratic institutions, such procedures are not only the first and foremost means of monitoring their implementation of international human rights standards, but are also a sort of expert assistance. Via individual complaints it is possible not only to discover details of any shortcomings and to react in good time, but also to cover areas which are usually outside the point of view of "big politics".

3. THE LEGAL NATURE AND IMPLEMENTATION OF DECISIONS TAKEN ON INDIVIDUAL COMPLAINTS

Judgments by the European Court of Human Rights and the decisions of the Committee of Ministers taken upon the reports of the European Commission of Human Rights are binding on states parties to the Convention. The Committee of Ministers not only determines itself whether the Convention has been violated or not, but also supervises the execution of the Court's judgments (Art. 54). The legal nature of the views of the HRC determined after the consideration of communications on their merits is not so clear. Article 5(4) of the Optional Protocol states only that the Committee "shall forward its views to the State Party concerned and to the individual". Their legal character is not mentioned and no follow-up is envisaged.

The very term "views", the attitude of some states ignoring these views and the lack of any enforcement mechanism may lead to a conclusion that these views are mere recommendations deprived of any legally binding force.

Such a conclusion is not, from my point of view, correct. As F. Pocar, the former Chairman of the HRC, observes, Article 5(4) has to be read together with Article 2(3) of the Covenant[21] which provides that each "State Party to the present Covenant undertakes: (a) To ensure that any person whose rights or freedoms as herein recognized are violated shall have an effective remedy, notwithstanding that the violation has been committed by persons acting in an official capacity". This means that when the HRC discovers a violation of the Covenant a state party is obliged under the Covenant to remedy that violation.

The views of the Committee in cases, where a violation of the Covenant has been found, do not only prescribe a remedy for the victim (e.g., the release of a prisoner or a payment of compensation, etc.) but also contain a standard formula that "the State Party is under an obligation to take measures to ensure that similar violations do not occur in the future".[22] This also includes, if necessary, adequate legislative measures.

A lack of effective enforcement procedures and sanctions is not so much a weakness but a characteristic of international law. Its effectiveness is to a great extent based on the principle of reciprocity (a threat of, for example, retortion and reprisals), which is not applicable in the field of human rights. Violations in one of the states parties to a human rights instrument does not mean that other states parties to the instrument are free from their obligations. Therefore other means of enforcement are needed.

One of the means by which to influence states found by the HRC to be in violation of the CCPR is the publication of the views of the Committee in its annual reports to the General Assembly. The Committee also raises issues of implementation of its views during the

---

[21]F. Pocar, "Legal Value of the Human Rights Committee's Views", *Canadian Human Rights Yearbook* (1991-1992) p. 119.

[22]See, for example, communication No. 238/1988, Aston Little *v.* Jamaica (Official Records of the General Assembly, 47th Sess., Suppl. No. 40, p. 284).

consideration of reports of countries which have not responded positively to the views of the Committee.

One of the novelties which the Committee has recently introduced is the nomination of a special rapporteur on the follow-up of views[23] (the first rapporteur is J. Fodor from Hungary) who has requested written information from the states parties on any measures taken in pursuance of the Committees views.

One of the possibilities of making the implementation of the CCPR including the views of the Committee more effective would be the use of regular meetings of states parties to the Covenant not only for the election of members of the Committee, but also for an overview of the implementation of the CCPR and the Optional Protocol. The Committee could prepare its proposals for such an overview.

States parties to the Optional Protocol should understand (most do, but not all) that their non-cooperation with the Committee on questions of individual communications or persistent denial of admissibility of communications and refusal to argue on the merits of cases is counter-productive not only for human rights protection, but also for the image of their country. First of all, the HRC considers communications even when a state party does not co-operate with the Committee (a state thereby violates its obligations under Article 4(2) of the Optional Protocol). If an author shows that he or she has exhausted all available domestic remedies and has also substantiated his or her claim, a state party runs a very high risk of losing the case simply by not co-operating with the Committee. For example, in one case the HRC observed that "the allegation that the victim was arrested and detained is confirmed by information, unexplained and substantially unrefuted by the State Party".[24] In another case, the Committee established that the state party had not refuted the

---

[23]See Official Records of the General Assembly, 47th Sess., Suppl. No. (A/47/40), para. 687.

[24]Human Rights Committee, *Selected Decisions under the Optional Protocol (Second to Sixteenth Sessions)* (New York: United Nations, 1985) para. 13, p. 109 at p. 112.

author's allegations that he was forced to sign false testimony against himself and that this testimony was used in the trial against him.[25]

Besides, it is necessary to stress that no state's prestige has suffered because of its recognition and implementation of the views of the HRC or the judgments of the European Court of Human Rights. Quite on the contrary, such states are often quoted as examples of the proper implementation of international human rights standards. But the stubborn refusal of some states to accept any criticism and references to interference in internal affairs as a shield from such criticism is a sure sign that something is wrong with human rights in a particular country.

4. PROBLEMS AND PERSPECTIVES

Some experts have warned that even successfully operating human rights bodies reach a stage when piecemeal and minor improvements in procedures undertaken by these bodies themselves are not enough.[26] P. Alston in his study for the UN writes:

> "Whatever terms may be used to characterize the present situation, however, it is generally agreed that the United Nations human rights treaty-monitoring system has reached a critical crossroads. Its successful future evolution demands that the gravity of existing problems be recognized, that the vital importance of effective solutions be pursued with energy and commitment".[27]

The HRC has recently changed its rules of procedure to expedite the consideration of individual communications. At its thirty-sixth session, the Committee decided to authorize the five-member working group on communications to declare communications admissible if all

---

[25]Ibid., para. 2.3, p. 88.

[26]See, R. Higgins, "The United Nations: Still a Force for Peace", 52, *Modern Law Review* (1989) no. 1, p. 20.

[27]UN Doc. A/44/668, p. 11.

members so agree. A special rapporteur on new communications was designated. He or she can transmit new communications to states parties, requesting information or observations relevant to the question of admissibility. All these measures have made the work of the HRC on communications more expeditious.

But here a new stumbling block has arisen. The Secretariat does not have sufficient staff to cope with the increased workload. I would like to emphasize that the Committee is extremely earnest and worried when reiterating its request to the Secretary-General to take the necessary steps to ensure a substantial increase in the number of staff, specialized in the various legal systems, assigned to service the Committee, and wishes it to be put on record that the work under the Optional Protocol continues to suffer as a result of insufficient secretariat resources.[28] It seems that very soon the time will come when the efforts of treaty bodies themselves and even the financial and administrative support by the Secretary-General will not be enough. Measures are necessary which only states parties to different human rights instruments can undertake.

One such measure would be the establishment of a "Super-Committee"[29] replacing each of the existing treaty-monitoring bodies. Such a committee would function permanently and consist of experts in different fields of human rights who would work mainly in chambers. The creation of such a body would be a complicated and time-consuming process and therefore the sooner states commence this process the better it will be for human rights. The UN World Conference on Human Rights[30] is a proper forum not only to raise the issue but also to explore practical ways of carrying it out.

The European human rights mechanism has to a certain extent become a victim of its own success. On the one hand, states parties to the Convention have come to see the Strasbourg institutions as a kind of nuisance.

---

[28]Ibid., para. 615.

[29]Ibid., para. 180.

[30]This conference will take place in Vienna in June 1993.

> "In recent years one may discern - even in contracting States which traditionally could be counted among the most Convention-minded ones - a growing dissatisfaction with and sometimes even obstruction to the consequences resulting from the judicial activism which the Court is alleged to practice".[31]

Such an attitude is not only detrimental to the human rights of peoples of European countries but may also serve as a bad example for other states with less developed domestic and international systems of human rights protection, which often look to the European system as a model not only for improving their own laws and practices but also to justify their own faults and attitudes. It is especially unacceptable because the interests of states are duly taken into account by the European human rights bodies, especially with the wide application of the doctrine of "the margin of appreciation".

On the other hand, in order to cope effectively with the increasing workload the European institutions have to be reformed. Protocol No. 8 to the Convention has already introduced some changes (consideration of cases in chambers and the setting up of committees to reject clearly inadmissible applications), the purpose being to expedite consideration of cases. But this is not enough. And though the Strasbourg secretariat has much more manpower[32] than the UN Secretariat's Communications Section, which deals with all individual communications sent to the UN on human rights matters, the strain is felt even in Strasbourg. Reform of the European institutions is also on the agenda.

Various proposed schemes to make the Strasbourg institutions more effective provide for the creation of either one permanent body (the Court) or to convert the Commission into a first instance court and

---

[31]Van Dijk and Van Hoof, op.cit. n. 2, p. 617.

[32]In 1991 the Commission was assisted by the permanent Secretariat of 39 lawyers, 24 administrative assistants, and two translators (Council of Europe. European Commission of Human Rights, *Survey of Activities and Statistics* (1991) p. 2).

the Court into a court of appeal.[33] As all applications have passed through different domestic hearings before being considered in Strasbourg a two-tier body would hardly be necessary there. An increase in the membership of the Council of Europe has already led and will certainly in the future lead to an increase in the membership of the Commission and the judges of the Court. This means that more work can and should be done in chambers or committees. The Parliamentary Assembly at the Council of Europe emphasizes that "the main point that has to be changed is the length of the Strasbourg procedures" and "it is evident that the creation of a single court would prevent the overlapping of work and also avoid certain delays which are inherent to the present system".[34]

This short analysis confirms the notion supported by many experts, human rights activists and shared by most European states that individual complaint procedures play a significant role in monitoring the compliance of internal laws and practices with international human rights standards.

For those states which are genuinely committed to improving human rights situations in their countries and which do not arrogantly think that they have nothing to learn from the experience of other countries and international bodies it is necessary to recognize procedures of individual complaints to international bodies, and first of all to ratify the Optional Protocol. For those countries which are not only paying lip service to human rights these procedures should become as natural as they are for the states parties to the European Convention, which in their turn have to face the reforms of the Strasbourg system in order to meet the challenges of the twenty-first century.

---

[33]See, e.g., Ryssdal, loc.cit. n. 15, p. 9.

[34]Recommendation 1194 (1992) of the Parliamentary Assembly of the Council of Europe on the Reform of the Control Mechanism of the European Convention on Human Rights, Strasbourg, December 1992, p. 10.

5. RECOMMENDATIONS

1. All European states, which have not yet done so, should adhere to the first Optional Protocol to the Covenant on Civil and Political Rights.

2. It is necessary to commence work on the reform of UN treaty bodies aiming at the creation of a UN Human Rights Committee (Court) dealing with the implementation of various UN human rights instruments.

3. Regular meetings of states parties to the CCPR should consider issues related to the implementation of the CCPR and the Optional Protocol.

4. It is necessary to substantially increase the staff and financing of the UN Centre for Human Rights in Geneva, especially that of the Communications Section.

5. The reform of the European human rights mechanisms should be expedited so that they may conform to new challenges, especially those which stem from the new enlarged Europe.

MONITORING THE CSCE HUMAN DIMENSION: IN SEARCH OF ITS EFFECTIVENESS

by Arie Bloed

1. BRIEF DESCRIPTION OF THE CSCE: Some basic features[1]

The Conference on Security and Co-operation in Europe (CSCE) is a unique phenomenon in international relations. It is based on an intergovernmental conference of all European states, the United States of America and Canada in the first half of the 1970s.[2] This conference resulted in the signature of the Final Act of Helsinki in August 1975. On the basis of the Final Act, an increasing number of CSCE follow-up meetings and specialized conferences took place which resulted in the CSCE nowadays being referred to as the 'CSCE process' or 'Helsinki process'.

The CSCE process started as a Cold War institution. Its main aim - at least from the Western perspective - was a gradual elimination of the artificial barriers in Europe. Although the East European states primarily aimed at official recognition of the territorial *status quo* in Europe, the Western states put most emphasis on agreements in the security field and in the area of human rights. The group of neutral

---

[1]A thorough analysis of the CSCE process up until 1989 is provided in: V.-Y. Ghebali, *La diplomatie de la détente; La CSCE d'Helsinki à Vienne (1973-1989)* (Brussels 1989). For reviews of the period thereafter reference may be made to the various issues of the quarterly *Helsinki Monitor*, published jointly by the Netherlands Helsinki Committee and the University of Utrecht.

[2]In the first period of the CSCE, all European states participated with the exception of Albania. Only in June 1991 did the latter state join the CSCE, following the demise of its communist regime. The original number of participating states was 35. In particular, after the dissolution of the Soviet Union and the disintegration of the former Yugoslavia, the number of participating states increased dramatically. At the time of writing (spring 1993) the CSCE process included 53 states, ranging from Vladivostok to Vancouver and San Francisco. One state (rest-Yugoslavia) was suspended. Macedonia was waiting for admittance to the CSCE ranks, which was blocked due to Greek opposition to the name 'Macedonia'. In comparison to the Council of Europe which has 27 member states, the number of CSCE states is nearly double.

A. Bloed et al. (eds.), Monitoring Human Rights in Europe, 45–91.

and non-aligned CSCE states played a useful role as 'bridge-builders' in order to facilitate the achievement of agreements between East and West. The CSCE started and developed as a diplomatic conference in more or less permanent session. Its main activity consisted of achieving agreements in the areas of the three 'baskets' of the CSCE: political and security issues, economic co-operation, and humanitarian and other questions (such as education and culture). The CSCE had no operational functions whatsoever, its main activity being standard setting. This is reflected in the basic features of the CSCE process.[3] One of its main features is its very light institutional structure. Until 1991 the CSCE structure consisted only of periodic meetings. Only after the collapse of communism in Eastern Europe was the CSCE granted more and more operational tasks - e.g., in the area of conflict prevention and conflict management - which required some permanent bodies as well. This resulted in 1991 in the establishment of three administrative organs with a minimum staff. The strict equality of all 53 participating states is another basic feature of the Helsinki process. This is reflected in particular in the principle of consensus in the decision-making process. Only recently have some exceptions to this basic rule been introduced.[4] Another basic feature is the dynamic, political character of the CSCE process. The process does not have a fixed constitutional basis: the 'constitution' of the CSCE is in a process of continuous development. Besides, the CSCE process has a strict political character, and does not encompass legally binding documents (see *infra* 2.2.2). An essential feature of the CSCE is also the interlinkage of the three 'baskets'. This has the effect that progress in one area has to be accompanied by more or less simultaneous progress in another area (progress in the less sensitive area of economic co-operation, for instance, was often used as a leverage for achieving progress in the highly sensitive area of human rights). This interlinkage has remained

---

[3]For a short survey of the basic features of the Helsinki process, see, e.g., the present author's "Institutional Aspects of the 'New' CSCE", in: A. Bloed and W. de Jonge, eds., *Legal Aspects of a New European Infrastructure* (Utrecht 1992) pp. 3-8.

[4]These exceptions relate, among other things, to the commencing of the Berlin emergency mechanism, the Moscow rapporteur system in the field of the human dimension, and the consensus-minus-one principle concerning serious violations of human dimension commitments (see *infra*).

a basic characteristic of the CSCE process until the present time, which is reflected, among other things, in the close relationship between security issues and human rights.[5] Although the CSCE is at present in a process of transition and although therefore the 'old' CSCE has to be distinguished from the 'new' one, the 'new' CSCE is still to a great extent determined by its Cold War origin. This is reflected, in particular, in the decision-making process.

2. BRIEF DESCRIPTION OF THE HUMAN DIMENSION OF THE CSCE

2.1 Introduction

The term 'human dimension of the CSCE' was only officially introduced in 1989. In the Concluding Document of the Vienna Follow-up Meeting of the CSCE (January 1989)[6] it was described as follows: "the undertakings entered into in the Final Act and in other CSCE documents concerning respect for all human rights and fundamental freedoms, human contacts and other issues of a related humanitarian character". The concept of the 'human dimension' is a very specific notion with very specific contents. I will not deal with all these issues. Instead I will try to outline some of the main characteristics of the CSCE human dimension: its comprehensive and far-reaching, sometimes even penetrating, nature; its political character; and the complementary value of the CSCE human dimension norms in comparison to other international human rights instruments.

---

[5]See, in particular, the sections in this study (*infra*) dealing with the High Commissioner on National Minorities.

[6]The official CSCE documents up to spring 1990 have been published in: A. Bloed, ed., *From Helsinki to Vienna: Basic Documents of the Helsinki Process* (Dordrecht, etc., 1990). A second edition with all documents up to the spring of 1993 and an updated introduction will be published by Martinus Nijhoff Publishers during the course of 1993.

2.2 Main characteristics

2.2.1 Comprehensive and far-reaching nature

Comprehensiveness is a characteristic feature of the CSCE human dimension. The CSCE has not only created standards in the 'traditional' field of civil and political rights and to a certain extent also in the field of economic, social and cultural rights, but it has also given birth to a great number of undertakings in the humanitarian area which go beyond the traditional field. The highly detailed character of many of the commitments is another characteristic element of the human dimension. The elaboration of freedom of expression into detailed rules concerning the working conditions for (foreign) journalists is one example.[7] Another example is the translation of freedom of movement into a great number of provisions about 'human contacts' (family reunification, marriages between citizens of different states, tourism, etc.). Worth mentioning separately are the commitments in the field of the protection of national minorities. The achievements in the latter field are unparalleled in comparison to other international instruments.

Even more important, however, is the fact that (a great number of) the commitments go far beyond the level which has been achieved in traditional human rights instruments. This far-reaching, sometimes even 'penetrating' character may be illustrated in two ways:

---

[7]This is reflected in the detailed rules in the third basket of the Helsinki Final Act and the subsequent documents of CSCE meetings. The most striking example of a further elaboration of the freedom of expression may be found in the Moscow Document of the Conference on the Human Dimension of the CSCE. In this document detailed rules about the protection of human rights in a state of public emergency have been laid down. In this context the CSCE states agreed that they "will endeavour to maintain freedom of expression and freedom of information" in a state of public emergency (para. 28.9 of the Moscow Document; text in: *Helsinki Monitor*, 1991, No. 4), a commitment going beyond the obligations in 'traditional' human rights instruments. See also the present author's 'Moscow Meeting of the Conference on the Human Dimension of the CSCE: A Critical Analysis', in: *Helsinki Monitor*, 1992, No. 1, pp. 9-10.

a) In the first place, the nature and the scope of the CSCE commitments go beyond the 'traditional' level which may be found in many human rights conventions and other international instruments. The latter deal predominantly with human rights in the strict sense of the term, encompassing in particular international obligations for the state regarding its relationship with (groups of) individuals. The means by which to implement these obligations is traditionally left to the discretion of the states concerned. However, the CSCE documents also contain a great number of rules in an area which is traditionally seen as belonging to the internal affairs of states, namely the political system of the states concerned. 'Traditional' human rights instruments do not deal directly with the constitutional system of states or the relationship between governmental agencies within the state. In other words, they do not directly address so-called rule-of-law concerns and the political system of the state.[8] International law comes into play only when national legal rules or constitutional principles would violate internationally guaranteed rights (for instance the independence of the judiciary); in other words: the rule of law and political pluralism is implied in the implementation of human rights. In this context it has to be observed that the European Convention on Human Rights and Fundamental Freedoms takes an 'intermediate' position between other 'traditional' human rights instruments and the CSCE human dimension. Rule-of-law issues, as well as issues such as free elections, are directly addressed in the Convention and its Protocols.

Within the CSCE the situation is different, certainly in comparison with universal human rights instruments. In the recent period a distinct CSCE order has been established, based on respect for human rights, rule of law and democratic pluralism. The scope of this order is much broader than the protection of human rights. It deals not only with the relation between the state and individuals, but it also deals extensively with the structure of government, the political system and the interaction between governmental institutions. The American expert Buergenthal, therefore, correctly observes that no

---

[8]T. Buergenthal, 'The CSCE Human Rights System", 25 *The George Washington Journal of International Law and Economics* (1991) No. 2, pp. 333-386 at p. 382.

domestic institution or norm is now beyond the jurisdictional reach of the CSCE:

> "Here the traditional domestic jurisdiction doctrine, which has tended to shield oppressive state practices and institutions from international scrutiny, has for all practical purposes lost its meaning. And this notwithstanding the fact that non-intervention in the domestic affairs of a state is a basic CSCE principle. Once human rights, the rule of law, and democratic pluralism are made the subjects of international commitments, there is little left in terms of governmental institutions that is domestic."[9]

In this way the myth that the political system of a state is irrelevant for adequate protection of human rights has been definitively discarded.

b) The human dimension commitments of the CSCE are also particularly penetrating in the internal situations of states in another respect. This relates to the sensitive issue of the relationship between the principle of respect for human rights and the principle of non-intervention in the internal affairs of states. In the past this constituted one of the most debated topics in the human dimension area, as the socialist states adhered to a very broad interpretation of the non-intervention principle in order to curb outside interference with the human rights position in their countries. This situation has changed fundamentally. In the most explicit terms, the CSCE states

---

[9] Idem.

agreed upon a 'banning' of the non-intervention principle in the framework of the human dimension.[10]

The general conclusion which may be drawn from this and other related statements in CSCE documents is that the non-intervention principle has lost its practical significance in the field of the human dimension of the CSCE process to a high extent.[11]

2.2.2 Political nature

Another distinctive feature of the CSCE human dimension commitments is their *political character*. As is well-known, the CSCE does not create legally binding norms and principles. CSCE documents are 'only' politically binding documents and CSCE commitments as such are not legally, but 'only' politically binding commitments. The difference should not be exaggerated, as the binding force of CSCE commitments is not seriously doubted. The Dutch lawyer Pieter van Dijk has correctly observed: "A commitment does not have to be legally binding in order to have binding force; the distinction between legal and non-legal binding force resides in the legal consequences attached to the binding force", not in the binding force as such.[12] Violation of politically, but not legally binding agree-

---

[10]The preamble of the Document of the Moscow Meeting of the Conference on the Human Dimension of the CSCE of October 1991 may serve as an example:

> "The participating States [of the CSCE] emphasize that issues relating to human rights, fundamental freedoms, democracy and the rule of law are of international concern, as respect for these rights and freedoms constitutes one of the foundations of the international order. They categorically and irrevocably declare that the commitments undertaken in the field of the human dimension of the CSCE are matters of direct and legitimate concern to all participating States and do not belong exclusively to the internal affairs of the State concerned".

[11]For a further discussion of this issue, see the present author's "The CSCE Human Dimension Commitments: Present and Prospects", in E. Decaux et al., eds., *La Dimension Humaine de la Conférence sur la sécurité et la coopération en Europe (CSCE)* (Paris, Actes du Centre de Droit International de Nanterre No. 8, 1993) (forthcoming).

[12]P. van Dijk, "The Final Act of Helsinki - Basis for a Pan-European System?", *Netherlands Yearbook of International Law* (1980) p. 110.

ments is as unacceptable as any violation of norms of international law. In this respect there is no difference between politically and legally binding rules.

This does not detract from the relevance of the fact that the human dimension commitments operate in an atmosphere which is different from the legal environment in which the 'traditional' human rights instruments function. This has its advantages and disadvantages. One of the major advantages of the political character of the human dimension commitments is its flexibility and dynamism in comparison to the more rigid nature of legal obligations. This is true both as far as the creation and as far as the application, interpretation, amendment or suspension of the rules are concerned. Due to its strictly political character the CSCE process is very suitable for finding quick solutions to new problems. One of the disadvantages of the political character of the human dimension commitments is that they are less stable and sometimes less specific than legally binding norms. Another disadvantage is related to the way in which CSCE negotiations are conducted. These negotiations often take place in a certain political climate which heavily influences the final outcome, the more so since the negotiations often have to be concluded in a very short time. That the CSCE documents are therefore not sometimes examples of (linguistic) beauty is a consequence of this procedure. This may have its negative effects, in particular if CSCE commitments deviate from the corresponding legal obligations which have been laid down in other international instruments.

2.2.3 Additional value of CSCE commitments

Finally, I want to draw attention to the *complementary value* of the CSCE norms in the field of the human dimension. First, it has to be realized that the (strictly political) sphere of operation of these norms within the CSCE context is different from the (legal) sphere of the corresponding legal norms. In a way one could say that these spheres do not overlap, but that they rather complement each other. This is reflected, in particular, in the supervisory procedures: within the CSCE an increasingly sophisticated system of supervision has been created which partly functions quite differently in comparison to the procedures which have been established in the context of 'traditional' legal instruments. The operation of CSCE procedures is characterized in particular by its great flexibility. Of course, it has to be observed that 'flexibility' is not synonymous with 'effectiveness'.[13]

Secondly, one has to bear in mind that the norms and principles as agreed upon in the CSCE framework are often characterized by their quite detailed character. In comparison to the corresponding rules in traditional legal instruments, CSCE rules are often not only much more detailed, but also often constitute a 'progressive development'.[14] The CSCE regime for emergency situations and that for the protection of national minorities are examples of this.

3. FUNCTIONING OF THE MONITORING MECHANISMS AND PROCEDURES

3.1 Introduction

Over the years a number of monitoring procedures (usually called "mechanisms") have been developed in the framework of the CSCE, some of which are exclusively aimed at the human dimension. In this study I focus on the human dimension mechanisms and leave aside the more general CSCE mechanisms which have been developed for other areas, although one has to bear in mind that these mechanisms may be of relevance for the protection of human rights as well.[15] Until the end of the 1980s, the monitoring of human dimension

---

[13]See, e.g., P. van Dijk, 'The Relation between the ECHR and the Human Dimension of the CSCE', in: *Helsinki Monitor*, 1991, No. 4, pp. 5-14.

[14]See, e.g., A. Heraclides, "Helsinki-II and the Human Dimension: Normative Commitments, the End of an Era?", *Helsinki Monitor*, Special Issue on Helsinki-II (1992) No. 4, pp. 65-76 at p. 66.

[15]These mechanisms are in particular the Berlin emergency mechanism (established in June 1991), the Vienna mechanism for unusual military activities (established in November 1990), the Valletta procedure for the peaceful settlement of disputes (January 1991 as amended in October/December 1992) and the related new Convention on Conciliation and Arbitration in the CSCE, and the High Commissioner on National Minorities (HCNM). The procedures for the peaceful settlement of disputes and the HCNM are dealt with briefly below.

commitments took place only at the periodic follow-up meetings and specialized conferences of the CSCE and in a rather unstructured way. In addition, issues could be raised at a bilateral inter-governmental level. Only in 1989 was this situation considerably improved by the introduction of the so-called Vienna mechanism, which in 1991 was further elaborated by and complemented with the Moscow mechanism. In 1992 the High Commissioner on National Minorities was established, although this instrument is not primarily aimed at the protection of the rights of (persons belonging to) national minorities (see *infra* 3.5).

3.2 Supervision at political CSCE meetings

In the Helsinki 1992 Document "*Challenges of Change*"[16] a new institutional structure for the human dimension of the CSCE has been established. The Conference on the Human Dimension (CHD) of the CSCE - which convened three times between 1989 and 1991 (in Paris in 1989, in Copenhagen in 1990 and in Moscow in 1991) and which resulted in an impressive set of new commitments (both substantive and procedural) in the field of the human dimension - was succeeded by regular Human Dimension Seminars on specific subjects and by biennial implementation meetings. The latter meetings will take place in the years between the biennial review conferences.[17]

The importance of monitoring the implementation of CSCE commitments was clearly emphasized in the Helsinki Document. The Helsinki Decisions determine that this task has to be fulfilled at "review conferences as well as at special meetings convened for this purpose at the ODIHR[18] and the CPC[19] ...".[20] The powers of

---

[16]Text in: *Helsinki Monitor*, 1992, No. 3, pp. 59-99.

[17]Since the adoption of the Helsinki 1992 Document in July 1992, the term 'review conference' is the official term for the CSCE conferences which in the past were officially labelled "follow-up meetings". Although the term has been changed, the mandate for these meetings *grosso modo* remained the same.

[18]CSCE Office for Democratic Institutions and Human Rights

[19]Conflict Prevention Centre in Vienna.

these meetings - with the exception of the review conferences - are limited: they are only entitled to refer questions of particular concern to the attention of the Committee of Senior Officials (CSO).[21] Only the biennial review conferences have substantial powers, although the document which these conferences are supposed to 'prepare' has to be adopted by the CSCE summit meetings.

Now focusing on the monitoring of human dimension commitments it has to be observed that in this area the main task has apparently been assigned to the biennial review conferences and implementation meetings. The Human Dimension Seminars have not been explicitly assigned with a review function, although it may be assumed that issues of particular concern may and will be raised at these seminars. The first seminar on tolerance in November 1992 was only minimally devoted to implementation issues.[22]

The function of implementation meetings is twofold: a thorough exchange of views on the implementation of human dimension commitments and an evaluation of the procedures for monitoring compliance with these commitments.[23] If the implementation meeting deems it necessary, it "may draw to the attention of the CSO measures to improve implementation", but it is clearly stipulated that this will not be done by producing "a negotiated document".[24] Therefore, for the time being it remains unclear how the implementation meetings will address the CSO. An important element of the functioning of the implementation meetings is the considerable

---

[20]Para. I.27 of the Helsinki Decisions of the Helsinki 1992 Document.

[21]Para. I.30 of the Helsinki Decisions reads as follows:
"Review should offer the opportunity to identify action which may be required to address problems. Meetings at which reviews of implementation take place may draw to the attention of the CSO any suggestions for measures to improve implementation which they deem advisable".

[22]See A. Bloed, "The First Human Dimension Seminar: Tolerance", *Helsinki Monitor* (1993) No. 1, pp. 15-21 at pp. 18-19.

[23]Para. VI.9 of the Helsinki Decisions.

[24]Paras. VI.10 and 11 of the Helsinki Decisions.

involvement of non-governmental organizations (NGOs) in its activities.[25]

In addition, the main political CSCE organs (Council of Ministers for Foreign Affairs and the CSO) have a role to play, in particular concerning major violations of human dimension commitments. One example is the intensive Council and CSO involvement in the Yugoslav crisis, resulting in the suspension of rest-Yugoslavia (Serbia-Montenegro) from participation in the CSCE on the basis of the so-called consensus-minus-one principle. Besides, the highest political CSCE bodies are deeply involved in several (potential and actual) conflicts relating to minority issues. In this context reference may be made to, for instance, the situation in and around Nagorno-Karabakh, in Georgia (in particular Ossetia and Abkhazia), in Moldova (in particular the situation in Trans-Dniestria), and in the Baltic states concerning the position of minority groups (e.g., Russians, Poles).

If we now focus the discussion on the main features of the monitoring functions and activities of the different political CSCE bodies, the following observations may be made.

In the first place it may be stated that supervision of the implementation of CSCE commitments has become a firm part of CSCE activities. This supervisory task has been more clearly structured on the basis of the decisions laid down in the Helsinki-II document "*The Challenges of Change*".[26] It has to be noted, however, that the emphasis of the CSCE activities concerned is in the security area. Although this is understandable in view of the increasing number of violent conflicts in the CSCE area, it results in a relative

---

[25]See, e.g., R. Brett, "NGOs and the Human Dimension of the CSCE", *Bulletin of the Office for Democratic Institutions and Human Rights* (1992/93), No. 1, pp. 1-5; R. Brett, "Non-Governmental Organizations and the CSCE", *Helsinki Monitor* (1992) No. 3, pp. 19-24.

[26]See, in particular, paras. I.26-30 of the Helsinki Decisions for implementation reviews in general and chapter VI for the review of the implementation of human dimension commitments.

decline in the importance of the human dimension, including its supervisory mechanisms.[27]

In the second place it has to be observed that the supervisory tasks of the political CSCE bodies in the field of the human dimension are fulfilled almost exclusively at the intergovernmental level. The involvement of independent bodies is almost lacking. The only exceptions are the reports of (independent) missions of experts or rapporteurs under the Human Dimension Mechanism or the human dimension aspects of the reports of other missions.[28] Besides, reference has to be made to the increasing influence of NGOs on meetings on the human dimension of the CSCE. At the new human dimension seminars, representatives of NGOs have *de facto* even almost the same status as official delegates as far as the right to participate in the debates and to distribute materials is concerned.[29] However, the supervisory tasks of these seminars seem to be of a rather cosmetic nature. Practice will show whether the NGO involvement in the biennial implementation meetings will be as substantial as that at seminars. However, NGOs have no official standing at the meetings of the most important political CSCE bodies: the Council and the CSO.

In the third place it is observed that the powers of the political CSCE bodies are rather limited. Seminars and implementation meetings are not even entitled to adopt negotiated concluding documents. Implementation meetings are only entitled to "draw to the attention of the CSO measures to improve implementation". Real decision-making powers concerning measures resulting from the exercise of the monitoring functions by the CSCE are vested in the CSCE Summit, the Council of Ministers and the CSO. However, decision making in

---

[27]This shift in emphasis within the CSCE is clearly demonstrated by the course of the last CSCE Follow-up Meeting in Helsinki (March-July 1992). Even the establishment of a separate working group on the human dimension was disputed at this meeting; see further Heraclides, loc.cit. n. 14, pp. 65-76.

[28]Examples of such missions are the CSCE missions which have been sent to all new participating States since 1991 and the first rapporteur mission to Nagorny-Karabakh in February 1992.

[29]See Bloed, loc.cit. n. 21, pp. 16-18.

these bodies requires consensus which may (and does) seriously hamper its effectiveness. Only in cases of "clear, gross and uncorrected violations" of CSCE human dimension commitments, may the Council or the CSO take "political" decisions also without the consent of the state concerned (the so-called consensus-minus-one principle).[30] So far, the consensus-minus-one principle has been applied only once: the suspension of (Serbia-)Yugoslavia from participation in the CSCE because of its aggression in Bosnia-Herzegovina. In other cases (for instance, concerning the Nagorno-Karabakh conflict) efforts to apply this principle have failed for political reasons. In this context, it also has to be observed that CSCE bodies do not have the power to take sanctions in cases of violations of human dimension commitments, the only exception being cases which fall under the consensus-minus-one regime. In the latter cases, however, the Council and the CSO are entitled to take political steps only.

Although the Council and the CSO are entitled to decide on follow-up measures in cases of violations of CSCE human dimension commitments, it has to be observed that these bodies mainly deal with very serious violations, in particular the violent, ethnic-based conflicts in the CSCE area. The Council and CSO agendas are so overloaded that these bodies have hardly any time left to deal with human rights violations of a less serious nature. All in all it has to be observed that the powers of the political CSCE bodies in relation to supervision of the implementation of human dimension commitments remain limited in theory and in practice. Practice will show whether the role of the implementation meetings[31] will be any different from this general picture.

[30]Para. 16 of the Prague Document on Further Development of CSCE Institutions and Structures, adopted at the Prague Meeting of the CSCE Council in January 1992; text in: *Helsinki Monitor* (1992) No. 2, pp. 71-77.

[31]The first implementation meeting will take place in September-October 1993. It will last for three weeks.

3.3 The Human Dimension Mechanism

3.3.1 Introduction

The CSCE Human Dimension Mechanism constitutes one of the major achievements in the area of supervision of CSCE human dimension commitments. Its basis was established during the third CSCE Follow-up Meeting in Vienna (1986-1989). In its Concluding Document (of 15 January 1989) a number of procedures are set out which may be used by all participating states in cases of alleged violations of human dimension commitments.[32] These procedures have become known as the *Vienna mechanism*.[33] The Vienna mechanism has been further elaborated and complemented several times. The most drastic further development in this area took place at the Moscow Meeting of the CHD. In addition, the Moscow Document (3 October 1991) also set out a new mechanism which is often referred to as the *Moscow mechanism*. Therefore, the present CSCE Human Dimension Mechanism consists of two pillars: the Vienna mechanism and the Moscow mechanism which are partly firmly connected.

3.3.2 The Vienna mechanism

The *Vienna mechanism* consists of four phases or, in other words, four different procedures. Its basis has been laid down in the Vienna Concluding Document. It has been further elaborated, in particular, at the meetings of the Conference on the Human Dimension in Copenhagen (1990) and Moscow (1991) and at the Helsinki Follow-

---

[32] See the chapter "Human Dimension of the CSCE" in the Vienna Concluding Document; published in: Bloed, op.cit. n. 6, p. 213. The Vienna Document does not refer explicitly to alleged violations of CSCE commitments; it speaks in more general terms about "questions relating to the human dimension of the CSCE", although it may be derived from the context that the drafters had alleged violations in mind. This is confirmed in practice.

[33] The term 'mechanism' is the usual diplomatic jargon, although the term itself is not used in the Vienna Concluding Document (January 1989). In the Report of the Copenhagen Meeting of the Conference on the Human Dimension of the CSCE (CHD) of June 1990, the term 'mechanism' was also officially used.

up Meeting (1992). At present the mechanism consists of the following elements:[34]

(1) To exchange information and to provide in as short a time as possible but no later than ten days, a written response to requests for information and to representations made to CSCE states by other participating states on questions relating to the human dimension of the CSCE. Usually, such communications are forwarded through diplomatic channels.

(2) To hold bilateral meetings with other participating states that so request, in order to examine questions relating to the human dimension of the CSCE, including situations and specific cases, with a view to resolving them. The date and place of such meetings will be arranged as soon as possible by mutual agreement through diplomatic channels, as a rule within one week of the date of the request. In the course of a bilateral meeting, the CSCE states shall refrain from raising situations and cases not connected with the subject of the meeting, unless both sides have agreed to do so. The ODIHR can serve as a venue for such bilateral meetings.

(3) Any participating state which deems it necessary may bring situations and cases in the human dimension of the CSCE, including those which have been raised at the bilateral meetings described in paragraph 2, to the attention of other participating states through diplomatic channels or through the ODIHR.

(4) Any participating state which deems it necessary may provide information on the exchanges of information and the responses to its requests for information and to representations (para. 1) and

---

[34]See the chapter on the Human Dimension of the CSCE in the Vienna Concluding Document, paras. 42.1 and 42.2 of the Copenhagen Report, para. 2 of the Moscow Document, and paras. VI.5 and 7 of the Helsinki Decisions. Text of the Copenhagen Report in : A. Bloed and P. van Dijk, eds., *The Human Dimension of the Helsinki Process; The Vienna Follow-up Meeting and its Aftermath* (Dordrecht/Boston/London 1991) pp. 243-268. Text of the Moscow Document in: *Helsinki Monitor* (1991) No. 4, pp. 66-83. Text of the Helsinki 1992 Document in: *Helsinki Monitor* (1992) No. 3, pp. 59-99.

on the results of the bilateral meetings (para. 2), including information concerning situations and specific cases, at CSCE meetings, in particular at meetings of the CSO, the biennial review conferences and at the biennial implementation meetings.

This mechanism - which resembles a system of inter-state complaint procedures - signified a major step forward in the area of CSCE supervision as it created a system of supervision which can function permanently, whenever any of the participating states thinks that there is reason for putting it into operation. Moreover, the mechanism is of a non-voluntary character.[35] When faced with requests for information from any of the CSCE states within the framework of the mechanism, the state concerned is under an obligation to provide an answer. It must also comply with a subsequent request to hold a bilateral meeting.

A major shortcoming of the Vienna mechanism was the lack of an independent element: the mechanism functioned at a strictly intergovernmental level. This shortcoming was 'repaired' at the Moscow CHD meeting (see *infra* 3.3.3). Another disadvantage is the lack of any sanctions in cases of proven violations of human dimension commitments.[36] The last phase consists of raising issues at CSCE meetings, but as decision making at these meetings requires consensus no actions against the will of the state(s) concerned are possible. The effectiveness of the Vienna mechanism was (and to a great extent still is) based on political pressure: the public application

[35]This follows from the words "The participating States ... have ... decided". However, since the Final Act of Helsinki is of a non-legally binding character, this also holds true for the concluding documents of subsequent meetings; the decision here under discussion therefore does not create legal, but only political obligations.

[36]Since January 1992 the consensus-minus-one principle may be used to introduce 'political' sanctions in cases of very serious violations (see *supra*). In cases of violations which are not covered by this regime - and *de facto* this concerns the great majority of cases of violations which are raised within the CSCE - the lack of possible sanctions remains to be felt.

of the mechanism hopefully leads to positive changes of behaviour by the state which is approached under it.[37]

3.3.3 Moscow Mechanism: missions of experts/rapporteurs

At the Moscow CHD meeting (September-October 1991) the Vienna mechanism was supplemented by a system of missions of independent experts or rapporteurs in the field of the human dimension of the CSCE. This system - often referred to as the *Moscow mechanism* - is rather complicated. It encompasses five separate procedures which may be used independently from one another to set up missions of rapporteurs or experts. Two of these procedures are linked to the Vienna mechanism: a) after the first or second phase of the Vienna mechanism, the initiating state may suggest that the other state should invite a mission of experts; b) if the other state refuses to do so, the requesting state may also initiate the establishment of a mission of rapporteurs against the will of the other state, if it receives the support of five other CSCE states.[38] In this way the possibility of an independent investigation into violations of human dimension commitments was created within the functioning of the Vienna mechanism. This implies a breakthrough in comparison to the previous strictly intergovernmental character of the mechanism.

Furthermore, the Moscow mechanism encompasses three other procedures which may be used to establish missions. These procedures, which are not linked to the application of the Vienna mechanism, are: a) the voluntary invitation of a mission of experts by a CSCE state; b) the decision by the CSO to establish a mission of experts or rapporteurs; c) the establishment of an 'emergency' mission of rapporteurs in cases of a "particularly serious threat" to the

---

[37]For an extensive discussion of the Vienna mechanism, see A. Bloed and P. van Dijk, "Supervisory Mechanism for the Human Dimension of the CSCE: Its Setting-up in Vienna, Its Present Functioning and Its Possible Development Towards a General Procedure for the Peaceful Settlement of CSCE Disputes", in Bloed and Van Dijk, op.cit. n. 33, pp. 74-108.

[38]Paras. 8 and 9 of the Moscow Document.

fulfilment of human dimension provisions.[39] These missions have to be composed of independent experts which are selected from a list which comprises the names of up to three experts appointed by each CSCE state.

The Moscow mechanism constitutes major progress. The system of human dimension missions of independent experts or rapporteurs is a first major deviation from the hitherto strictly intergovernmental supervisory procedures.

The powers of these missions may vary according to the procedure which gave birth to these missions. In general it may be noted that the powers of missions of experts go beyond those of missions of rapporteurs.[40] The powers of missions of rapporteurs are mainly related to fact-finding and the rendering of advice or proposals for the solution of the questions raised.[41] Missions of experts have a broader mandate: their mandate aims to facilitate "resolution of a particular question or problem relating to the human dimension of the CSCE". For that purpose they may gather information "and, as appropriate, use its good offices and mediation services to promote dialogue and co-operation among interested parties". The exact terms of reference for each mission of experts have to be settled on an *ad hoc* basis.[42] Only the CSO is entitled to decide on any follow-up action, but in these cases the consensus principle is applicable (with the consensus-minus-one principle as the only, largely theoretical exception). All this means that the Moscow mechanism has not made the application of sanctions more likely in the CSCE framework. However, the application of the possibility to establish "emergency missions" in cases of "particularly serious threats" to the implementation of CSCE commitments would in itself contain elements of sanctions, as the establishment of such a mission would

---

[39]Paras. 4, 12 and 13 of the Moscow Document.

[40]Missions of experts are established in cases where the receiving CSCE state invites such missions. Missions of rapporteurs are established when the receiving state refuses to invite a mission. The CSO may establish both types of missions.

[41]Para. 11 of the Moscow Document.

[42]Para. 5 of the Moscow Document.

certainly be interpreted in the international arena as *prima facie* proof of very grave behaviour on the part of the state concerned.

The Moscow mechanism contains very penetrating, even 'intrusive' elements. The fact that missions of rapporteurs may be sent with the support of (a total of) six CSCE states after the application of the first or second phase of the Vienna mechanism, also against the will of the state concerned, is already a procedure which may be seen as quite penetrating. The possibility of "emergency missions", however, contains a still more intrusive character, as in this case even the phase of prior consultation with the state concerned may be skipped, which is highly unusual in international relations.[43]

For the sake of completeness it must also be observed that the political character of the functioning of CSCE mechanisms has not so far been changed. This makes the functioning of CSCE missions highly flexible.

A final remark concerns the confidentiality of the reports which are created under the Moscow mechanism. Due to this confidentiality - which is only lifted when the report of the mission and the comments of the state(s) concerned are brought to the attention of or discussed by the CSO[44] - the co-ordination of the activities of these CSCE missions with the activities undertaken by other international institutions may be hampered, in any case during the period of confidentiality which may last a few months.

---

[43]This fact has resulted in criticism of the Moscow mechanism in scholarly writings. See, e.g., the present author's 'Moscow Meeting of the Conference on the Human Dimension of the CSCE: A Critical Analysis', *Helsinki Monitor* (1992) No. 1, pp. 4-16 at p. 14.

[44]See paras. 7 and 11 of the Moscow Document. The only examples so far (March 1993) are the reports on Estonia and Croatia. The report on Croatia was made public in the autumn of 1992. In February 1993 the CSO decided at its 19th meeting to make the report on Estonia public. See *infra* in the present study.

3.4 *Ad hoc* Missions

During the course of the recent period the CSCE process has created a considerable number of *ad hoc* missions outside the framework of the Moscow mechanism. Most of these *ad hoc* missions were sent to states which applied for participating state status. The first mission of this type was sent to Albania in 1991, aiming at a thorough investigation of the fulfilment of CSCE commitments by Albania. In 1992, in particular, a great number of these missions were established as a result of the drastic increase in the number of CSCE states after the dissolution of the Soviet Union and Yugoslavia. Such missions were recently sent to the Czech Republic and the Slovak Republic (March 1993), after the dissolution of Czechoslovakia. Although these missions covered all three baskets of the CSCE, particular attention was given to the human dimension.[45]

In January 1992 the CSCE also decided to establish a special mission of rapporteurs which was sent to Nagorno-Karabakh, mainly with a fact-finding task. Although the main focus was on the security dimension of the conflict, the human dimension was covered as well. Similar missions were also established at later stages, although only now and again (e.g., in the case of the conflicts in Georgia).

An *ad hoc* mission of rapporteurs whose main task was in the field of the human dimension was the so-called Thomson mission to Yugoslavia. The mission, headed by Ambassador Sir John Thomson, was established by the CSO in August 1992. It was asked "to investigate allegations of human rights abuses" in the former Yugoslavia. The CSO decided that "its primary tasks should be, in close co-ordination with the International Committee of the Red Cross and the United Nations Commission on Human Rights, to ensure that all alleged places of detention are inspected within the shortest possible time".[46]

---

[45]A very useful survey of all CSCE missions, including their composition, may be found in: *CSCE Missions, A Summary Prepared by the Staff of Commission on Security and Cooperation in Europe, 1 September 1992.*

[46]15-CSO/Journal No. 2, Annex 1 (14 August 1992).

Another new phenomenon in the CSCE framework was the establishment of so-called long-term missions in trouble areas. Such missions (which are stationed for a period of at least six months in the area concerned) were established, in particular, in the former Yugoslavia: in Kosovo, Vojvodina and Sanjak. Moreover, such missions were stationed in the neighbouring countries of the former Yugoslavia: in Albania, Bulgaria, Romania and Hungary. Outside the context of the Yugoslav conflict, such long-term missions were also sent to Georgia (to monitor a cease-fire in Ossetia), Moldova and Estonia. All of these missions have mainly a security function, although the link with the human dimension is very strong.[47] In Estonia, in particular, this connection is very obvious, as the mission is charged with promoting stability, dialogue and understanding between the communities in Estonia, which means in particular dialogue and understanding between the Estonian authorities and the Russian minority.

Another recent type of CSCE mission is the so-called sanctions assistance missions (SAMs) which are located in countries neighbouring the former Yugoslavia.[48] Their aim is to assist the neighbouring states in implementing the UN-imposed sanctions on Yugoslavia. Some of these states appeared to have considerable difficulty in implementing the UN embargoes. As these missions have hardly any relationship to the CSCE human dimension, I will not deal with them further.

---

[47] The mandate for the long-term mission to Moldova, for instance, specifically refers to the 'observance of international obligations and commitments regarding human and minority rights'; Annex 3 of Journal 3 of the 19th CSO Meeting (4 February 1993), published in: *Helsinki Monitor* (1993) No. 1, p. 93.

[48] Sanctions assistance missions have been established in co-ordination with the European Community (EC) at the request of the London Conference on Yugoslavia. The first EC/CSCE SAMs were established in Bulgaria, Romania and Hungary followed by a mission in Macedonia. See the 'Decision on sanctions monitoring', adopted by the CSO at its 16th meeting of 16-18 September 1992, 16 *CSO/Journal* No. 3, Annex 1 (published in: *Helsinki Monitor* (1992) No. 4, p. 95).

3.5 The High Commissioner on National Minorities

In July 1992 the Helsinki Summit decided on the establishment of a CSCE High Commissioner on National Minorities (HCNM). His mandate is laid down in the Helsinki 1992 Document "*The Challenges of Change*". In December 1992 the former Foreign Minister of the Netherlands, Mr. Max van der Stoel, was appointed as the first High Commissioner. Although the activities of the HCNM have a strong link with the human dimension of the CSCE, it has to be observed that the HCNM has been designed as a 'security instrument'. This determines both his mandate and his functioning to a high extent. His mandate, as described in the Helsinki Document, is to:

> "provide 'early warning' and, as appropriate, 'early action' at the earliest possible stage in regard to tensions involving national minority issues which have not yet developed beyond an early warning stage, but ... have the potential to develop into a conflict within the CSCE area, affecting peace, stability or relations between participating States, requiring the attention of and action by the Council or the CSO".[49]

In other words: the CSCE has conceived the HCNM as an instrument of strictly preventive diplomacy. This is clearly reflected in the functions of the HCNM: he is charged not with the promotion and protection of the rights of national minorities,[50] but with "early warning" and, if needed, "early action".[51] The major task of the High Commissioner is to function as an independent and impartial instrument for the early investigation and resolution of ethnic tensions

---

[49]Para. II.3 of the Helsinki Decisions.

[50]This is clearly reflected, *inter alia*, in para. II.5(c) of the Helsinki Decisions, in which it is clearly stipulated that the High Commissioner is not allowed to "consider violations of CSCE commitments with regard to an individual person belonging to a national minority". In this way the CSCE aimed at excluding the possibility that the High Commissioner would become an "ombudsman" for national minorities.

[51]For an analysis of the mandate of the High Commissioner, reference may be made to: K.J. Huber, 'Preventing Ethnic Conflict in the New Europe: The CSCE High Commissioner on National Minorities', in: *Minority Rights and Responsibilities: Challenges in the New Europe* (forthcoming, to be published by the Institute on East-West Studies, New York 1993).

through quiet and flexible means.[52] The emphasis in the activities of the High Commissioner must be in a preliminary phase of tensions, aimed at de-escalation and resolution of (potential) conflicts through a process of dialogue, confidence building and co-operation between the parties concerned.

One of the consequences of the mandate of the HCNM, as laid down in the Helsinki Document, is the fact that national minorities in the CSCE area are, to a certain extent, dealt with unequally. Only in cases of tensions which have the potential to develop into a (violent) conflict, is the HCNM entitled to pay attention to violations of the rights of national minorities. Although the concept of "tensions" in the terms of the Helsinki Document certainly allows for flexible interpretation, it goes without saying that cases of evidently manifest violations of minority rights which clearly do not involve "tensions" in CSCE terms are outside the scope of the HCNM's mandate.[53]

Another 'inequality' in the treatment of national minorities by the HCNM might ensue from the 'escape clause' in his mandate: the High Commissioner is not entitled to "consider national minority issues in situations involving organized acts of terrorism".[54] Although this was the compromise achieved at the Helsinki Follow-up Meeting in order to overcome the serious reservations of certain CSCE states (such as Turkey, Spain, and the United Kingdom) against the establishment of the High Commissioner,[55] it may lead to an unwarranted limitation of the HCNM's room to manoeuvre. On the other hand, practice must indicate whether this 'terrorism clause' will

---

[52]Huber, ibid.

[53]A (theoretical) example could be possible violations of the rights of indigenous peoples of North America. Even if such violations would result in "tensions", it might well be that such "tensions" are not tensions which "have the potential to develop into a conflict within the CSCE area, affecting peace, stability or relations between participating States, requiring the attention" of the CSCE, as laid down in the HCNM's mandate.

[54]Para. II.5(b) of the Helsinki Decisions. Moreover, in para. II.5(c) it is laid down that the HCNM may not consider violations of CSCE commitments with regard to an individual person belonging to a national minority.

[55]See, e.g., the present author's review of the Helsinki-II meeting in: *Helsinki Monitor* (1992) No. 3, pp. 37-50 at pp. 47-48.

indeed be an obstacle for the proper functioning of the High Commissioner. If a CSCE state were to refuse to receive the High Commissioner on the basis of the allegedly terrorist character of the acts of the national minority concerned, it would undoubtedly result in negative publicity. It is not to be excluded that states would consider it more proper to receive a HCNM mission with all the possibilities to influence the HCNM's opinion than to refuse such a visit with all its negative consequences in world public opinion.

An important element of the powers of the HCNM is his right to "collect and receive information regarding the situation of national minorities and the role of parties involved therein from any source, including the media and non-governmental organizations".[56] Moreover, the High Commissioner may receive "specific reports" from "parties directly involved", both governmental and non-governmental.[57] In this respect it must be observed that NGOs and individuals are not dependent upon specific requests from the High Commissioner; they are entitled to send any information on their own initiative. This individual "right of communication and information", however, has been subject to a serious limitation: "The High Commissioner will not communicate with and will not acknowledge communications from any person or organization which practices or publicly condones terrorism or violence".[58] Here again it has to be observed that this was the price for the consent of some CSCE states to the establishment of the High Commissioner. Although one may object to this provision as a matter of principle, practice should reveal whether the clause might indeed hamper the functioning of the High Commissioner.

The creation of the right of communication for individuals and non-governmental organizations which is an indispensable element of the functioning of the High Commissioner has been a remarkable development within the CSCE process: for the first time in the CSCE the individual has been granted a direct 'right' in relation to CSCE

---

[56]See para. II.23(a) of the Helsinki Decisions.

[57]Paras. II.23(b), 24 and 26 of the Helsinki Decisions.

[58]Idem, para. II.25.

bodies.[59] However, this 'right' has only a limited scope, as the right of communication is not connected with a right to receive a reply or decision on the issue concerned. It is hard to evaluate the effectiveness of this right of communication so far, due to the limited time which has passed since the High Commissioner took office. A first impression points to a considerable use of this instrument by non-governmental groups connected with national minority issues.

3.6 Peaceful settlement of disputes

Although the issue of peaceful settlement of disputes has been on the agenda of the CSCE since its very inception, the results of the various rounds of negotiations on the establishment of new procedures have, until recently, been disappointing.[60] Only after the Cold War could substantive progress be achieved. At a meeting of experts at Valletta (Malta) in January and February 1991, the CSCE states succeeded in adopting a CSCE procedure for the settlement of disputes, which became known as the so-called *Valletta mechanism*. It provides for political instruments for the settlement of certain disputes between CSCE states. It has to be observed, however, that the Valletta mechanism is subject to a number of major weaknesses which account for its inoperativeness so far. The major weakness is the fact that a number of possible disputes are exempted from its application: disputes which raise "issues concerning its territorial integrity, or national defence, title to sovereignty over land territory, or competing claims with regard to the jurisdiction over other areas".[61] Any

---

[59]The only comparable situation may be found in the Moscow rapporteur system which provides for a right of missions of experts "to meet freely with officials, non-governmental organizations and any group or person from whom it [the mission of experts; A.B.] wishes to receive information. The mission may also receive information in confidence from any individual, group or organization on questions it is addressing" (para. 6 of the Moscow Document).

[60]See, e.g., A. Bloed, "A European System of Peaceful Settlement of Disputes?", 18 *Polish Yearbook of International Law* (1989-1990) pp. 113-127; G. Tanja, 'Peaceful Settlement of Disputes within the CSCE: Bridge over Troubled Water', *Helsinki Monitor* (1993) No. 1, pp. 22-33.

[61]Section XII of the Provisions for a CSCE Procedure for Peaceful Settlement of Disputes. The text was published in: *Helsinki Monitor* (1991) No. 2, pp. 27-33.

disagreement concerning the question whether a certain dispute touches upon such issues is decided by the relevant CSCE state itself. So far, the Valletta mechanism has not been used by any CSCE state.

At the end of 1992 further progress was achieved. In October a meeting of experts in Geneva achieved consensus about a package of measures. These measures contained a strengthening of the Valletta mechanism, *inter alia*, by adding a procedure for 'directed conciliation',[62] and, on the other hand, a Convention on Conciliation and Arbitration in the CSCE. The texts were formally adopted by the CSCE Council of Ministers at its Stockholm meeting in December 1992.[63] It is hard to predict whether these new procedures will have any impact upon the implementation of human dimension commitments. On the one hand, doubts exist whether these new procedures will be effective at all: the Valletta mechanism has never been used so far, and one can hardly expect a more positive approach on the part of the CSCE states towards the mechanism after its further elaboration at the Stockholm meeting; the use of the Convention seems unlikely in view of the fact that other legal instruments for the peaceful settlement of disputes[64] are also not used. On the other hand, one may also raise the question whether these procedures will be used for human dimension issues, in particular in view of the fact that for that area other CSCE mechanisms have been specifically designed (see the above-mentioned mechanisms). If the new procedures, as decided upon at the Stockholm meeting of the Council of Ministers, will indeed be used in the future, one may assume that they will be applied to (try to) settle serious political disputes. In the field of the human dimension one may theoretically assume that national

---

[62]'Directed conciliation' provides for the possibility that the Council of Ministers or the CSO may "direct any two participating states to seek conciliation to assist them in resolving a dispute". Decisions may be taken, if necessary, without the consent of the two parties to the dispute concerned (the so-called consensus-minus-two rule). See Art. 1 of the Provisions for Directed Conciliation; text in: *Helsinki Monitor* (1993) No. 1, p. 77.

[63]The texts of these documents were published in: *Helsinki Monitor* (1993) No. 1, pp. 62-77. The Council decided to open the Convention for signature. During the Stockholm meeting 29 CSCE states signed the Convention which will enter into force after ratification by twelve parties.

[64]Such as the 1957 European Convention for the Peaceful Settlement of Disputes.

minority issues might be a topic for 'peaceful settlement' by way of the newly developed CSCE procedures.

3.7 Practice

3.7.1 Introduction

An important question is, of course, the effectiveness of the monitoring procedures and mechanisms which have been developed within the CSCE. In general it has to be observed that most procedures have only been developed in the post-Cold War period. Due to the short time which has elapsed since their establishment, their effectiveness is hard to assess. In this section, a few remarks will be made concerning the practical application of the procedures and mechanisms which have been specifically established for monitoring and supervising CSCE commitments in the field of the human dimension. Corresponding questions concerning the practice of political CSCE bodies have already been dealt with above.[65]

3.7.2 The Vienna mechanism

The 'oldest' supervisory procedure is the *Vienna mechanism* which was established in January 1989 in the era of *glasnost* and *perestroika*. It was applied immediately after its establishment[66] and on a great number of occasions thereafter. Although official records concerning its application do not exist, the Vienna mechanism was applied approximately 110 times during the first two years of its existence.[67]

---

[65] See *supra* 3.2 of the present study.

[66] It was first applied by the Netherlands in January 1989 which started the mechanism in relation to Czechoslovakia because of the arrest of the dissident writer Vaclav Havel. Havel and many others were arrested and prosecuted because of their participation in a public demonstration in commemoration of the death of Jan Palach in 1968. See on this case: F. Coomans and L. Lijnzaad, "Initiating the CSCE supervisory procedure: The cases of the Netherlands and Czechoslovakia", in: Bloed and Van Dijk, op.cit. n. 33, pp. 109-127.

[67] S. Lehne, *The CSCE in the 1990s; Common European House or Potemkin Village?* (Laxenburg 1991), p. 86; Bloed and Van Dijk, loc.cit. n. 36, pp. 79-80.

A striking feature of the application was its predominantly East-West character: the mechanism was used by Western countries in particular to raise violations of human rights and other human dimension commitments in East European states.[68] The number of cases in which East European states applied the mechanism in relation to Western states was considerably lower. The first instance of application of the mechanism within the Eastern bloc occurred in November 1989, when Hungary approached Romania to raise the issue of violations of the rights of the Hungarian minority in Romania.

After the collapse of communism in Eastern Europe the Vienna mechanism was resorted to much less frequently. It has been invoked only now and again to raise serious situations, such as the civil war in Yugoslavia or the bloody military actions by the Russians in Lithuania in 1991, aimed at suppressing the independence movement in the Baltics.[69]

So far, most Western countries have refused to invoke the Vienna mechanism in their relations with other Western states. This refusal was/is substantiated by reference to procedures within the framework of the Council of Europe - such as the complaint procedures under the European Convention on Human Rights and Fundamental Freedoms - which are considered to be better suited for raising human rights issues in relations with other member states of the Council of Europe. This reasoning has been contested, *inter alia*, on the grounds that the CSCE mechanisms and the Strasbourg procedures do not overlap, but are complementary in nature, each having its distinct value. The Western reasoning becomes still more peculiar when looking at the practice: proposals to apply the CSCE mechanisms to raise issues in, for instance, Turkey are rejected on the ground that the Council of Europe with its supervisory procedures which are based on legally binding instruments is much better equipped for such issues. At the same time, however, it has to be observed that the member states abstain from applying Council of

---

[68]See Bloed and Van Dijk, loc.cit. n. 36, pp. 79-80; Lehne, op.cit. n. 66, p. 86

[69]Lehne, op.cit. n. 66, p. 86.

Europe procedures.[70] This type of behaviour certainly does not contribute to a positive development of the CSCE human dimension order and its supervisory mechanisms: it only leads to a more and more painfully felt distinction between, on the one hand, 'civilized' CSCE participating states which are members of the Council of Europe[71] and which allegedly do not need the 'political' CSCE procedures for their mutual relations, and, on the other, the 'new democracies', in particular states such as the former Soviet republics and Albania. Such a distinction between 'first class' and 'second class' CSCE participating states could affect the legitimacy of the CSCE order and, in particular, its supervisory mechanisms.

Therefore, the fact that in March 1992 Austria raised the treatment of the Kurdish minority in Turkey under the Vienna mechanism constituted a major step forward.[72] It heralded a first application of the mechanism in inter-Western relations which might constitute a precedent for future use. However, the 'precedent' itself was not very convincing, as Austria decided not to continue the case after the first phase of the mechanism (exchange of information). Formally, Austria reserved its right to start the second phase of the mechanism when it feels it appropriate to do so,[73] but it is highly unlikely that this will happen.[74] Therefore, the Austrian-Turkish case may even be

---

[70]On the relationship between CSCE and Council of Europe procedures, reference may be made to the study by M. Scheinin and M. Pentikäinen in the present volume. See also Van Dijk, loc.cit. n. 13.

[71]With the exception of the USA and Canada which cannot join the Council of Europe because of their geographical situation.

[72]The Austrian *démarche* concerned the bloody military operations of the Turkish army against Kurds in the eastern part of Turkey during the celebration of the Kurdish New Year (21 March). As a kind of 'retaliatory' action, Turkey invoked the Vienna mechanism in order to raise the alleged Austrian support of 'terrorists' on its territory. Although Turkey did not specify the nationality of these 'terrorists', it apparently meant people of Kurdish origin. This case was also stopped after the first phase of the mechanism.

[73]Oral information from Austrian diplomats.

[74]After spring 1992 several instances of major violations of the rights of the Kurdish minority could have led to a continuation of the procedure, but Austria apparently decided not to do so. See the reports on Turkey of NGOs such as Amnesty International and Helsinki Watch.

construed as a precedent that the Vienna mechanism does *not* work in inter-Western relations.

3.7.3 The Moscow mechanism

The *Moscow mechanism* only entered into force in May 1992 after the registration of the names of 45 experts at the ODIHR in accordance with paragraph 3 of the Moscow Document. It explains the fact that to date the mechanism has been applied on only a few occasions. So far two missions of experts and one mission of rapporteurs have been established. At the invitation of the states concerned, the missions of experts visited Estonia and Moldova. A mission of rapporteurs visited Croatia and Bosnia-Herzegovina. In addition, some efforts have been undertaken to establish some other missions, but due to the refusal of the states concerned and the lack of support from other CSCE states these efforts have so far failed.

One of the first efforts to apply the Moscow mechanism took place in June 1992. In that month the Russian Federation asked Estonia to invite a mission of experts in order to investigate the Estonian legislation on citizenship.[75] This request was made after the application by Russia of the Vienna mechanism in this same case (exchange of information). In August 1992 Moscow made another effort to persuade Estonia to invite a mission of experts which would have had a mandate which slightly differed from the previous request, but again Estonia refused to comply with the Russian request. Russian efforts to get the support of other CSCE states for its action failed.[76] Thereupon, in the autumn of 1992 Estonia decided independently of any request from another CSCE state to invite a mission to study Estonian legislation in the areas of citizenship and language, especially regarding minority rights. The mission visited the Baltic state in December. In February 1993 the CSO decided on the

---

[75]This request was made through the ODIHR in accordance with para. 8 of the Moscow Document.

[76]In accordance with para. 9 of the Moscow Document, the Russian Federation needed the support of at least five other CSCE states to send a mission of rapporteurs to Estonia.

establishment of a six-month CSCE mission to Estonia with the objective begin "to promote stability, dialogue and understanding between the communities in Estonia".[77] Although there exists a connection between both missions, the decision on the long-term mission to Estonia had already been taken before the mission under the Moscow mechanism had reported to the CSO.

The mission of experts, invited by Moldova under the Moscow mechanism, aimed to investigate current legislation and implementation of minority rights and inter-ethnic relations. This mission visited Moldova from 31 January to 3 February 1993. The mission of rapporteurs to Croatia and Bosnia-Herzegovina was established upon the initiative of the United Kingdom on behalf of the European Community (EC) states with the support of the USA on the basis of paragraph 12 of the Moscow Document. This first "emergency" mission of the CSCE visited Croatia from 30 September to 5 October 1992.[78] At its 17th meeting in November 1992, the CSO decided to transmit the report of the mission to the UN and the Co-chairmen of the International Conference on the former Yugoslavia (Vance and Owen). Besides, the report was released after this CSO meeting.[79] At its Stockholm meeting in December 1992, the CSCE Council of Ministers authorized the mission of rapporteurs to refine its proposals on personal accountability, including by way of the establishment of an *ad hoc* war crimes tribunal.[80]

Due to the fact that the Moscow mechanism has so far been applied only a few times, it is difficult to assess its effectiveness. However, some observations may be made on the basis of this limited practice. A first observation relates to the membership of missions. This membership is limited to the experts who are registered in the list in which each CSCE state may appoint up to three experts and which is

---

[77]Annex 1 of Journal No. 2 of the 19th CSO meeting.

[78]Because of security reasons the mission did not visit Bosnia-Herzegovina at this time. At the time of writing (spring 1993), this latter visit is still pending.

[79]17-CSO/Journal No. 1 (5 November 1992).

[80]Para. 14 of chapter 1 of the Summary of Conclusions of the Stockholm Council Meeting; text in: *Helsinki Monitor* (1993) No. 1, p. 81.

kept at the ODIHR. The present list comprises persons of varying background, quality and capabilities. Although most of the appointed experts have academic or practical experience in the field of human rights, it has to be observed that the membership of missions of experts or rapporteurs has additional requirements. Missions are not only engaged in fact-finding, but may also become involved in negotiation and mediation processes which require quite distinct qualities. It must be observed that several experts on the CSCE roster apparently have no experience in this area. This might affect the success of future missions to a certain extent. An outstanding human rights academic, for instance, is not necessarily an outstanding negotiator or mediator in acute political problems. In contrast, a skilful diplomat is not necessarily the best candidate for solving human rights problems with predominantly legal implications. The limited practice of missions under the Moscow mechanism indicates that this observation appears to be correct. This is also true if the practice of *ad hoc* missions is taken into account as well.[81] This would lead to the suggestion that the formal requirements for membership of missions under the Moscow mechanism should be more flexible, so as to make possible the invitation of experts who are not on the ODIHR list in case this is considered necessary.[82]

A second observation concerns the preparation of missions. It seems that members of missions have hardly any time left for thorough preparation, partly due to the urgency of the missions and partly due to a lack of time because of their normal work. It goes without saying that this may have negative effects on the effectiveness of missions. This state of affairs may partly be improved by introducing special

---

[81]This observation concerning the membership of *ad hoc* missions is less pertinent in the context of this paragraph which deals with the Moscow mechanism for which strict formal requirements - i.e., registration on the ODIHR list - have been laid down. The membership of *ad hoc* missions is more flexible and in practice more or less dependent upon the will of CSCE states and of the CSCE Chairman-in-Office. However, the observation concerning the qualities of members of missions is equally valid for the latter type of missions.

[82]This flexibility also appears to be important in view of the fact that the High Commissioner on National Minorities may decide to request the assistance of experts in specific cases. According to para. II.35 of the Helsinki Decisions, the High Commissioner may only select experts from the ODIHR list.

training for all experts on the ODIHR list, for instance. In this way the experts may acquire the necessary skills for effective participation in future missions. Besides, thorough preparation concerning the specific issues at stake remains, of course, of paramount importance for the effectiveness of missions. Another element which is connected to the issue of preparation of missions is the fact that as a rule missions spend only a few days on on-site visits. During this limited time the mission must gather enough material to draw up its conclusions and/or recommendations. It is self-evident that in order to avoid superficiality the need for thorough preparation becomes ever more urgent.

A third observation relates to the confidentiality of the reports of the missions. The Moscow Document prescribes that the reports will remain confidential "until brought to the attention of the Senior Officials". This implies a certain delay in the release of reports of missions. So far, the complete reports on Croatia and Estonia have been published. The situation concerning the reports of *ad hoc* missions has not been formally regulated at all. In these circumstances the CSO or the Council of Ministers may take any decision according to its discretion. As an example reference may be made to the report of the Thomson Mission of the CSCE to Yugoslavia which was only partly made public: in September 1992 the CSO approved the public release of only the descriptive parts of the report.[83] In this way the desirable transparency of CSCE mission activities in the field of the human dimension is hampered. Normally CSCE mission reports remain confidential, at least for a certain time. The highly necessary *timely* co-ordination of CSCE mission activities with corresponding activities of other international institutions may be hampered in this way. This makes it unlikely that duplication or overlap of activities between different institutions may be avoided.

A fourth observation concerns the co-ordination of CSCE activities under the Moscow mechanism with other CSCE activities in the same area. The Moldova mission, for instance, was deeply involved in issues

---

[83] 16-CSO/Journal No. 3, Annex 1 (published in *Helsinki Monitor* (1992) No. 4, p. 93).

concerning national minorities, but the mission reportedly did not pursue a prior co-ordination of its work with the activities of the High Commissioner on National Minorities before the on-site visit. Although this may be understandable in the present transitionary stage of many CSCE bodies and also because of the different aim of the activities of the mission and the High Commissioner, a better co-ordination of activities is nevertheless urgently needed.[84]

A fifth observation is related to the follow-up of the missions. It is one thing to establish a mission and to draft a report with conclusions and/or recommendations, but equally important is the question of the follow-up: what effect is given to the results of the missions? The question of the follow-up of mission reports under the Moscow mechanism has been dealt with in the pertinent chapter of the Moscow Document of 1991. In paragraphs 7 and 11 it is stipulated that the reports of missions of experts or rapporteurs with the attached comments of the state(s) concerned[85] *may* be discussed by the CSO, which "may decide on any possible follow-up action". This implies that the CSO is not obliged to deal with the mission reports.

The practice of the reports of missions under the Moscow mechanism is so far too limited to draw any general conclusions. The report of the Estonian mission played a role in the CSO decision to establish a long-term mission in this Baltic state, although the decision had already been taken before the mission report was submitted to the

---

[84]Estonia may provide another example. After the mission under the Moscow mechanism in December 1992, the High Commissioner visited Estonia in January on the first mission since he took office. In February 1993 the CSO decided on the establishment of a long-term mission in Estonia. All these activities are related to the same subject: the status of, in particular, the Russian minority in Estonia. A clear co-ordination of all these activities is necessary, both for substantive and for financial reasons. The Estonian example is of a clearly transitionary nature, as the mission under the Moscow mechanism was established prior to the operationalization of the High Commissioner. In the case of the long-term mission in Estonia, a proper co-ordination with the High Commissioner has been agreed upon in the spring of 1993.

[85]In the case of missions of experts, invited by the state(s) concerned, these comments should include a description of any action which the state has taken or intends to take upon the observations of the mission (para. 7). In the case of missions of rapporteurs, the Moscow Document only refers to "observations on the report" which may be submitted by the states concerned (para. 11).

CSO.[86] The impact of the Moldova mission has to be awaited. It was clear, however, that the CSCE followed different tracks in the Moldova crisis as well: the activities of the Personal Representative[87] of the Chairman-in-Office of the CSCE led to the despatch of a long-term mission to Moldova; the mission under the Moscow mechanism was established independently from this first range of CSCE activities.

The "emergency" procedure under the Moscow mechanism which allows for the despatch of emergency missions to another CSCE state in case of allegations of "a particularly serious threat to the fulfilment of the provisions of the CSCE human dimension" has been applied only once so far. This first CSCE "emergency" mission was despatched to Croatia and Bosnia-Herzegovina in September-October 1992. The mission report contained a detailed description of atrocities, committed not only by Serbian forces, but also by Croatian authorities. In a balanced way the mission report contains proposals for the establishment of a system for storing information concerning the cruelties in the former Yugoslavia and for the creation of an international tribunal for prosecuting the perpetrators of war crimes. After the release of its well-received report in November 1992, the Stockholm Ministerial authorized the mission to refine its proposals on making the principle of personal accountability effective. This authorization has to be put in the context of the debate on the possible establishment of an international crimes tribunal for the prosecution of persons who commit(ted) international crimes in the Yugoslav conflict. At the time of writing this study, it is impossible to predict the impact of the proposals of the CSCE mission.

Since the entering into force of the Moscow mechanism in 1992, a few cases have been made public concerning refusals to apply (elements of) the mechanism. During the Helsinki Follow-up Meeting of the CSCE from March to July 1992, Austria requested Turkey to invite a mission under the Moscow mechanism. This procedure has been provided for in the Moscow Document: under certain

---

[86]The CSO already decided at its 18th meeting in December 1992 to establish a long-term mission in Estonia.

[87]The Director of the Stockholm International Peace Research Institute (SIPRI) and former Polish diplomat, Dr. Adam Rotfeld.

conditions, a CSCE state may take the initiative to enquire whether another CSCE state would agree to invite a mission.[88] In the case of Turkey, this was refused, among other things, because Austria had already invoked step one of the Vienna mechanism and because Turkey considered a mission of experts to be unnecessary as it supposedly only had problems with terrorism by Kurdish nationalists.[89] In January 1993, at the initiative of the USA, the CSCE Chairman-in-Office approached Uzbekistan with a request to invite an ODIHR mission of experts to investigate problems in the human rights field. Perhaps because of lack of concrete knowledge about the nature of the CSCE mechanisms, the Uzbek government refused to comply with this request on the grounds that this would imply an interference in the internal affairs of Uzbekistan. If Uzbekistan would have consented, it would have resulted in the establishment of a special *ad hoc* ODIHR mission.[90] So, from a formal point of view, the 'Uzbek case' is not related to the Moscow mechanism as such.

3.7.4 High Commissioner on National Minorities

Although the *CSCE High Commissioner on National Minorities* may not be considered to be a human dimension instrument, but must be viewed in terms of security, it is an undisputable fact that a close link exists. Therefore, a few remarks on the functioning of the High Commissioner in practice appears to be appropriate. So far, the High Commissioner has visited the Baltic states and Moscow (first mission in January 1993), Slovakia and Hungary (second mission in February 1993), and (again) Latvia, Estonia and Moscow (March/April 1993).

---

[88]Para. 8 of the Moscow Document.

[89]R. Brett, *The Challenges of Change. Report of the Helsinki Follow-up Meeting of the Conference on Security and Co-operation in Europe (CSCE) (24 March - 10 July 1992)* (Papers in the Theory and Practice of Human Rights, Number 2, University of Essex, 1992), p. 14.

[90]The real background to the unsuccessful effort directed towards Uzbekistan seems to have been the fact that it had been badly prepared by the USA, resulting in a 'surprise attack' on the Central Asian republic. At the time of writing (spring 1993), efforts are still being made to have a mission sent to Uzbekistan.

It is too early to draw any conclusions on the effectiveness of the High Commissioner's operations. It is clear, however, that the High Commissioner has to function within an institutional environment which has not (yet) adapted to independent posts such as that of the HCNM. The co-ordination of the activities of the High Commissioner with overlapping activities by other CSCE bodies and by other international organizations is an issue which requires much attention. In this context the relationship of the High Commissioner with the CSCE Chairman-in-Office (the "CSCE super-coordinator") and the new post of CSCE Secretary-General will require the most attention. Another important issue is the follow-up to the activities, undertaken by the High Commissioner. Finally, it is worth mentioning that the "strict confidentiality" of the activities and reports of the High Commissioner may make the desirable co-ordination with overlapping activities within and outside the CSCE somewhat problematic.

3.7.5 *Ad hoc* missions

Finally, a few remarks have to be made about the *ad hoc* missions of the CSCE.

An important question in relation to the establishment of CSCE missions in general is related to the results of these missions. It is one thing to establish a mission, but quite another to give effect to its recommendations. In this context a distinction can be made between the reports of *ad hoc* missions which were sent to the new participating states of the CSCE and the reports of missions to trouble areas. The country reports of the former type of missions had only a very limited follow-up. Only at the Helsinki Follow-up Meeting in 1992 was a special meeting of the working group on the human dimension convened to discuss these reports,[91] but its effect seemed to be unspectacular. Maybe this is connected to the substance of these reports which deal with a great variety of subjects which often do not call for specific follow-up actions at the CSCE level. Moreover, the nature of these reports varied considerably, apparently depending on

---

[91] Brett, op.cit. n. 88, pp. 14-15.

the qualifications and the knowledge of the members of the missions concerned.

As far as the follow-up is concerned, the *ad hoc* CSCE missions to trouble areas were more successful. If this was not a consequence of the quality of the reports themselves, the follow-up was certainly due to the serious nature of the conflicts at stake. The Yugoslav conflict, the civil war in Georgia, the violent conflict in and around Nagorno-Karabakh, and the bloody conflict in Moldova (Trans-Dniestria) may serve as examples. The fact that these missions did not result in any successful solutions to these conflicts was certainly not due to these missions alone, but more in particular to the lack of powers of the political CSCE bodies and the lack of political will of the parties to the conflicts concerned. The reports of the missions concerned were seriously discussed at meetings of, in particular, the CSO, resulting in a variety of decisions and recommendations.[92] However, the CSCE has no possibilities to enforce the implementation of these decisions. The impossibility of implementing the decision to organize a peace conference on the Nagorno-Karabakh conflict in the Belorussian capital Minsk is a sad example of this. It appears to be impossible even to start the conference due to a deadlock in the preparatory talks which are taking place in Rome.[93]

In the context of the present study the *ad hoc* Thomson mission to the former Yugoslavia deserves special attention, as it focused mainly on the human dimension aspects of the conflict. The mission appears to have played a significant role in the political debate concerning the Yugoslav crisis. Its report contained detailed descriptions of the

---

[92]The CSO decisions, based on the interim-report of the rapporteur mission to Nagorny-Karabakh of February 1992, may serve as an example. Subsequent to the recommendations of the mission, the CSO called upon the parties to impose a cease-fire and 'requested' a number of conservatory measures (such as an embargo on arms transfers and the establishment of 'humanitarian corridors'). In addition, the CSO suggested a number of procedural steps which the parties to the conflict might take to achieve a peaceful solution of the conflict; 7 *CSO/Journal* No. 2, Annex 1 (28 February 1992). See the pertinent decisions of the CSO, adopted at its 7th meeting in February 1992. The text of the interim-report was published in: *Helsinki Monitor* (1992) No. 2, pp. 50-64.

[93]Rome is the meeting place for the preparatory talks because of the Italian chairmanship of the envisaged peace conference.

atrocities, committed by all sides in the on-going civil war. However, its concrete impact upon the decision-making process within the CSCE and in other international institutions is hard to assess. The impression is that the frightening findings of the atrocities during the hostilities between the various camps in the former Yugoslavia had a distinct impact upon the decision-making process within the CSCE.

4. RECOMMENDATIONS/CONCLUSIONS

In the preceding paragraphs a number of conclusions have already been submitted and it does not make much sense to repeat them here. What follows are a few general observations which have relevance for the CSCE system of monitoring the human dimension commitments as a whole. These observations are related to, *inter alia*, the institutional aspects of the CSCE system, including co-ordination with other international bodies, the functioning of the system of missions of experts and rapporteurs, and a streamlining of the individual mechanisms which have been developed within the CSCE. A preliminary point has to be made, however, concerning the official CSCE jargon. It has to be observed that in the CSCE there is a tendency to use terms rather loosely and sometimes even to deviate from normal usage in international law practice. This is reflected in the fact that CSCE concepts as a rule are badly defined, if at all. The concept of the 'human dimension of the CSCE' itself is already an undefined concept. Besides, the rather loose CSCE wording may lead to confusion, in particular by those who are not familiar with the CSCE. An example is the term 'fact-finding' which in the CSCE has a slightly different meaning to that in international law. In the CSCE fact-finding may also encompass the giving of advice or recommendations sometimes, which is alien to the traditional concept of fact-finding. Another example is offered by the very term 'missions of experts': such missions may not only function as expert groups, but also be engaged in mediation, conciliation and other activities which are certainly not the normal tasks of expert groups at all. At the same time it should be observed that this rather loose wording allows for flexible interpretations, focused on the specific features of individual cases.

General [94]

1. The monitoring of human dimension commitments has been one of the main issues at meetings of political CSCE bodies since its inception. After the collapse of communism in the states of Central and Eastern Europe, however, security issues have become of paramount importance on the CSCE agenda. This has resulted in a relative decline in the significance of the human dimension, which is reflected in the fact that at present human dimension commitments are often considered in security terms. The recent establishment of the CSCE High Commissioner on National Minorities as a security instrument is a clear reflection of this changing emphasis.

   It has to be observed that the interlinkage between the three baskets of the CSCE has always been one of the basic features of the process. Therefore, a strong connection between security and human rights issues within the CSCE is not a new development. During the present period, however, the human dimension has certainly been losing ground to the security field. This development contains certain risks. The fact that the main political decision-making bodies of the CSCE are hardly involved in strictly human dimension issues may result in a further downplaying of these issues. This is further promoted by the fact that the newly created CSCE organs for the human dimension - biennial implementation meetings and human dimension seminars - have been granted only limited powers in the area of monitoring the implementation of CSCE commitments by the participating states. Only the biennial review conferences appear to have further-going powers, although these have also not been specifically defined. This development may have negative effects upon the CSCE human dimension.

   In order to curb this development, a strengthening of the powers of the human dimension bodies appears to be necessary. Proce-

---

[94] I do not deal with the highly important role of NGOs in the CSCE process, as this subject is covered by the contribution of R. Brett in the present volume.

dures have to be developed to channel the results of implementation meetings and seminars to the political decision-making bodies in order to retain a close link between the human dimension bodies and the other CSCE organs. A possible solution could be found in granting these bodies the right to adopt a (non-binding) document.

In order to strengthen the link between human dimension seminars and the CSCE as a whole, implementation of CSCE commitments should also become a fixed point on the agenda of such seminars. Although the monitoring of the implementation of human dimension commitments is the main task of the biennial implementation meetings, measures have to be taken to avoid these meetings ending up as non-committal gatherings. In this context one of the procedures to be considered may be a scrutinizing of the human dimension record of all individual CSCE states resulting in concrete conclusions and/or recommendations.

2. In the recent period the CSCE has established an increasing number of procedures and mechanisms. Part of these mechanisms have been created specifically for monitoring human dimension commitments, others have a more general scope. Although this is a development to be welcomed, it has also resulted in certain drawbacks. One of the problems is the increasing complexity. The CSCE system has become so complex that only a very limited number of people are aware of all its peculiarities and specific features, even in the 'traditional' CSCE states. The knowledge of CSCE in the new participating states which joined the process after the revolutionary developments of past years, is minimal. This increasing complexity and the more or less simultaneously decreasing knowledge of the CSCE monitoring system may seriously hamper its application in practice, in particular by the new participating states such as the former Soviet republics. In order to curb this worrisome development, a streamlining of the presently existing CSCE procedures and mechanisms should be

considered. Besides, due attention should be given to an information campaign for the new participating states.[95]

3. Another major problem, resulting from the creation of an increasing number of specific mechanisms, is that of co-ordination. The CSCE should pay due attention to establishing a firm co-ordination between the various activities, undertaken under the different mechanisms in order to avoid overlapping of activities and frictions. In particular, co-ordination appears to be necessary between the activities of the High Commissioner on National Minorities, of personal representatives of the CSCE Chairman-in-Office, of human dimension missions under the Moscow mechanism, and of *ad hoc* missions (such as long-term missions in various trouble areas).

Specific supervisory mechanisms

4. The *Vienna mechanism* was used very frequently in 1989 and 1990. Since the collapse of communism the mechanism has been applied only now and again. In particular Western states have refused to apply the mechanism in their mutual relations, among other things because of the fact that the Council of Europe would offer better possibilities for raising human rights problems. This state of affairs has to be regretted. The monitoring procedures and mechanisms, as developed within the framework of the Council of Europe and the CSCE, may not be considered as overlapping or competing, but they are of an evidently complementary nature. The political, flexible character of the CSCE mechanisms offers certain advantages in comparison with more rigid, (quasi-)legal procedures. If the CSCE mechanisms are applied almost exclusively in the relations between Western states

---

[95]In the Helsinki 1992 Document a special chapter is devoted to this issue. The "Programme of Co-ordinated Support for Recently Admitted Participating States" (chapter XI) envisages, *inter alia*, the organization of special meetings and seminars for the new CSCE states concerning CSCE matters. The ODIHR, in particular, has been entrusted with special tasks in this area. Practice shows the urgent need of a speedy implementation of this programme. One may wonder, however, whether the minimum staff of CSCE bodies, in particular also the ODIHR, is able to fulfil all the pertinent needs of the increasing number of new participating states.

and the "new democracies", the risk exists that this would undermine the general applicability and therefore the legitimacy of these mechanisms. The application of CSCE mechanisms almost exclusively in relation to the new participating states may lead to a humiliation of these states which would seriously undermine the CSCE monitoring system as a whole. In particular, Western states should therefore carefully consider the application of the CSCE mechanisms in addition to or as a substitute for the procedures as developed in the Council of Europe, depending upon the political circumstances of the specific cases. This holds true, in particular, for the Vienna mechanism and the Moscow mechanism, and also for other political CSCE procedures. At the same time, the former socialist states should be encouraged to apply the various mechanisms in their international relations as well.

In order to enhance the transparency of the application of the Vienna mechanism, a central registration of all actions, undertaken under the mechanism, by the ODIHR should be promoted. The present situation in this respect has to be considered unsatisfactory.[96]

5. The *Moscow mechanism* which became operational during the course of 1992 has been applied only a few times. Therefore, it is hard to define its effectiveness. The system as such constitutes major progress in the area of monitoring human rights, in particular the 'emergency' system which enables the despatch of missions of rapporteurs in cases of particularly serious threats to the implementation of human dimension commitments. The system is not hampered by any procedural requirements which are so typical for legal proceedings. The first indications from the so far limited practice of the system lead to a positive evaluation. Although the concrete impact of missions on the developments of

---

[96]In the Helsinki 1992 Document, it was laid down that the CSCE states which invoke the first or second step of the Vienna mechanism "*may* provide information" on its actions to the other CSCE states through the ODIHR (para. VI.7 of the Helsinki Decisions). This is only a small step forward in comparison to the previous situation in which no regulation on information existed at all.

(potential) conflicts is hard to assess, they seem to play a useful role.

However, it may be observed that the functioning of the Moscow mechanism could be further enhanced if the system would be further elaborated along the following lines. In the first place a better co-ordination with other CSCE activities in relation to the same problem area should be established. In addition, more attention should be given to a proper formulation of the mandates which are given to the missions. Another significant element would be a more thorough-going preparation which would also include a longer period for on-site visits in order to be better able to avoid superficiality. In this context the CSCE states should also consider the introduction of special training for experts which have been registered on the list at the ODIHR. It goes without saying that the functioning of an expert or a rapporteur in CSCE missions under the Moscow mechanism requires technical skills which most people do not have. The most practical solution would be the organization of periodic training by the ODIHR in Warsaw.

An important innovative element would also be the abolition of the restriction on states to select experts or rapporteurs only from a list which contains the names of up to three persons nominated by each CSCE state. This would allow for a more flexible composition of missions, depending upon the concrete cases. In this way the problem of the presently rather varying quality and capacities of the experts/rapporteurs on the CSCE list could be solved. Of great importance for the success of missions under the Moscow mechanism would be a stricter procedure for the follow-up to recommendations of the missions. Reports of such missions should become a fixed point on the agenda of political CSCE bodies. A final point to be mentioned is the fact that the confidentiality of reports of missions during a certain period may not only hamper co-ordination within the CSCE, but also co-ordination with activities in the same area which are undertaken by other international institutions (in particular the UN, the Council of Europe, and the European Community). A timely exchange of information may have positive effects.

Ad hoc missions

6. To a great extent the above-mentioned problems in relation to missions under the Moscow mechanism *mutatis mutandis* also apply to CSCE *ad hoc* missions. In relation to these *ad hoc* missions, established by the CSO or the Council of Ministers, due attention has to be given to issues such as the composition of the membership of missions; the preparation of the members of missions; confidentiality; a well-defined mandate; the follow-up of missions; and co-ordination with other CSCE activities and corresponding activities of other international organizations.

   With reference to *ad hoc* missions sent to trouble areas, it may be observed that the political CSCE bodies do pay due attention to the follow-up of missions. In other cases more attention from these bodies appears to be warranted, in particular in cases of missions to new participating states.

Co-ordination

7. In the recent period there is a tendency to create missions and follow-up missions in an ever-increasing number. This is a consequence of the increasing number of violent or potentially violent, ethnic-based conflicts in the CSCE area. This may result, however, in a rather chaotic situation. So, for instance, various missions under different CSCE banners may visit a specific area; but these missions apparently do not yet co-ordinate their activities. At the same time, the same area may be visited by several missions, despatched by other international organizations, such as the Council of Europe, the EC or the UN.[97] The exchange of information between all these institutions, let alone any proper co-ordination, appears to be almost absent. This situation undoubtedly leads to a certain weariness on the side of the visited

---

[97]States such as Estonia (and also the other Baltic states), Moldova and the Caucasian states are frequently visited by missions from various intergovernmental institutions as well as from a number of non-governmental organizations. A similar picture is offered by the former Yugoslav republics.

countries which does not contribute to the success of the efforts undertaken. At the same time it results in an 'inflation' of the significance of international missions.

In order to avoid an undermining of the effectiveness of the system of monitoring missions in the field of human rights in the CSCE area, a well-organized timely exchange of information concerning planned activities and the results of missions have to be considered as a minimum requirement. It would be desirable to envisage also a co-ordination of activities between the CSCE and other international institutions.[98] A possible solution would be the establishment - by agreement between the international institutions concerned - of a database of human rights missions in the CSCE area which could be created at the ODIHR in Warsaw or at the UN in Geneva. This also requires a flexible application of the hindering CSCE rules on confidentiality.[99]

---

[98]In view of the cherished autonomy of these institutions, however, such a co-ordination might not be the most realistic proposal at the present time.

[99]For other suggestions concerning the relationship between the CSCE and other European organizations, in particular the Council of Europe, reference may be made to the contribution of M. Pentikäinen and M. Scheinin in the present volume.

A COMPARATIVE STUDY OF THE MONITORING MECH AND THE IMPORTANT INSTITUTIONAL FRAMEWO FOR HUMAN RIGHTS PROTECTION WITHIN THE COUNCIL OF EUROPE, THE CSCE AND THE EUROPEAN COMMUNITY

by Merja Pentikäinen and Martin Scheinin

1. INTRODUCTION

There exist three regional and separate arrangements that are of importance in a discussion on the promotion and protection of human rights at the European level: the Council of Europe, the Conference on Security and Co-operation in Europe (CSCE) and the European Community (EC). There are currently 26 European member states of the Council of Europe, 12 of which also belong to the EC. And altogether 53 states, including all member states of the Council of Europe, participate in the pan-European system of the CSCE.

For the Council of Europe human rights are one of the primary concerns, since one of the main reasons for the establishment of this organization was the need to devote special attention to human rights protection in Europe. The Council's work has resulted in the adoption of numerous human rights instruments, and among those legally binding instruments which are of primary importance are the European Convention for the Protection of Human Rights and Fundamental Freedoms (ECHR) with its Protocols, the European Social Charter (and its Additional Protocol of 1988) and the European Convention for the Prevention of Torture and Inhuman or Degrading Treatment or Punishment (ECPT). Since the two last mentioned are discussed in other contributions to this publication,[1] our focus regarding the Council of Europe is on the mechanisms set up by the ECHR. References are nevertheless made to the European Social Charter and the ECPT when necessary. Regarding both the CSCE and the EC, human rights have a rather different position compared

---

[1]On the European Social Charter, see the contribution of A. Eide in the present volume. On the ECPT, see the one of M. Nowak and W. Suntinger.

A. Bloed et al. (eds.), Monitoring Human Rights in Europe, 93–119.

to that in the Council of Europe, since in the CSCE and the EC "internal" human rights protection is closely interconnected with the other objectives pursued within their framework. In the following pages more light is shed on this distinction when presenting the human rights monitoring mechanisms and the institutions involved in these three contexts. The focus of this article is on a comparison of special features, advantages, disadvantages and the interrelationship of the systems and on conclusions that can be drawn from these observations.

2. PRESENTATION OF THE MECHANISMS AND THE VARIOUS INSTITUTIONAL FRAMEWORKS

2.1 The Council of Europe, in particular the European Convention for the Protection of Human Rights and Fundamental Freedoms (ECHR)

The international monitoring mechanisms to secure compliance with human rights obligations accepted by the contracting states to the ECHR are a reporting system and complaint procedures for interstate and individual applications. The task of initiating the reporting system has been entrusted to the Secretary-General of the Council of Europe, and the ultimate means at his disposal for the monitoring is publicity: the replies submitted at his request can be brought to the attention of governments and made public. So far, this ECHR reporting system has, however, been resorted to on only a few occasions.[2] This can be partly explained by the fact that the interstate and individual complaint procedures, in which the European Commission of Human Rights, the European Court of Human Rights and the Committee of Ministers share the responsibility for ensuring human rights protection, constitute and offer far more developed mechanisms for monitoring. The possibility of submitting interstate applications follows *ipso facto* the ratification of the ECHR, whereas the individual petition procedure was made optional and required the declaration

---

[2]For more details on the reporting procedure, see the contribution of V. Dimitrijević in the present volume.

of acceptance of the Commission to receive such petitions. The present situation when all the states parties to the ECHR have also made this declaration has contributed to the fact that in practice the latter has turned out to be the most successful and the most resorted to supervisory mechanism of the ECHR, thus forming the cornerstone of its monitoring system. Most of the material rights and freedoms laid down in the ECHR and in its Additional Protocols are so-called civil and political rights, albeit at least some of them also require positive state action (e.g., the right to a fair trial). The right to education enunciated in the First Protocol represents an extension to the field of economic, social and cultural rights, which within the Council of Europe system can otherwise be found in the European Social Charter.

2.2 The Conference on Security and Co-operation in Europe (CSCE)[3]

The CSCE constitutes a unique phenomenon in intergovernmental co-operation between states, providing CSCE states with the political means to monitor human rights. Unlike the Council of Europe and the EC, the CSCE is not an international organization, but a political process. It follows from this that the absence of an institutional structure comparable to that in international organizations remains one of the essential characteristics of the CSCE.[4] As far as the political nature of the CSCE is concerned, it also boils down to the proper understanding of the functioning and significance of this process. The political nature of the CSCE, of its commitments, as well as of the human rights monitoring within its framework should not be

---

[3]For more details, see the contribution by A. Bloed in the present volume.

[4]Before the Paris Summit of November 1990 (the Paris Meeting of the Heads of State or Government of the CSCE states) the CSCE's work was carried out at the meetings which were held at irregular intervals within the framework of the process. The decisions made in Paris and laid down in the Charter of Paris for a New Europe resulted in the creation of the first CSCE institutions (e.g., the CSCE Council, the Committee of Senior Officials, the CSCE Secretariat). The process of institutionalizing the CSCE has continued, and, therefore, the structure of the CSCE can nowadays be said to resemble more and more that of intergovernmental organizations. The juridical basis, however, still differs.

viewed, as is often the case, as negating the binding force of CSCE commitments and decisions. The mere fact that the CSCE documents include clear statements of states' determination to act in accordance with the commitments laid down is evidence that these commitments are also expected to be complied with.[5]

In addition to the political character of the CSCE, a close interrelationship between the matters considered and commitments adopted within its framework should be looked at. The mere fact that the CSCE documents contain commitments on a variety of issues, in addition to human rights (human dimension issues), touching upon such matters as security, economics, science, technology and the environment, makes the perspective of CSCE human rights protection somewhat different from that of international human rights treaties. A close linkage has characterized human rights and security issues in particular, so that they are often made dependent on one another in the way that progress or stagnation in one area has usually affected the other, producing the equivalent progress or stagnation. Due to this strong interlinkage, human rights commitments cannot be separated from the other objectives of the CSCE, but they must be interpreted taking particularly the CSCE security commitments into account. To this end the inclusion of numerous express and implied references in other human rights instruments in the CSCE documents is also important. With these references the CSCE states are encouraged to adhere to international human rights treaties, i.e.,

---

[5]See also the contribution of A. Bloed in the present volume. The political binding force of the CSCE commitments does not exclude legal implications attached to them. CSCE commitments acquire legal significance when they can be seen as the restatement of existing international legal obligations. The inclusion of a right or freedom in the CSCE documents may also lead to a strengthening of the normative force of weak norms contributing to the formation of new norms of customary international law. On the domestic level CSCE commitments may have interpretive effect in the application of national legal norms. For more details, see, e.g., M. Pentikäinen, *Human Rights Commitments within the CSCE Process: Nature, Contents and Application in Finland*, Publication no. 3 of the Finnish Advisory Board for International Human Rights Affairs (1992) pp. 11-14.

legally binding human rights instruments.[6] These references must not be interpreted as diminishing the value of CSCE human rights protection, but merely as enunciating the priority of treaty-based systems in the field of international human rights protection. Regarding the CSCE this priority is understandable when viewed against the background of the different starting points of the systems: within the CSCE human rights are viewed as part of a broader context of European peace and security, whereas human rights treaties are clearly focused on promoting the essential rights and freedoms of individuals. Despite this different emphasis, the CSCE human rights system nevertheless shares the same aim with all the other human rights systems: the promotion and protection of human rights. The CSCE merely provides the CSCE states with a separate and different kind of process, which has its own human rights norms and mechanisms for supervising their implementation. As Arie Bloed puts it in his article, the CSCE commitments operate in a political atmosphere which differs from the legal environment in which the "traditional" human rights instruments are functioning. In addition, within the CSCE human rights form part of a wider group of commitments, the so-called human dimension of the CSCE. The CSCE human dimension also comprises, together with human rights commitments, other matters of importance for the general protection of human beings: commitments of a humanitarian character (e.g., human contacts)[7] and express commitments relating to democracy and the rule of law.[8] When looking at the material human rights norms adopted within the CSCE, it may be observed that most CSCE undertakings concern so-called civil and political rights, whereas economic and social rights are also recognized and dealt with, but usually in

---

[6]Among the express references are those made to the United Nations International Covenants on Human Rights (in the Helsinki Final Act) and the ECHR (in the Document of the Copenhagen Meeting of the Conference on the Human Dimension of the CSCE).

[7]The concept "humanitarian" used in the CSCE context has a meaning all of its own, i.e., a different form that is connected with the protection of human beings in times of armed conflict. In the CSCE process this concept is used to refer to the area of humanitarian affairs defined in the CSCE documents.

[8]See also the contribution of A. Bloed in the present volume.

very general terms and without defined commitments.[9] In connection with the commitments on migrant workers and persons belonging to national minorities, however, more concrete undertakings of an economic and social nature can be discerned. Most of the civil and political rights enumerated in the CSCE documents can also be found in the ECHR (as well as in the United Nations International Covenant on Civil and Political Rights). Some CSCE human rights undertakings can also be seen as clearly more elaborate and detailed when compared to the provisions of the general human rights conventions.[10] As far as the whole sphere of the CSCE human dimension is concerned, many of the CSCE commitments extend beyond the treaty obligations which are binding upon the CSCE states. And it is especially in those areas where the CSCE undertakings gain special significance by providing the states with important supplementary norms.

Among the achievements of the CSCE process in the field of international human rights is the departure from the principle of non-intervention in the internal affairs of states with regard to human rights, since it was first within the CSCE that states clearly held that human rights matters do not belong solely to their internal affairs, but are subject to international scrutiny. The international monitoring of compliance with the CSCE human rights (dimension) commitments had been entrusted to different meetings arranged within the framework of the process. Also separate mechanisms have been created to serve the same end, of which the Vienna and Moscow mechanisms were designated to operate in the field of the CSCE human dimension.

[9]See, e.g., the very general references to economic and social rights in the CSCE Helsinki (Principle VII), Vienna (paras. 12 and 14), Copenhagen (para. 23) and Paris Documents.

[10]More elaborate CSCE undertakings concern, e.g., freedom of movement, freedom of religion, the rights of persons belonging to national minorities. In particular, the CSCE commitments on the proclamation of a state of public emergency and the protection of human rights during such an emergency go clearly beyond the scope of the treaty-provisions. For more details, see Pentikäinen op.cit. n. 5, pp. 32-33.

2.3 The European Community (EC)

At first sight it could be argued that human rights have no role to play within the EC. This impression results from the fact that a specific human rights catalogue comparable to those adopted by the Council of Europe and the CSCE listing the rights and freedoms protected is lacking in the EC. This absence can be explained by the mere observation that the EC is not a human rights organization, but an entity which focuses on economic unity within the geographical area of its member states. Despite the economy-oriented emphasis of the EC and the promotion of objectives relating to that end, a broad set of human rights nevertheless receive protection within the framework of the Community. A limited set of fundamental rights emerge from of the treaties establishing the Community, and the Treaty of Maastricht includes some elements for a Community Bill of Rights in the institution of the Citizenship of the Union (a new Part Two to the Treaty of Rome).

So far it has been mainly the dynamic work of the European Court of Justice (ECJ) which has primarily taken the responsibility for the incorporation of fundamental rights in the Community legal order as general principles of Community law. The ECJ's case-law shows that in order to define the rights belonging to the category of fundamental rights, the ECJ has resorted to customary international human rights law, human rights treaties ratified by the EC member states (the ECHR in particular) and the constitutional traditions common to the member states. This development has now also been institutionalized in Article F of the Common Provisions in the Treaty of Maastricht.[11]

Although, in the light of the Court's practice, most pertinent rights can be said to be the same as those found in international human rights treaties, especially the rights laid down in the ECHR, there seems to be no common understanding on the contents and limits of

---

[11]Common Art. F, para. 2: "The Union shall respect fundamental rights, as guaranteed by the European Convention for the Protection of Human Rights and Fundamental Freedoms signed in Rome on 4 November 1950 and as they result from the constitutional traditions common to the Member States, as general principles of Community law."

these rights. The Court's case-law gives no precise list of rights which have found their way into the Community legal order, but rights such as the right to property, freedom of movement, the prohibition of discrimination (especially because of nationality or sex), freedom of expression, freedom of association, certain procedural rights and the prohibition of retroactive punishment[12] can be said to be among the fundamental rights protected as being general principles of Community law. It must be noted, however, that the ECJ's references to fundamental rights mostly have the character of *obiter* statements and that currently there is no clear understanding of the material contents of international human rights law within the EC framework. This problem is underlined by the fact that the bodies applying EC law do not seem to have enough expertise in international human rights law, probably simply because of a lack of information on, for example, the case-law of the Strasbourg organs. Simultaneously, it is also interesting to note that in spite of the weak general position of human rights norms within the EC framework, Community law sometimes goes beyond the protection offered by the ECHR, the prohibition of gender discrimination in the workplace being probably the clearest example.

The position of economic and social rights within Community law illuminates additional problems. Because economic life is what EC law is all about, workers' rights become an issue of primary importance when the role of human rights within Community law is approached. Also the cases in which "traditional" civil and political rights are invoked in the EC context very often touch upon workers' rights. So far, the European Social Charter (of the Council of Europe, the ESC) has not achieved a position comparable to that of the ECHR in the case-law of the ECJ. The Treaty of Maastricht demonstrates an open controversy within the EC on this issue, and creates further confusion concerning the role of economic and social rights. While the Single European Act of 1986 included in its preamble an explicit reference to both the ECHR and the ESC, Common Article F of the Treaty of Maastricht does not even have an

---

[12]Probably the ECJ's strongest human rights case is Regina *v*. Kirk (Case 83/83, Judgment of 10.7.1984) which related to the prohibition of retroactive criminal punishment.

implicit reference to international treaties on economic and social rights. It is true, however, that there is a separate Protocol on Social Policy, making further reference to an Agreement on Social Policy between eleven member states.[13] It remains to be seen how the eleven states can "have recourse to the institutions, procedures and mechanisms" of the European Union in order to give effect to the Agreement, when the Protocol and the Agreement are at the same time explained as being "without prejudice to the provisions" of the Treaty of Maastricht.

In addition to the adoption of human rights norms of a legal nature, numerous legally non-binding documents (proposals, declarations, resolutions, etc.) have also been adopted by the Community organs, by the European Parliament in particular. The Joint Declaration on Human Rights (1977), the Parliament's Declaration of Fundamental Rights and Freedoms (1989) and the Community Charter of the Fundamental Social Rights of Workers adopted by the Heads of State or Government of eleven member states (1989) have been considered as constituting steps towards a juridical EC human rights catalogue.

To sum up, it is correct to conclude that human rights and their protection have become relevant within the EC. Significant human rights are characterized, however, by the fact that they must relate in some way or another to economic life, i.e., they must touch upon the scope of Community law. Human rights protection is thus closely linked to the structure and objectives of the Community. This also has an impact on the interpretation of human rights norms, which is dictated and directed by the demands of European integration.[14]

Furthermore, the nature of EC law and its supremacy over national law also highlights another less developed dimension, e.g., in the system under the ECHR. When a threat to human rights has traditionally been considered as emanating from states and their legislative

---

[13]That is, all the present EC member states except the United Kingdom.

[14]The European Court of Justice has categorically stated that "The protection of ... rights, whilst inspired by the constitutional traditions common to the Member States must be ensured within the framework of the structure and objectives of the Community" (*Internationale Handelsgesellschaft*, Case 11/70, Judgment of 17.12.1970).

and executive powers, within the EC a real threat originates from Community law itself and the enjoyment of its economic freedoms by companies and other private actors. It follows from this that within the EC the protection and monitoring of human rights is necessary in respect of the actions of the member states, of the Community organs and of private actors. The problem of third-party effect (the so-called *Drittwirkung* phenomenon) is hence of greater importance than under "traditional" human rights law. As the ECJ has stated, at least some fundamental community rights apply to both national authorities and private bodies.[15] The extension to the latter, i.e., to the relationship between private persons, can be said to constitute a remarkable opportunity for development in the field of human rights protection in general. The concept of third-party effect is not unknown in international human rights treaties either, but as the main international mechanism for human rights protection under, e.g., the ECHR, rests on individual complaints against states, the Commission and the Court are, as a rule, faced only with the indirect aspect of the state's duty to ensure human rights between private subjects also.

3. A COMPARISON OF THE PROCEDURES

The three contexts studied not only provide for separate institutional frameworks and procedures but they also offer different possibilities for human rights protection and monitoring. When comparing the human rights mechanisms under these systems, numerous differing features can be seen. In our opinion, a proper understanding of their role for human rights protection in Europe is primarily to be found in the quite different methods by which human rights are protected within them. In addition, the mere fact that the geographical scope of application differs - within the CSCE extending from Vancouver to Vladivostok when comprising the USA, Canada and the states of the Commonwealth of the Independent States - gives the separate arrangements their distinct value. In the following pages the different procedures are described and a few observations are made both relating to them individually and to some common aspects.

---

[15]See, e.g., the case *Defrenne II*, Case 43/75 (1976).

3.1 Procedures provided

3.1.1 The Council of Europe, in particular the ECHR

The Strasbourg organs are competent to consider complaints that relate to the rights and freedoms set out in the ECHR and its protocols accepted by the state party to a dispute. Any state party to the ECHR may refer to the Commission any alleged breach of the treaty provisions accepted by the other contracting state. The admissibility of an individual complaint is dependent on a specific requirement as far as the victim is concerned: the complaint may be considered by the Commission only if it has been lodged by the victim of the alleged violation. The procedure for both interstate and individual complaints follows the same basic patterns. The admissibility of the complaint is preconditioned by the prior exhaustion of domestic remedies as generally required under international law. Once the complaint has been declared admissible and investigated by the Commission, the case can still be forwarded to the Court by the Commission or the state party to the dispute - on condition that the Court's jurisdiction has been recognized.[16] If the case is not referred to the Court, the Committee of Ministers gives its decision on the alleged breach. The supervision of compliance with the judgment of the Court or the decision of the Committee of Ministers, to which the states parties are legally bound, has been assigned to the Committee of Ministers. The procedure before the Commission is confidential and is conducted mostly in writing ending with the publication of a report. The Court's proceedings as a rule include a public and an oral hearing. The proceedings before the Committee of Ministers, in which the state representatives participate, are held in camera. Furthermore, regarding the applicable law before the Strasbourg organs, it is worth mentioning that in addition to the provisions of the ECHR and of those protocols the state party to a dispute has accepted, it has been held that Article 15 of the ECHR also brings humanitarian law within the scope of the applicable law.

---

[16]The Ninth Protocol to the ECHR adopted in 1990 will also allow, when it enters into force, access to the Court for those individuals or groups of individuals who have submitted a petition to the Commission under Art. 25 of the ECHR.

Within the ECHR monitoring system the emphasis is on the so-called "Judicial Review" model: after the exhaustion of all available legal remedies on the domestic level a complaint is examined by the independent human rights experts of the Commission and the Court. The ECHR system operates by legal precedent and is based on juridical interpretation and case-law. Also the accessibility of complaints depends on legal and procedural criteria, not on political considerations or on the quantitative number or qualitative gravity of human rights violations in a given country. Political elements nevertheless come clearly into play in connection with interstate applications and proceedings before the Committee of Ministers.

When considering the advantages of the ECHR system, the fact that the major supervisory bodies (i.e., the Commission and the Court) are independent of the respective governments, the fact that the complaint procedures end with decisions which are legally binding upon the states parties and that the injured party can be provided with compensation must be emphasized. The possibility to make reservations, derogations and limitations to the rights and freedoms laid down can be viewed as weakening the optimal human rights protection also affecting the effectiveness of the system. The escape clause inherent in the optional character of the Court's jurisdiction and the individual petition procedure, on the other hand, are not of practical importance as long as all the contracting states accept them both, as they have now done. Among the weaknesses of the ECHR system are also the limited results of the interstate complaint procedure following from the states' reluctance to resort to it. This reluctance boils down to political implications attached to filing an interstate complaint that might be viewed by some governments as an act of unfriendly diplomacy.

Regarding individual petitions, only a small proportion (some 10% of registered applications and clearly fewer than this of all the complaints addressed to the Commission) are declared admissible. This is partly due to the strict procedural requirements which are essential for the functioning of the system, but at the same time having the consequence that many serious human rights violations end up never being considered by the ECHR system. The expanded workload of the supervisory bodies over the years has in many serious cases also caused a far too lengthy handling time, sometimes more than of five years having elapsed before the report of the Commission is eventually drawn up. This is undoubtedly one of the most serious drawbacks of the present procedure. The heavy case-load of especially the Commission has also contributed to the prevailing situation in which it is difficult to devote attention to the urgency of human rights violations. This is in spite of the existence of systems of interim measures of protection and the possibility of giving priority to a particular case, providing for some flexibility in this direction. The requirement of the exhaustion of domestic remedies may also be a high threshold: the requirement of taking a case before all ordinary court instances and a constitutional court on the domestic level before commencing the international complaint mechanism bars a great number of genuine human rights cases from ever being declared admissible by the Commission, and even for the few remaining cases the total length of domestic and Strasbourg procedures will be something like ten years.

Both the strength and the weakness of the ECHR system may be attached to the Judicial Review model. The Commission and the Court have made a tremendous contribution in developing international human rights law. Their case-law not only has the role of precedent within the system itself, but it also operates as a normative standard for the domestic application and interpretation of human rights law and for other international human rights mechanisms as well. At the same time, the fact that the system operates by legal precedent, and not by the actual monitoring of the situation in a given country, makes it slow, sporadic and even random. This situation causes at least a potential threat to the legitimacy of the ECHR system. For how long will it be tolerated that the Court attaches more attention to appeals against administrative decisions concerning the licensing of economic life in Sweden than to widespread torture in Turkey?

The rights protected within the ECHR system represent only a certain, albeit important, part of international human rights. The absence of a general non-discrimination clause and an article on minority rights are two clear disadvantages in comparison to the International Covenant on Civil and Political Rights. On the other hand, the position of social, economic and cultural rights can be identified as the weak side of human rights protection within the context of the Council of Europe due to the far less strong protection of social and economic rights under the European Social Charter compared to the protection offered by the ECHR system. This statement can be verified by referring to the absence of an individual complaint system in the Charter system, to the fact that the organs heavily involved in the Charter's monitoring mechanism are political by nature, and to the fact that the Charter organs are not entitled to give decisions which are binding upon states.

3.1.2 The CSCE

Regarding the possibilities for human rights monitoring within the CSCE, we refer to Arie Bloed's article in the present volume which gives an overview on the existing options. Consequently, we will merely summarize some relevant points to be taken into consideration in our comparative analysis.

The international monitoring concerning compliance with the CSCE human dimension commitments takes place by bringing up human dimension issues at the CSCE meetings, at biannual review conferences and implementation meetings in particular, and by resorting to the CSCE mechanisms. Also the CSCE Council and the Committee of Senior Officials have a role to play. The institution of the High Commissioner on National Minorities, which was established in Helsinki in 1992, can also be said to be connected with CSCE human rights monitoring, even though it is primarily designated to serve the conflict prevention machinery of the CSCE. With the Helsinki decisions the High Commissioner was conferred with the right to collect information, to visit states, to communicate with the parties concerned, and - this is an interesting new development within the CSCE - to receive communications from private citizens and organizations concerning national minority issues.

The CSCE commitments operate only between states, establishing no enforceable rights of international petition for individuals or groups of individuals. This means that only the CSCE states can resort to the monitoring mechanisms set up within the framework of the process, and that only these states may raise human rights issues at the CSCE meetings and seminars. Individuals and their groups have no formal right to initiate the mechanisms and discussions. This observation does not lead, however, to the total exclusion of possibilities of participation for individuals and groups of individuals in the monitoring of CSCE commitments. Persons and groups whose rights have been violated may namely call their own governments into account on the basis of written commitments, which may result in taking up and solving individual cases at CSCE meetings by means of diplomatic contacts. To the same end and worth noting are the recently expanded possibilities for non-governmental organizations (NGOs) to participate in the CSCE as they have been granted the right to take part in debates and to distribute their own materials in connection with some CSCE meetings.[17] Even though this development can be viewed as representing a departure from the strictly intergovernmental character of the CSCE process, for the time being the CSCE human rights (dimension) monitoring takes place almost exclusively at the intergovernmental level. In addition to this observation, it should be added that the powers of the monitoring organs are also rather limited, since only some of them are entrusted with real decision-making powers.[18] Furthermore, a decision on a matter considered within the CSCE is only made if the states manage to reach a consensus.[19] Consequently, the powers of the CSCE with regard to the supervision of the implementation of the human dimension commitments can be said to be quite restricted.[20] Regarding the CSCE human dimension mechanisms, they can be initiated by any CSCE state that is of the opinion that another state has violated its human dimension commitments.

---

[17]See the contribution of A. Bloed in the present volume.

[18]These are the CSCE Summit, the CSCE Council and the Committee of Senior Officials. For more details, see the contribution by A. Bloed in the present volume.

[19]The consensus-minus-one principle is applicable in respect to matters concerning the most serious violations of the CSCE human dimension commitments. See the contribution of A. Bloed in the present volume.

[20]See also the contribution by A. Bloed in the present volume.

The CSCE meetings and mechanisms provide CSCE states with a monitoring system in which political considerations play a significant role and greatly affect the outcome of the process. Due to this political character of the CSCE, on the other hand, the CSCE monitoring mechanisms offer a flexible means by which to address human dimension violations, since procedural admissibility considerations comparable to those to be taken into account in juridical procedures do not come into play. The criteria for action reside in the urgency and importance of human rights problems, making it possible to consider an alleged human rights violation expeditiously within the framework of the CSCE. Another side of the coin is that the political nature of the process and especially the ordinarily required consensus in the decision-making, even though conferring on the CSCE decisions a specific value when indicating the states' political will to comply with them, have also turned out to effectively bar the CSCE work. The inability to agree on considered matters easily results in paralysing of the functioning of the CSCE, an example of which was the 1992 Helsinki Follow-up Meeting in connection with the Yugoslavia crisis. It is precisely this kind of deadlock that evidences the close interlinkage between the efficiency of the CSCE and the prevailing political climate. This linkage has also contributed to the departure from the consensus principle in CSCE decision-making. In addition, the fact that the CSCE organs cannot impose any sanctions on the state that has violated its CSCE commitments, but are only entitled to take political actions, has an impact on its effectiveness. CSCE practice also shows that the human rights matters brought to the consideration of the CSCE usually touch upon serious violations of the protected rights and freedoms.

3.1.3 The EC

Alleged human rights abuses may be dealt with by the different Community organs (e.g., the Commission), but the ECJ has evolved into the most important body to secure their protection. Human rights issues may be considered by the Court in connection with a complaint submitted to it by the Community organs, by a member state or, in the case of a decision directly affecting an individual case, also by a natural or legal person. In addition, human rights issues may arise in the ECJ through the system of preliminary rulings on the basis of a request made by a domestic court, also following action by private individuals or groups of individuals having a legal interest in the matter.[21]

The absence of a defined catalogue of rights to be protected within the EC not only causes confusion and leaves the basis of human rights protection vague, but it also results in cautiousness in the judicial review of member state action aimed at compatibility with human rights norms. In order to depart from this cautiousness, there have been debates on the adoption of legally binding human rights instruments and on the possible accession of the EC to the ECHR, and possibly to other international human rights treaties as well. The direct effect of Community law makes it possible to address even human rights violations by private bodies in the proceedings before the ECJ. These proceedings, however, have not been designed to offer human rights protection but to ensure uniform application of Community law. This of course affects the practical possibilities of bringing cases with human rights implications to the ECJ.

3.2 General observations

When comparing the contexts studied the first characteristic to be underlined is the *differing nature of the systems, institutions and norms*. The Council of Europe and the European Community are international organizations whose existence and very functioning are based on legal instruments, whereas the CSCE is a political process. Accordingly, the human rights norms adopted within their frameworks are also of a different nature. A few conclusions can be drawn based

---

[21]It is also worth noting in this context that according to the European Parliament's rules of procedure every citizen of the Community has the right to address written petitions to the European Parliament concerning the rights set out in the Parliamentary Declaration of Fundamental Rights and Freedoms, which proclaims a number of both "traditional" civil and political rights and social rights. This procedure cannot, however, result in legally binding decisions. This right has also been pronounced in the Maastricht Treaty as one of the rights stemming from the Citizenship of the Union (Arts. 8 D and 138 E of the Treaty of Rome).

on this juridical/political dichotomy. In general, political commitments and procedures can be characterized by their flexibility. Therefore, in comparison to juridical obligations the political commitments of the CSCE can be viewed as possessing greater flexibility in adapting to new developments: the CSCE commitments can be adopted and modified expeditiously compared to legal obligations since amendment of and supplements to the rules and procedures become effective as soon as consensus has been reached. The observation that the creation, as well as the termination, of non-legal commitments is in general simpler than those of legal obligations, due to the fact that the preparation of treaties may be rather time-consuming and the termination of treaties is often made dependent upon the expiration of a defined term of notice, should also be taken into consideration when choosing the means of regulating state behaviour. It should also be emphasized that the violation of a political commitment is just as inadmissible as a violation of a legal obligation. The difference between these undertakings of a different nature resides in the consequences of their violation so that a failure to comply with political commitments does not result in state responsibility, and accordingly, does not allow legal sanctions against the state (a claim for reparation or even punitive actions in some cases). Compared to judicial mechanisms, the political CSCE mechanisms may also offer a flexible means of obtaining direct results through the means of silent diplomacy. In addition, political decision-making can be viewed as being less formal than judicial decision-making. The absence of rigidity has also provided possibilities for the informal involvement of NGOs and individuals in the CSCE process. The direct involvement of the governments and the central role of political considerations also leave room for political pressure. A problematic side of this feature is, however, a certain instability connected with political undertakings. Within the Council of Europe the Commission and the Court are of a juridical character composed of independent human rights experts, whereas the Committee of Ministers is the Council's governing organ, and a political body whose members are the representatives of their governments. Accordingly, in the Council of Europe political elements come to play, additionally in connection with interstate complaints, in the proceedings before the Committee of Ministers.

The existing human rights norms: The traditional dichotomy between civil and political rights and economic and social rights, can be viewed as characterizing the Council of Europe's system. The mere fact that two separate conventions have been adopted to regulate these two sets of rights (the ECHR and the European Social Charter) is evidence of this observation. Furthermore, in the light of the structure of the European Social Charter (the nature of the organs involved and the decisions given) it can be argued that economic and social rights have so far been given subsidiary significance within the Council of Europe. The CSCE documents on their part do not separate civil and political rights and economic and social rights as such, but most human rights adopted concern those belonging to the first category, whereas economic and social rights are usually touched upon in very general terms. In addition, the CSCE human dimension commitments gain a specific complementary value in the areas where they extend beyond the scope of the legal obligations which are binding upon the CSCE states. Within the European Community the lack of a Bill of Rights leaves the body of protected rights unclear, but sometimes Community law can be said to go beyond the protection offered by human rights treaties, the ECHR included. In most cases, however, the normative framework for protecting fundamental rights is clearly less developed than in the Council of Europe.

Some systems provide for escape clauses from the undertakings adopted by allowing *reservations, limitations and derogations*. Reservations are admissible in respect of the ECHR and its protocols, but they are not possible with regard to CSCE commitments, nor regarding the provisions of the ECPT. Limitations to and derogations from the undertakings on their part are usually regarded as accessible. The right to derogate from the protected rights and freedoms is nevertheless not absolute, since derogations are not allowed in respect of some rights viewed as being of a fundamental character. It is notable that in times of war or public emergency none of the systems provide for a special supervision system for the observance of a state's compliance with human rights. The ECPT, however, may provide valuable guarantees during emergency situations due to the fact that derogations from the Committee's right to visit cannot be made on one side only by the state concerned.[22] Within the context of European Community law, the lack of a catalogue of protected fundamental rights is highlighted by the case of limitations or derogations. The economic freedoms established by the Treaty of Rome might in practice be understood as having precedence in relation to human rights and as justifying limitations for example. The role of the ECJ as a proponent of economic integration and the lack of traditions in applying and interpreting international human rights law form additional reasons for concern.

When comparing the mere wording of the instruments concerned, it can be seen that *the expectations of compliance* with respect to certain obligations or commitments are higher than those regarding others. This observation applies to both the formulation of legal obligations and political commitments, but it can be said to be particularly visible in CSCE commitments. It is true that the texts of the CSCE documents have become increasingly specific year after year, but in spite of that the language used therein can still be considered as "soft" compared to the texts of human rights treaties. This contributes to the fact that states are given a broader margin of appreciation in the implementation of their commitments.

A different position of human rights in the systems at hand should still be emphasized: the Council of Europe and its conventions focus clearly on the protection and promotion of human rights; the CSCE human dimension commitments are interlinked with the other CSCE commitments, in particular those relevant to security issues; and within the EC the important human rights are those rights or aspects of rights that operate in the field of Community law application. Furthermore, attention should be paid to the to some extent *differing coverage of human rights protection* offered. Under the ECHR and the CSCE protection is extended to everyone under the jurisdiction of the state in question. The rights protected within the EC on their part are

---

[22]This can be said to hold true irrespective of its Art. 9, which allows the state to make representations on the Committee's visits in exceptional circumstances.

often made dependent on the nationality of one of the member states.[23]

Also *the position of individuals* in the proceedings being studied varies. Before the Strasbourg organs an individual complainant participates in the proceedings before the Commission, at least in theory, on an equal footing with the state party to the dispute. Before the Court and the Committee of Ministers formal standing is for the time being reserved only to the states and the Commission. The situation in respect of the Court's proceedings, however, will change as soon as the Ninth Protocol to the ECHR will enter into force, enabling access to the Court for individuals or groups of individuals also. In the CSCE individuals or groups of individuals do not have a formal right to initiate the mechanisms and discussions, but as already stated, this does not totally exclude their participation in the monitoring of the CSCE commitments. Also the recent improvements concerning the informal involvement of NGOs in the CSCE can be viewed as signifying a step forward in the process of strengthening the position of groups of individuals within the framework of the CSCE. Regarding the EC and individuals, the lack of any special human rights machinery within the framework of the Community is to be noted. The possibilities for an individual to bring an action against someone who seeks authorization to infringe human rights within Community law, largely depends on the circumstances of the particular case. In principle, violations by both the Community organs and by various actors under Community law can be taken to the ECJ, either directly or through a request by a national court. The direct effect of Community law creates possibilities for also addressing human rights violations by private bodies.

The *effectiveness* of the monitoring systems is one of the most difficult aspects to measure. It can be observed in general that the fact that decisions are not made independently of governments influences the

---

[23]The ECPT does not make any distinction between nationals and non-nationals. The rights enshrined in the European Social Charter apply to foreigners only in certain conditions. (According to the Appendix to the Social Charter reciprocity and lawfully staying in the territory of the contracting party concerned are among these conditions).

systems' efficiency. This is clearly visible in the CSCE process in which the effectiveness of the mechanisms and decisions made is strongly based on political pressure, which on its part depends on the existing political climate. It also follows from this that under politically favourable circumstances the CSCE forum may turn out to be a powerful instrument for protection. The required consensus in CSCE decision-making can nevertheless be viewed as decreasing the efficiency of the CSCE work. The effectiveness of the monitoring systems of a legal nature, even though they are not dependent on political considerations in the way comparable to the CSCE, is also ultimately connected with the states' will to comply with their obligations. Furthermore, in general the possibility of making reservations, derogations and limitations to the rights and freedoms agreed upon has an impact on the effective functioning of the systems.

It can still be observed that *confidentiality* attached to the monitoring mechanisms and the work of the organs involved is one of the common characteristics. Access by the public to the proceedings is, generally speaking, rather restricted, and deliberations are usually conducted in camera with the exception of those before the European Court of Human Rights. Information concerning the cases under consideration is usually not made available before the final decisions have been given. The ECPT system represents one extreme by making access to information gathered dependent on the consent of the state party involved. Furthermore, in order to establish the facts in individual cases the different systems have created possibilities to conduct *on-the-spot enquiries* (the ECHR, the ECPT, the CSCE), of which the ECPT with the visits of its Committee can be regarded as the most regulated and far-reaching.

Decisions and judgments: The judgments of the European Court of Human Rights and the decisions of the Committee of Ministers are formally binding in relation to any state party in a given case. The Committee of Ministers has also been entrusted with the more general duty of ensuring that the Court's rulings are observed. In many states the judgments of the Court can by themselves form the basis of domestic measures. In addition, the ECHR system influences domestic courts and authorities through the system of precedent, thus contributing towards a common understanding of the contents of human rights law. The supremacy of Community law in relation to domestic law and the powers of the Commission and the ECJ to ensure this supremacy also create possibilities for effective implementation of human rights, if the position of human rights norms should become firmer in Community law than it is at present. Political CSCE decisions may be used as an interpretative aid at the domestic level when standards are needed to interpret international human rights norms which have also become relevant on the domestic front.

Within European Community law in general, the strong role of the European Court of Justice and the system of precedent characterize the system. Similarly to the ECHR system, also Community law represents the so-called Judicial Review model described above. The ambiguous position of human rights within European Community law and the various alternatives for altering the situation have been the starting-point for discussions not only on the possibilities for strengthening the role of human rights within the existing framework but also on complementing the Judicial Review model itself. Within the human rights project of the European University Institute it has been demonstrated that courts or court-like procedures might not be the most effective ones in addressing *all* kinds of human rights problems. Collective and "new" human rights in particular might never reach the courts or international bodies by way of the traditional Judicial Review approach. The alternative or complementary Access to Justice Approach starts from the basic observation that different human rights might need different methods of protection. In addition to the possibility of taking individual cases to court according to the Judicial Review model, institutions like class action, "jumping the queue", legal aid schemes, grants for test cases and information schemes should be developed.[24]

---

[24]See A. Clapham, *Human Rights and the European Community: A Critical Overview* (European Union - The Human Rights Challenge, vol. I), and A. Cassese, A. Clapham and J. Weiler, eds., *European Union - The Human Rights Challenge*, vols. II-III (Baden-Baden 1991).

4. CONCLUSIONS AND RECOMMENDATIONS

When drawing conclusions from the aforementioned observations and when thinking of recommendations for improving human rights protection, attention should be paid particularly to the differences in the procedures and institutions of the systems studied. Within the European context we have human rights protection systems of a differing nature, treaty-based systems creating legal obligations upon states and the political system of the CSCE, the EC on its part constituting a distinct entity. Taking the differences of the systems into consideration, it may be important which forum is chosen for dealing with a certain human rights case or situation. Possibilities within these systems vary.

For the time being *the Council of Europe's system* is more inclined to offer protection for individual victims of violations than solving interstate human rights disputes. Due to states' reluctance to file complaints against other states, resorting to the interstate complaint procedure has remained exceptional. *The CSCE*, which functions almost exclusively at the intergovernmental level, provides the CSCE states with possibilities to concentrate on human rights violations needing urgent consideration. In addition, the CSCE offers a good forum especially when expeditious solutions to new situations or problems are needed. In practice the CSCE has been used for discussions on patterns of serious human rights violations. An interesting new development in the CSCE process is the establishment of the institution of the High Commissioner on National Minorities. What the impact of his authority to receive communications from individuals will be, remains to be seen, but it is conceivable that this may lead to a change in the individual's position within the CSCE framework by opening the door to an individual petition system. This, on its part, might contribute towards the more juridical nature of CSCE human rights commitments and their monitoring mechanisms in the future. Within *the EC system*, the application of human rights norms for the evaluation of decisions by the EC bodies is entrusted with the ECJ, which is a body dependent on aspirations concerning the effective implementation of Community law. From the viewpoint of effective protection of human rights, the ECJ is far too involved in

Community law as a proponent for tighter harmonization and integration.

Not only due to the different role of human rights within the Council of Europe, the CSCE and the EC, but also due to the differing geographical scope of application, the existence of human rights protection procedures within all these three systems should not be seen as a problem of duplication or repetition. It is clear that together these different systems have a greater normative value and a stronger effectiveness than individually. The political forum of the CSCE is an essential complement to other mechanisms, however developed they become. Therefore, the existence of parallel international mechanisms to pursue remedies for a specific human rights violation cannot be regarded as a drawback from the point of view of effective human rights protection. Special attention should be paid, however, to avoid conflicting human rights norms.

In respect of the ECHR there have already been for quite some time demands to review and streamline its system. The role of the Committee of Ministers has been criticized for politicizing human rights protection. And the vast workload of the organs has triggered off suggestions for merging the Commission and the Court, for example. Regarding the European Social Charter, recent suggestions for developing a collective complaint procedure can be viewed as an attempt to strengthen the monitoring mechanism within its framework. International discussions on and examples of enabling individual complaints in the case of economic and social rights should also be examined at the European level.

In relation to discussions concerning the position of human rights protection within the European Community, a line of development which is also highly interesting for the European context in general is the "Access to Justice" approach. The elaboration of this approach within the European University Institute Human Rights Project is an important complement to the already traditional discussion on the EC either adopting a human rights catalogue of its own or becoming a party to the ECHR (and, possibly, to the ESC as well). The positive contribution of the EC to human rights protection in general might lie in the identification of "new" rights (consumer rights, environmental rights, etc.) and the elaboration of specific solutions for making these new rights and some less developed aspects of more traditional rights effective - along the lines of the Access to Justice Approach. This approach might also be used to complement the assessment of the Council of Europe and the CSCE mechanisms.

When recommending improvements to the systems considered in order to strengthen human rights protection within them, we are of the opinion that it is better to concentrate on the existing systems of protection than to suggest clear institutional changes to the prevailing situation, e.g., by establishing new institutions. The starting point is the acknowledgement of the value of the existing systems and their potentials. The special characteristics relating to each of them should be highlighted, and the strengths of the systems should be emphasized in order to help make them more effective.

Concerning the individual systems considered,[25] in order to strengthen the efficiency of *the ECHR system* some structural improvements aimed, in the first place, at eliminating the unbearable case-load, e.g., the suggested merger of the Commission and the Court, should be made. Among the possibilities for improving the human rights implementation machinery is also the development of the advisory opinion system of the Strasbourg Court. National authorities (courts) should be authorized to request advisory opinions or even binding preliminary rulings. The strength of the ECHR system lies in the accumulating case-law and the system of precedent, representing the traditional Judicial Review approach. In order to ensure that emerging new types of human rights problems are addressed under a system which is burdened by a very heavy case-load, some complementary measures representing the Access to Justice approach might be worth considering. A special fund could, for example, be created for the purpose of giving financial aid to "test cases", representing "new" human rights or new aspects of "traditional" rights.

---

[25]Regarding the CSCE, see the contribution of A. Bloed in the present volume. We also strongly support A. Bloed's recommendation concerning the application of the CSCE system in inter-Western relations, also among the member states of the Council of Europe.

Within *the EC* the absence of a Bill of Rights is a source of confusion. The reference to the ECHR in the Treaty of Maastricht represents a partial solution, but is not as such satisfactory. In order to avoid double standards, the accession of the EC to the ECHR and the ESC to us seems to be the proper solution, compared to the possibility of adopting a separate Community catalogue of fundamental rights, monitored by the Community bodies themselves. It could be conceivable that the EC should become a party to all those human rights conventions to which all the member states are already parties. The accession of the EC to the treaties of the Council of Europe might require specific technical solutions, e.g., the authorization of the European Court of Human Rights or one of its particular Chambers to issue advisory opinions to the ECJ (and possibly to other EC bodies as well). This is in order to avoid double standards. This might also be a partial answer to the problematic role of the ECJ in the integration process.

When making recommendations in order to strengthen *the interrelationship of the three systems considered*, closer co-operation among existing systems is needed in order to avoid unnecessary duplication of work and in order to reach at least elementary coherence in the interpretation of various substantive rights. An exchange of information and know-how would benefit each system separately and also the effectiveness of human rights protection within the European context in general. A concrete step forward on the road to a better co-ordination of the separate systems would, for example, be the setting up of a joint data bank in which the information gathered in connection with fact-finding could be collected.

THE CONTRIBUTION OF NGOS TO THE MONITORING AND PROTECTION OF HUMAN RIGHTS IN EUROPE: AN ANALYSIS OF THE ROLE AND ACCESS OF NGOS TO THE INTER-GOVERNMENTAL ORGANISATIONS

by Rachel Brett

The focus of this paper is the role of non-governmental organisations (NGOs) in relation to inter-governmental organisations (IGOs). However, the contribution of NGOs to the promotion and protection of human rights cannot be adequately covered without considering their role and position within their own countries since the most effective implementation of human rights is at the domestic level; the international system can only be a back-up. Accordingly, Section 1 examines the roles of human rights NGOs and their domestic position. Section 2 considers and critically analyses their status in relation to IGOs. Section 3 recommends improvements.

1. ROLES OF NGOs IN MONITORING AND PROTECTING HUMAN RIGHTS

The roles which NGOs fulfil in the field of human rights are fact-finding[1] and monitoring in their own or in other countries, investigating and reporting on human rights abuses, lobbying national governments and international bodies, mobilising interest groups, educating the public about human rights matters and the work of international organisations, representing clients in their dealings with national officials, courts, or international bodies, and providing ideas, information and expertise to national governments and international

[1]See also H. Thoolen and B. Verstappen, *Human Rights Missions: A Study of the Fact-Finding Practice of Non-Governmental Organisations* (Dordrecht 1986).

A. Bloed et al. (eds.), Monitoring Human Rights in Europe, 121–144.

bodies.[2] Which of these functions is performed, and how, varies from country to country and from NGO to NGO.[3]

More specifically, the most relevant NGO roles in relation to intergovernmental organisations are:

a) Participating in the setting of human rights standards by initiating and drafting proposals, and making oral statements and written submissions to relevant bodies;

b) Supplying information about human rights abuses to the organisations, including to thematic and country rapporteurs, delegates and the public;

c) Providing ideas, information and expertise in written or oral form to the organisations, or to members of committees or delegations individually. This includes constructive criticism of the organisations themselves, and the raising of politically sensitive issues;

d) Bringing cases before human rights bodies, or providing expertise or legal assistance in bringing such cases.[4]

An area which NGOs have neglected until recently is monitoring violations of human rights during armed conflicts. However, the current focus of attention on the relationship between human rights and armed conflict has encouraged the development of the "Humanitarian Law Fund", based in Belgrade, and has led to

---

[2]See also D. Weissbrodt, "The Contribution of International Nongovernmental Organizations to the Protection of Human Rights", in T. Meron, ed., *Human Rights in International Law* (Oxford 1984) p. 403; F. Ermacora, "Non-governmental Organizations as Promoters of Human Rights", in F. Matscher and H. Petzold, eds., *Protecting Human Rights: The European Dimension* (Cologne 1990) p. 171; C.M. Eya Nchama, "The Role of the Non-governmental Organizations in the Promotion and Protection of Human Rights", *UN Bulletin of Human Rights*, 90/1 (1991) p. 50.

[3]See H.J. Steiner, *Diverse Partners: Non-Governmental Organizations in the Human Rights Movement* (Cambridge, Massachusetts 1991).

[4]See H. Hannum, "Implementing Human Rights: An Overview of Strategies and Procedures", in H. Hannum, ed., *Guide to International Human Rights Practice*, 2nd ed. (Philadelphia 1992) p. 19.

suggestions for an international NGO which would apply international humanitarian law,[5] thus operating parallel to the International Committee of the Red Cross.

The existence of NGOs is essential for the effective protection of human rights at both national and international levels as it is NGOs which create the public understanding of human rights as well as monitoring and seeking to rectify violations. NGOs have usually been the first to draw public attention to human rights violations; a reading of the reports of the various Special Rapporteurs of the United Nations (UN) Commission on Human Rights shows their heavy reliance on NGO input for both facts and ideas. Moreover, the link between democracy and human rights, and the fundamental role of NGOs in democratic societies have now been accepted, for example by the European Council Resolution (November 1991) on Human Rights, Democracy and Development, which commits the European Community (EC) and its member states, when providing aid to other countries, to give high priority to active support for "promoting the role of NGOs and other institutions which are necessary for a pluralist society". That is not to say that every group which calls itself an NGO is essential. NGOs which are lobbies for particular groups, which are not scrupulous in their fact-finding, and are not politically impartial or are not willing to abide by the organisational rules not only damage their own reputations, but also reinforce negative perceptions of NGOs in general and thus tend to undermine their status.

One of the ironies for human rights NGOs is that their very existence implies a certain level of human rights, since they themselves are dependent on the availability of the rights to freedom of assembly, association and expression. At the most fundamental level there is, therefore, a need for the right of such groups to exist and to function.[6] This presupposes recognised, generally accepted, indepen-

[5]For further information on the applicability of international humanitarian law see the contribution by A. Rosas in the present volume.

[6]Y. Beigbeder, *The Role and Status of International Humanitarian Volunteers and Organisations* (Dordrecht 1991).

dent and impartial principles for the national legal and financial framework necessary to enable NGOs to exist and operate[7] since there is a tendency for governments, particularly those with a poor human rights record or where there is no tradition of voluntary associations, to view human rights NGOs as being anti-government or worse. The question of funding from outside the country of origin is particularly sensitive but may be essential for the survival of domestic NGOs. For example, in the UK NGOs whose purpose is to change the law, including Amnesty International, are considered to be political, not "charitable", and therefore do not benefit from the tax advantages of charities, while in Turkey the Associations Act of 1983 bans associations which are politically active, as well as prohibiting contact with foreign associations thus precluding the establishment of national branches of international NGOs.

General criteria for international NGOs seeking consultative status with the UN are specified in Resolution 1296(XLIV) of 23 May 1968 of the UN Economic and Social Council (ECOSOC). To obtain consultative status, NGOs must have aims and purposes which conform with the spirit, purposes and principles of the UN Charter; undertake to support the work of the UN and promote knowledge of it; be international in structure, of representative character and of recognised international standing, with basic resources derived in the main part from its national affiliates, other components or from individual members. In addition, specific criteria for human rights NGOs are contained in paragraph 17.[8] These are that the NGO "should have a general international concern" with human rights, "not restricted to the interests of a particular group or persons, a single nationality or the situation in a single State or restricted group of States". A strict application of these rules, suitably adapted for national NGOs, together with the internationally recognised restrictions on freedom of expression and of assembly and on activities

[7]See also *The Role of Voluntary Organisations in Emerging Democracies* (Report of a Workshop held in Prague, Czechoslovakia, 21-24 June 1992, by the Danish Centre for Human Rights, and the Institute of International Education, New York).

[8]See also L.S. Wiseberg, "Protecting Human Rights Activists and NGOs", 13 *Human Rights Quarterly* (1991) p. 524.

aimed at the destruction of the rights and freedoms of others,[9] should be adequate as a general definition of the boundaries of acceptable NGO activity.

The draft UN "Declaration on the right and responsibility of individuals, groups and organs of society to promote and protect universally recognised human rights and fundamental freedoms" (known as the "draft declaration on human rights defenders") seeks to cover such matters as the rights to form a group, to meet, to seek and impart information, and to solicit funds both within the country and across national frontiers.[10] Completion of the declaration will not, however, end the process; unless and until such provisions are enshrined in domestic legislation they will remain principles only and not legally enforceable rights.

The European Convention on the Recognition of the Legal Personality of International NGOs, which came into force in 1991, provides for mutual recognition by the states parties of the legal personality and capacity as acquired by an NGO in the party in which it has its statutory office. For the purposes of the Convention, an NGO must have a non-profit-making aim of international utility, be established by an instrument governed by the internal law of a party, carry on its activities with effect in at least two states, and have its statutory office in a party and the central management and control in the territory of that party or another party (Art. 1). The Convention is a step forward in that it provides legal rights to at least a limited group of NGOs, but it does not address the question of domestic requirements for the establishment and protection of NGOs.

---

[9]For example, International Covenant on Civil and Political Rights, Arts. 5, 19 and 21; European Convention for the Protection of Human Rights and Fundamental Freedoms, Arts. 10, 11 and 17.

[10]N.S. Rodley, "The Work of Non-governmental Organizations in the World-wide Promotion and Protection of Human Rights", *UN Bulletin of Human Rights*, 90/1 (1991) p. 84 at p. 92.

2. THE STATUS OF NGOS WITH INTERGOVERNMENTAL ORGANISATIONS CONCERNED WITH HUMAN RIGHTS IN EUROPE

The inter-governmental organisations which are particularly relevant to the promotion and protection of human rights in Europe are: the UN and its Specialised Agencies, especially the International Labour Organisation (ILO) and the United Nations Educational, Scientific and Cultural Organisation (UNESCO); the Council of Europe; the European Community; and the Conference on Security and Co-operation in Europe (CSCE). The role and access of NGOs to each of these institutions is considered briefly in 2.1 to 2.5. The question of NGO access to human rights treaty implementation bodies is considered separately in 2.6. Although this will summarise the formal position, it should be remembered that much input by NGOs is made indirectly or informally, through their influence and contacts with their own or other governments, or with individual delegates or experts. In addition, whatever the formal arrangements may be, the attitude of the Secretariat makes a significant difference. If the Secretariat is favourably disposed to NGO involvement, an informal system can work reasonably well, whereas an antagonistic or obstructive Secretariat can place obstacles against the operation of even a formalised system.

2.1 The United Nations

From the outset, it was recognised that NGOs could make an important contribution to the work of the UN. Article 71 of the UN Charter empowers ECOSOC to "make suitable arrangements for consultation with non-governmental organisations which are concerned with matters within its competence", and the current position of NGOs is governed by ECOSOC Resolution 1296(XLIV).

There are three categories of consultative status. Category I (NGOs concerned with most of the activities of ECOSOC, such as the World Federation of United Nations Associations) is the only one which permits the proposal of items for the agenda of ECOSOC. Category II (NGOs having a special competence in a few of the fields covered by

ECOSOC) enables representatives to attend meetings of ECOSOC and its subsidiary bodies with full access to delegates and documentation produced for them, to submit written statements for circulation as UN documents, and to speak. The third category, the Roster, is for those NGOs which can make occasional useful contributions to the work of ECOSOC. International human rights NGOs satisfying the criteria come within Category II, but in practice there is little distinction between the categories.[11] ECOSOC Rule 80 set up a Committee on NGOs which decides on consultative status and receives the reports which NGOs are required to submit every four years. In addition, NGOs can gain access to information by joining the mailing lists of the UN Centre for Human Rights, the UN Department of Public Information and the United Nations Children's Fund (UNICEF).

NGOs, like delegates, suffer from the late availability of much UN documentation. For example, the reports by Special Rapporteurs are often made available only just before the item is due to be discussed, making it impossible to read and consider them properly. In addition, NGOs often find themselves speaking late at night when there are few delegates to hear them. It has been suggested that the need for night sessions of the Commission on Human Rights is due to the number of NGOs wishing to speak. However, the International Service for Human Rights has monitored NGO statements to the Commission over the last few years and claims that the total time taken by them has not increased significantly. The increase in the size of the membership of the Commission, the number of observer states who participate in the debate, and the number of visiting speakers (Foreign Ministers and others) are at least as plausible an explanation for the increasing pressure on available time at the Commission.

The subsidiary bodies of ECOSOC include the Commissions on Human Rights, the Status of Women, and Crime Prevention and Criminal Justice; the Sub-Commission on Prevention of Discrimi-

---

[11]See also D. Weissbrodt and P. Parker, *Orientation Manual: The UN Commission on Human Rights, Its Sub-Commission, and Related Procedures* (Minneapolis 1993); N.S. Rodley, "United Nations Non-Treaty Procedures for Dealing with Human Rights Violations", in Hannum, ed., op.cit. n. 4, p. 60.

nation and Protection of Minorities (hereafter referred to as "the Sub-Commission"); and the Committee on Economic, Social and Cultural Rights. NGOs can and do exercise their right to submit documents to these bodies and to attend and make oral statements at their public meetings. In addition, they receive requests for information from the Secretariat in the course of the production of reports requested by the Commission on Human Rights and the Sub-Commission, and many of the resultant reports rely heavily on information supplied by NGOs.

Most human rights NGOs concentrate on civil and political rights which are in any case in practice predominant within the UN system. The fact that the system relies heavily on NGOs which themselves give greater attention to these rights, reinforces the tendency to neglect economic and social rights. Other NGOs, in fields such as development and trade unions, may be working on issues which fall within the latter area but without using the human rights approach or necessarily being aware of the relevant standards. In general, NGOs have had little contact with international financial institutions. A new development is the possibility of consultative status with the World Bank, although how influential its Committee of 26 NGOs will be in policy matters remains to be seen. The International Monetary Fund has yet to indicate an interest in involving NGOs. The European Bank for Reconstruction and Development pays special attention to democracy and has *ad hoc* contact with NGOs, which could usefully be institutionalised.

In addition, the rights of women as distinct from universal human rights are marginalised both in substance and institutionally. The location of the Women's Division in Vienna, and of the meetings of the Commission on the Status of Women and the Committee on the Elimination of Discrimination against Women there and in New York means that they are isolated from the mainstream human rights work in Geneva, and that many human rights NGOs ignore or lack the resources to attend these meetings. The rights of women will never be integrated into the mainstream of human rights until the bodies dealing with them are situated where human issues are considered and the majority of human rights NGOs are based.

NGOs participate in some of the working groups of the Human Rights Commission and Sub-Commission and contributed significantly to the drafting of, for example, the Convention on the Rights of the Child and the Draft Declaration on Indigenous Populations. Representatives of indigenous groups (whether or not in consultative status) were assisted, so that they could attend the meetings of the latter working group, by funding from the UN Voluntary Fund for Indigenous Populations.[12] This involvement was of mutual benefit since it helped to publicise the situation of indigenous peoples and to enhance awareness of the drafting process. (Indigenous NGOs were also allowed to participate in the drafting of the ILO conventions on this subject by making written and oral submissions, but not to vote. They do not have direct access to the system governing implementation of these ILO conventions.)

NGOs contribute information to the various "country" and "thematic" rapporteurs and working groups such as those on torture and disappearances. Furthermore, NGOs "acting in good faith in accordance with recognised principles of human rights not resorting to politically motivated stands contrary to the provisions of the Charter of the United Nations and having direct and reliable knowledge of such violations" are entitled to submit "communications" under the "1503 procedure" (relating to situations which appear to reveal a consistent pattern of gross violations of human rights).

The UN Security Council and General Assembly are not, of course, subsidiary bodies of ECOSOC. NGOs thus have no special status but have access to their public meetings, to delegates and to documentation.

The UN High Commissioner for Refugees (UNHCR) grants to each NGO the consultative status that it has with ECOSOC, as well as using NGOs as "implementing partners" to provide services to refugees.

---

[12]The Fund was established by General Assembly resolution 40/131 of 13 December 1985.

A new development for the UN is that the NGOs entitled to participate in the World Conference on Human Rights, to be held in Vienna in June 1993, are not confined to those in consultative status with ECOSOC. NGOs which are active in the field of human rights and/or development, and have their headquarters in the relevant region, in prior consultation with the countries of the region (the latter phrase was only accepted after the Secretariat had clarified that it did not give individual countries a veto) may participate in the regional preparatory meetings of the world conference (held in Africa, Latin America and Asia), and any which do so are entitled to participate in the World Conference itself, as may all NGOs in consultative status. It is to be hoped that special arrangements will be made for NGOs in those areas where no regional preparatory meeting has been held. This may be a model for future NGO involvement in UN activities.

2.2 UN Specialised Agencies

The UN Specialised Agencies each have their own arrangements for NGOs. The two most relevant to the subject of human rights in Europe are UNESCO and the ILO.

2.2.1 UNESCO

UNESCO has three categories of relations with international NGOs: "mutual information" (Category C); "information and consultation" (Category B); and "consultation and association" (Category A). The latter covers a limited number of NGOs who have contributed regularly and significantly to the work of UNESCO, and entitles the organisation to participate in the UNESCO General Conference. The UNESCO Communications Procedure,[13] established in 1967, allows communications concerning violations of human rights within the competence of UNESCO in the fields of education, science, culture

---

[13]See also S.P. Marks, "The Complaint Procedure of the United Nations Educational, Scientific and Cultural Organization", in Hannum, ed., op.cit. n. 4, p. 86.

and information, not only from "a person or a group of persons who it can be reasonably presumed are victims" but also "from any person, group of persons or NGO having reliable knowledge of those violations" - knowledge which must not be based exclusively on information disseminated through the mass media. This procedure has been used by NGOs but its slowness and total confidentiality limit its effectiveness.

2.2.2 ILO

The tripartite nature of the ILO is unique, providing for the full participation of non-governmental occupational organisations in all ILO deliberative bodies and activities, as well as in the drafting of ILO conventions and recommendations and in their implementation; the latter including the right (Art. 24, ILO Constitution) to make "representations" that a member state has failed to observe a convention. Unfortunately such participation is limited to workers' and employers' organisations only, not extending to NGOs in general who are, therefore, limited to submitting information through a member organisation. Exceptionally, the Commission of Inquiry into Romania (1989-90) invited a few NGOs to provide information. NGOs can apply to the ILO Director-General to be placed on a list of organisations whose objectives are in harmony with the ILO, which entitles them to receive documentation and notice of meetings and, with special permission which is rare, to distribute documents and make oral interventions at some meetings.[14]

Article 23(2) of the ILO Constitution requires governments to send copies of their reports to the most representative employers' and workers' organisations in their countries. This procedure enables those organisations to submit observations concerning the measures taken by their governments to meet their obligations, particularly as regards the practical application of ratified conventions. "The

---

[14]See also L. Swepston, "Human Rights Complaint Procedures of the International Labour Organisation", in Hannum, ed., op.cit. n. 4, p. 99; V. Leary, "Lessons from the Experience of the International Labour Organisation", in P. Alston, ed., *The United Nations and Human Rights* (Oxford 1992) p. 580.

supervisory bodies have always encouraged the submission of such observations, and... experience has shown that observations from employers' and workers' organisations which call for greater compliance with ratified conventions are frequently followed up by the governments concerned".[15]

2.3 Council of Europe[16]

The Council of Europe provides for consultative status with international NGOs "particularly representative in the field of their competence"[17] and capable of contributing to the achievement of greater unity between the Council's member states. "International" means that the organisation has members or branches in "a reasonable number" of Council of Europe countries.

As part of their consultative status, NGOs undertake to publicise the Council's work and report periodically on how they have done this, to inform the Secretariat of their activities, to admit Secretariat observers to their meetings, and to furnish information, documents or opinions relating to their own field of competence as requested by the Secretary General. Council of Europe bodies may consult NGOs in consultative status on questions of mutual interest, and the NGOs may submit memoranda to the Secretary General who, if she sees fit, transmits them to a committee of the Parliamentary Assembly or a committee of governmental experts.

NGOs may be invited by an Assembly committee to express their views orally or in writing on a question included in that committee's agenda. This happens on an *ad hoc* basis depending on a member of the relevant committee being alert to the expertise of a particular

---

[15] F. Wolf, "Human Rights and the ILO", in Meron, ed., op.cit. n. 2, p. 279 at pp. 279-280.

[16] For further information on the Council of Europe and the European Community see the contribution of M. Pentikäinen and M. Scheinin in the present volume.

[17] Council of Europe, *Relations between the Council of Europe and International Non-Governmental Organisations* (Strasbourg 1976) p. 1.

NGO in the area concerned. NGOs receive agenda and public documents of the Assembly and may send observers, without the right to speak, to public sittings of the Assembly. NGOs, whether or not in consultative status, may attend as observers at meetings of the Steering Committees on Human Rights and on Crime Problems, and other inter-governmental committees by invitation of the relevant committee ratified by the Committee of Ministers. The invitation may be for one agenda item, one meeting, or a general invitation. Currently, three NGOs attend the meetings of the Steering Committee on Human Rights. NGO observers are required to respect the confidentiality of such meetings. They, and other NGOs, are hampered by the lack of access to documents, including drafts to the Committee of Ministers and reports of country visits by Committees of the Parliamentary Assembly, because they are deemed to be confidential.

The NGOs in consultative status elect a Committee and have twice-yearly meetings with members of the Secretariat. This is a useful forum for briefing NGOs on recent developments, but does not help to integrate NGOs into the decision-making processes of the Council. On the other hand, the Council has institutionalised the provision of independent information about the human rights situation in some of its member countries by paying recognised national human rights institutes to report directly to it.

2.4 European Community

NGOs, except those working in the area of development, have no official status with the European Community but the Commission has funded some NGO activities and has established an informal consultation mechanism. NGOs can attend public meetings of the European Parliament and many of its members welcome informed comment on the issues before them. The Council of Ministers meets in private and its working papers are confidential although forthcoming meetings are listed and press releases are issued before and after each meeting. Since it consists of representatives of national governments, input is more likely to be effective if made in advance at the national level. The Economic and Social Committee is an advisory body of 189 members, representing employers, trade unions and "other interests", which in practice means consumer and professional associations. The Commission is required to consult the Committee on most legislative proposals but is not obliged to act on its opinions. As it usually reaches a consensus position, the Committee's opinions tend to carry considerable weight with the Commission but it is no substitute for consultative status for NGOs.[18]

Some decisions on issues with major human rights significance, such as those in relation to refugees and asylum seekers, are made on a purely inter-governmental basis behind closed doors and are not, therefore, subject to the usual checks by other European Community institutions, let alone public opinion.

2.5 CSCE[19]

Before 1992, there was no formal input of NGOs into the CSCE process. However, some NGO representatives had been included in governmental delegations and were thus allowed to make oral presentations, and NGOs had held "parallel meetings", had made informal contact with delegates and had distributed materials. NGOs still do not have access to meetings of the CSCE Council (of Foreign Ministers) or the Committee of Senior Officials where many significant decisions are taken, including, for example, the sending of and follow-up on missions to CSCE states.

The Vienna Human Dimension Mechanism (adopted in 1989) makes no provision for any direct input from or access by NGOs. It is a purely inter-governmental procedure. The Moscow Human Dimension Mechanism (adopted in 1991) can also be activated by governments only, but expert missions under the Mechanism are empowered to "gather the information necessary for carrying out their tasks,

---

[18]See M. Zwamborn, "Human Rights, a Community Concern?", *ECAS: The European Citizen*, No. 9 (1991) p. 9; See also *ECAS: The European Citizen*, Nos. 8, 9 and 11 (1991) *passim*.

[19]For further information on the CSCE see the contribution by A. Bloed in the present volume.

including receiving information in confidence",[20] thus enabling input from NGOs within the territory of the state visited and more generally.

Since the "Helsinki Decisions" of 1992, NGOs (defined as "those who declare themselves as such according to existing national procedures"[21], but excluding any which use or publicly condone terrorism or violence)[22] have had access to all plenary sessions of human dimension implementation meetings and seminars, and the possibility of access to informal sessions being granted. In fact, the only seminar held since Helsinki 1992 (the Warsaw seminar on Tolerance, November 1992), allowed access to all sessions by NGOs and provided them with equal participation in the discussions.

As far as the annual human dimension implementation meetings are concerned, NGOs are invited to make written submissions, and "may be invited by the implementation meeting, on the basis of their written presentations, to address specific questions orally".[23] Until this procedure has been tried out, it is not clear how it will work in practice.

Finally, NGOs can provide information to the new High Commissioner on National Minorities about national minority situations which have the potential to develop into a conflict within the CSCE area. The CSCE has not defined the term "national minorities".

---

[20]Document of the Moscow Meeting of the Conference on the Human Dimension of the CSCE (1991), para. I.5.

[21]Document of the Moscow Meeting of the Conference on the Human Dimension of the CSCE (1991), paragraph III.43, amended by the CSCE Helsinki Document 1992, para. IV.16.

[22]It is important to clarify that the terrorist exception is not about safety at meetings since all participants, including governmental representatives, are in any case subjected to security checks.

[23]CSCE Helsinki Document 1992, para. VI.16.

2.6 Human Rights Treaty Implementation Bodies

Three human rights treaties have been agreed within the Council of Europe: the European Convention for the Protection of Human Rights and Fundamental Freedoms (ECHR), the European Social Charter, and the European Convention for the Prevention of Torture and Inhuman or Degrading Treatment or Punishment. In addition, all the international human rights treaties drafted under the auspices of the UN are relevant, except the International Convention on the Suppression and Punishment of the Crime of Apartheid.

2.6.1 ECHR

Under the ECHR, Article 25, the High Contracting Parties may recognise the competence of the European Commission of Human Rights to receive petitions "from any person, non-governmental organisation or group of individuals claiming to be a victim of a violation" of any of the rights recognised in the Convention. Thus an NGO may lodge a petition only if it claims itself to be the victim of a violation, and not in the form of an *actio popularis*, as is available under Article 44 of the American Convention on Human Rights, which states, "Any person or group of persons, or any non-governmental entity legally recognised in one or more member States of the Organisation [of American States], may lodge petitions with the Commission containing denunciations or complaints of violation of this Convention by a State Party." Furthermore, this provision is obligatory upon ratification of the American Convention, whereas the wording of the weaker provision in the ECHR is optional. However, the significance of this distinction has diminished now that all the original members of the Council of Europe have accepted Article 25 and new applicants are required to agree to both the right of petition and the jurisdiction of the Court before being accepted as members.

Notwithstanding the restrictions, NGOs have been able to make some contributions to the case law of the ECHR by assisting applicants, and the European Court of Human Rights has accepted the submission of *amicus curiae* briefs by NGOs (e.g., by the International Press Institute, Amnesty International and Art. 19).[24]

2.6.2 European Social Charter[25]

The implementation procedure under the European Social Charter was revised by the Protocol of 1991. The revised procedure takes account of some of the shortcomings encountered under its predecessor, but will need time to demonstrate its effectiveness.

Revised Article 23 of the Charter requires a contracting party to send a copy of its report to "such of its national organisations as are members of the international organisations of employers and trade unions" and these are invited to be represented at the Governmental Committee which receives the reports of the Committee of Independent Experts and prepares decisions for the Committee of Ministers. The organisations may send comments on the reports to the Secretary General, who then forwards them to the Committee of Independent Experts and to the state concerned, which is entitled to respond if it wishes. In addition, the Secretary General sends copies of the reports to international NGOs in consultative status with the Council of Europe which "have particular competence in the matters governed" by the European Social Charter. Such NGOs may also be consulted directly by the Governmental Committee (revised Art. 27).

---

[24]K. Boyle, "Europe: The Council of Europe, the CSCE, and the European Community", in Hannum, ed., op.cit. n. 4, p. 133 at p. 150.

[25]For further information on economic, social and cultural rights and the European Social Charter see the contribution by A. Eide in the present volume.

2.6.3 European Convention for the Prevention of Torture and Inhuman or Degrading Treatment or Punishment[26]

NGOs are able to submit information directly to the European Committee for the Prevention of Torture about situations in places of detention which give cause for concern, thus alerting the Committee to countries or particular places to which a visit might be advisable. In practice the Committee relies on prior information from NGOs such as the Association for the Prevention of Torture (formerly the Swiss Committee Against Torture).

2.6.4 International Human Rights Treaties

The relevant treaties are the International Covenants on Economic, Social and Cultural Rights and on Civil and Political Rights (and its two Optional Protocols), and the Conventions on the Elimination of All Forms of Racial Discrimination, on the Elimination of All Forms of Discrimination against Women, against Torture and Other Cruel, Inhuman or Degrading Treatment or Punishment, and on the Rights of the Child.

Each of the above treaties requires states parties to submit reports to a supervisory committee.[27]

The official position is that, with three exceptions, there is no provision for NGOs to be involved in providing information in relation to, or to be involved in the consideration of, these reports. The Committee on Economic, Social and Cultural Rights, being a subsidiary body of ECOSOC, allows NGOs to make both written and oral submissions. Article 45 of the Convention on the Rights of the Child authorises the Committee on the Rights of the Child to invite "the specialised agencies, UNICEF and other competent bodies" to

---

[26]For further information on the European Convention for the Prevention of Torture and the International Convention against Torture see the contribution by M. Nowak and W. Suntinger in the present volume.

[27]See also *UN Manual on Human Rights Reporting* (New York 1991).

provide expert advice, and this has been interpreted as including written and oral statements from NGOs on matters other than the examination of state reports. The Committee Against Torture allows NGO submissions in writing only.[28] Nonetheless, information from NGOs has also been made available to, and used by, members of the other committees in their capacity as individual experts. Indeed, without information from NGOs, the committees would be severely hampered in their efforts to assess the actual situation with regard to implementation of the treaty provisions since governments are notoriously reluctant to display their shortcomings in public. A change of policy was instituted in October 1992, when the meeting of chairpersons of the treaty bodies urged both national and international NGOs "to seek to provide as much relevant information as possible to the treaty bodies and to do so on a systematic and timely basis".[29]

The compilation of a file of information on each state party containing not only NGO material but also relevant documents from UN sources and those of other international or regional bodies would be of great assistance to Committee members. Furthermore, the failure to involve NGOs in the reporting procedure reduces the domestic effect since the public often are unaware that their government is producing the report, of what is being said about the situation, or of the discussion of the report in the relevant committee. Opening the procedure to NGOs should enhance greater publicity and public debate both before and after, as well as contributing to informed consideration of the report by the treaty body. Some states Parties have chosen to involve NGOs in the preparations of their reports. For example, the Netherlands has encouraged NGOs to submit critical comments directly to the relevant committee. Norway has created a body comprised of NGOs, independent scholars, relevant ministries and parliamentarians, by which draft contributions for the report are discussed before they are finalised.[30] The Austrian Government has approached the Ludwig Boltzmann Institute of Human Rights (an

---

[28]S. Coliver, "International Reporting Procedures", in Hannum, ed., op.cit. n. 4, p. 173 at p. 189.

[29]*Human Rights Monitor*, No. 19 (1992) p. 13.

[30]J. Egeland, *Impotent Superpower - Potent Small State* (Oslo 1988) p. 154.

independent Austrian human rights centre) about the Institute producing the report instead of the Government itself. Although this might produce an interesting and informative report, it raises questions about the governmental engagement in the reporting process. The Dutch system avoids censorship or influence by the state as regards the contents of NGO submissions, or the fear of this on the part of NGOs; and with the change of policy by the committees NGO information will be circulated to committee members by the UN.

An optional right of complaint by individuals claiming to be victims of violations is available in relation to the Covenant on Civil and Political Rights and its Second Optional Protocol, the Racial Discrimination Convention, and the Convention against Torture (CAT).[31] NGOs do not have the right to use these procedures, but Article 20 of the Convention against Torture empowers the CAT to act of its own volition if it "receives information which appears to it to contain well-founded indications that torture is being systematically practised in the territory of a State Party". The Committee has received and taken account of information from NGOs, including Amnesty International, in reaching this conclusion in relation to Turkey - the first such case. States can, however, opt out of Article 20 at the time of signature, ratification or accession to the Convention (Art. 28). Furthermore, the confidential nature of the procedure may limit its effectiveness.

---

[31]See also S. Lewis Anthony, "Treaty-Based Procedures for Making Human Rights Complaints Within the UN System", in Hannum, ed., op.cit. n. 4, p. 41.

3. RECOMMENDATIONS

The foregoing account of the limits of NGO access to IGOs points to a number of suggestions which could be made for increasing their effectiveness.

A fundamental dilemma is, however, that (with the limited exception of the ILO) in so far as NGOs are allowed to participate in inter-governmental bodies, they do so on sufferance - that is, they do so on the terms laid down by the bodies themselves and the permission to participate may be withdrawn unilaterally. Given that those genuinely concerned about human rights recognise that without the contributions of NGOs, the ability of inter-governmental bodies to promote, monitor and protect human rights would be severely hampered, this calls into question the reality of the commitment to human rights by many governments. Accordingly, it must be recognised that many proposals which might seem obviously desirable would be politically unacceptable, for example that members of the Sub-Commission should be drawn exclusively from the ranks of NGOs in consultative status and academic institutions.

It is not recommended that NGOs should be directly involved in the consideration of individual cases or in the preliminary stages of the 1503 Procedure, although the latter would benefit from a reduction in the number of such stages with the consequent time lag between the submission of material and any action being taken on it, and from the process becoming public after the initial sifting of information.

The specific recommendations which do emerge are:

1. Efforts should be made to assist the establishment or development of NGOs within Eastern Europe to enhance the knowledge and understanding of human rights in both principle and in daily practice at every level, as "'real changes' can be brought about only by people in a country, not by 'outsiders looking through windows'".[32]

[32]Steiner,op.cit. n. 3, pp. 61-62.

2. Instruction in international humanitarian law should not be confined to armed forces but should be considered as part of any education about human rights. In this way, its dissemination to groups who might subsequently become involved in armed conflict would be enhanced, and human rights NGOs would be better informed about, and more likely to apply applicable humanitarian law as part of their criteria for judging human rights violations.

3. Priority should be given to completing the drafting of the Declaration on Human Rights Defenders and consideration given to the best means of providing legal protection for such individuals and groups.

4. States should be encouraged to become parties to the European Convention on the Recognition of the Legal Personality of International NGOs.

5. NGOs, in particular international NGOs, should provide equal emphasis in practice as well as in theory to economic, social and cultural rights.

6. The international financial institutions should involve NGOs in their policy and decision-making procedures.

7. The Commission on the Status of Women, the Committee on the Elimination of Discrimination Against Women and associated parts of the UN Secretariat should be moved to Geneva to facilitate the integration of the rights of women into the mainstream of UN and NGO human rights work.

8. The ILO should find ways to make it possible for human rights NGOs to participate in its activities, including taking NGO information into account and direct access of NGOs to ILO procedures. NGOs should likewise be encouraged to take account of the ILO and its conventions in their work, and to seek ways of influencing the ILO both in the setting of standards and in their implementation.

9. NGOs should be given a recognised status with the European Community. The recognition by the European Community of the role of NGOs in the promotion of democracy and human rights in third countries should be extended to the EC itself. In addition, intergovernmental decision-making within the EC on issues with human rights implications should be made more transparent and accessible to NGOs.

10. The role of NGOs in CSCE Human Dimension Implementation Meetings should be monitored with a view to enabling oral statements by NGOs as of right as well as written submissions.

11. NGOs should be involved in the reporting procedures under all international human rights treaties. First, to ensure that NGOs, and through them the public, know that a state is reporting and when the report will be considered, and to stimulate awareness and discussion of the condition of human rights in the country concerned. Secondly, since governments are reluctant to publicise their failings or difficulties, to ensure that the treaty monitoring bodies receive information from non-governmental sources. Reporting states should be questioned about the means by which national NGOs were informed of the report and the possibility of providing information to the relevant committee; failure to notify NGOs should be the cause of adverse comment by the committee. Thirdly, NGOs should be informed promptly about the consideration of the report to enable effective NGO follow-up.

12. The relevant secretariat should compile a dossier for each state party to human rights treaties which have a reporting procedure, consisting of information relevant to its human rights record from all official inter-governmental sources, including, as relevant, UN (reports to and of treaty bodies, rapporteurs, etc.), regional bodies (including reports of the European Human Rights Commission and Court and of the Committee for the Prevention of Torture), CSCE (reports of expert missions), and from NGOs in consultative status with ECOSOC.

13. A provision similar to that contained in Article 44 of the American Convention on Human Rights should be included with all rights of individual petition to enable NGOs to submit communications concerning violations of human rights.

Finally, since armed conflict frequently arises from human rights violations as well as being a cause of them, NGOs with experience of non-violent conflict resolution should be encouraged and given the opportunity to share their knowledge and skills at all levels of society, particularly, but not exclusively, in areas where there are minorities, including minority groups such as migrant workers, refugees and asylum seekers.

INTERNATIONAL MECHANISMS FOR THE PREVENTION OF TORTURE

by Manfred Nowak and Walter Suntinger

1. INTRODUCTION

A look at the human rights protection scheme at the global and the regional level shows that since the end to the Second World War an impressive level of international standard setting has been achieved and that a variety of enforcement mechanisms for these standards have been created. This observation is particularly true in the case of the prohibition of torture, which is contained in all general human rights instruments, considered to be part of international customary law and to belong to the rules of *ius cogens*.[1] Several instruments at the universal and the regional level provide for mechanisms to enforce this prohibition.

Nevertheless, torture is practised worldwide, and for those concerned with combating "this plague of mankind" the following fundamental question arises: how can the successes reached at the international level be transferred to the national level "where only failures can be recorded",[2] as the United Nations (UN) Special Rapporteur on Torture has observed.

Torture constitutes the most direct attack at the very essence of human dignity and often causes irremediable damage, as the experience of those concerned with the rehabilitation of torture victims shows. Keeping this effect and the gravity of this violation of human rights in mind, one has to think of possibilities to prevent the occurrence of torture.

---

[1]See, e.g., Report of the UN Special Rapporteur on Torture, UN Doc. E/CN.4/1991/17, para. 278; M. Nowak, "Recent Developments in Combating Torture", 19 SIM Newsletter (1987) p. 24.

[2]Report of the UN Special Rapporteur on Torture, UN Doc. E/CN.4/1992/17, para. 288.

A. Bloed et al. (eds.), Monitoring Human Rights in Europe, 145–168.

While in the broader field of the realization of human rights the preventive approach has been gaining ground only recently, efforts to implement this approach in the field of torture are already "old", partly due to the recognition of the described gravity of its effects.

What does prevention mean and which preventive mechanisms do actually exist? Prevention is basically the identification and the eradication of the underlying causes leading to violations of human rights. If torture is understood as the final link in a long chain which starts where respect for the human dignity is taken lightly,[3] its prevention means having to identify the links of the chain which precede torture and to break the chain before it reaches its final link.

The experience and practice of the many international mechanisms dealing with torture have contributed to the identification of the links of the chain which have to be worked on in order to prevent torture. A special nexus exists between the prohibition of torture and the right to liberty and security, since mis-treatment usually takes place when persons are deprived of their liberty. But the risk of torture is diminished considerably if special safeguards exist for persons deprived of their liberty. It seems, therefore, that for the effective prevention of torture one has to look at the circumstances and the rules relevant to the state's power to arrest and detain. But the identification of causes is only the first step, the second step is the eradication of these causes.

This article looks at different mechanisms which serve the task of preventing torture. Special importance is, of course, given to the most courageous approach in this respect, the institution of a purely preventive system of visits to places of detention, as is already in force in Europe (European Convention for the Prevention of Torture and Inhuman or Degrading Treatment or Punishment) and is under consideration at the universal level (the Draft Optional Protocol to the UN Convention against Torture and Other Cruel, Inhuman or Degrading Treatment) (2.) In addition, the preventive elements in other mecha-

---

[3]Report of the UN Special Rapporteur on Torture, UN Doc. E/CN.4/1993/26, para. 582.

nisms whose main thrust is other than pure prevention are analysed (3.). Further, the ways in which these mechanisms coexist or possibly overlap are highlighted (4.), and in the final part concrete recommendations both of a substantive and procedural nature with a view to strengthening the effective prevention of torture are given (5.).

2. PREVENTIVE SYSTEMS OF VISITS TO PLACES OF DETENTION

2.1 Basic Notion

The basic notion is a very simple one: states should accept that an international body carries out visits to places within their jurisdiction where persons are deprived of their liberty by a public authority. This international body should then draw up a report on its findings and make, if necessary, recommendations for the improvement of the treatment of these persons.

By this system, which provides for a non-judicial review of the conditions which can be conducive to torture, these illicit acts will be forestalled. In addition, the mere fact that an international body has the right to inspect any place of detention without previous notice has a deterrent effect on those responsible for torture.

Yet, the creation of an international convention providing for such a system of visits has far-reaching implications: It is the most intense limitation of state sovereignty ever conceived of in the field of human rights protection by international law and the most advanced and penetrating form of supervision.[4]

[4]See A. Cassese, "A New Approach to Human Rights: The European Convention for the Prevention of Torture", 83 *AJIL* (1989) p. 151.

2.2 History and realization of the notion

The idea of creating a preventive system of visits to places of detention was launched by the Swiss lawyer and humanist, Jean-Jacques Gautier, in 1976, who drew his inspiration from the system of visits carried out by the International Committee of the Red Cross. Originally, a draft convention at the universal level was prepared. Since this idea coincided with the drafting of the UN Convention against Torture and Other Cruel, Inhuman or Degrading Treatment (CAT) which was primarily aimed at the criminal prosecution of torturers, the International Commission of Jurists (ICJ) and the Swiss Committee against Torture (SCAT) decided to propose the system of preventive visits as a draft Optional Protocol to the draft Convention against Torture. In 1980 the Government of Costa Rica officially submitted this text to the Commission on Human Rights.[5] It was agreed, however, to discuss this draft (known since then as the Costa Rica Protocol) only after the UN Convention would be completed. Although the Convention against Torture had been adopted by the General Assembly in 1984, the Commission on Human Rights again postponed consideration of the Costa Rica Protocol in 1986 and in 1989.[6]

As the perspectives of the universal draft being adopted at the universal level within a reasonable period of time were highly uncertain, upon the initiative of the above-mentioned non-governmental organizations (NGOs) the Parliamentary Assembly of the Council of Europe invited the Committee of Ministers to adopt a European Convention in 1983.[7] In 1986 the Committee of Experts for the extension of the rights embodied in the European Convention on Human Rights had already submitted a preliminary draft to the Steering Committee for Human Rights, which completed the text in November of the same year. On 26 June 1987 the Committee of Ministers of the Council of Europe adopted the *European Convention*

---

[5]UN Doc. E/CN.4/1409.

[6]Comm-Res. 1986/56, Comm-Dec.1989/104, respectively.

[7]Rec. 971 (1983).

for the Prevention of Torture and Inhuman and Degrading Treatment or Punishment (ECPT).[8]

Attempts to establish regional conventions providing for such systems of visits were also made in other continents. In the Americas where, in 1985, the General Assembly of the Organization of American States (OAS) had already adopted the Inter-American Convention to Prevent and Punish Torture,[9] a group of experts discussed the project at two meetings in Montevideo in April 1987 and in Sao Paolo in October 1988.[10] A similar initiative was also envisaged for the African region.

2.3 The main features of the system

States have the *obligation to permit visits to any place within their jurisdiction* where persons are deprived of their liberty by a public authority. The term "any place" includes not only prisons and police detention centres, but also those places where persons are interned for medical reasons, where minors are detained by a public authority and where foreigners are held pending deportation.

The *visits* are carried out *by a committee of experts*, who shall be independent and impartial and shall serve in their individual capacity. These experts are not only lawyers, but also, e.g., experts in the field of prison administration and in various medical fields. After having notified the state of its intention to carry out a visit the committee may without further notification visit any place at any time. On this occasion it may interview in private any person deprived of his or her liberty and may communicate with all persons who can supply relevant information. The visits can take place on a periodic and on an

[8]CE Doc. H (87) 4.

[9]AG/Res. 783 (XV.-085); for the text see 19 SIM Newsletter (1987) p.83.

[10]The Prevention of Torture in the Americas, Visits to Persons deprived of their Liberty, Report of the Meeting of Experts, Montevideo, April 1987. Draft Inter-American Convention to protect persons deprived of their liberty from torture and other ill-treatment, adopted by the Committee of Experts for the Prevention of Torture in the Americas (CEPTA) on 14 October 1988.

ad hoc basis, if circumstances so require. After the visits the committee draws up a *report* of its findings and may make any *recommendation* it deems necessary for improving the protection of persons deprived of their liberty. These recommendations are not legally binding.

The established machinery is strictly *non-judicial*: Unlike judicial or quasi-judicial bodies the committee does not, *ex post facto*, establish that violations of international norms have been committed and then denounce this fact. The committee's task is not to react to the occurrence of ill-treatment, but to act in order to prevent such practices.

The first step of prevention, the identification of indicators showing the future risk of torture, must, however, to a certain degree involve looking at past events. This implies a thorough investigation of the general and specific conditions of detention, of the legal framework within which the arrest and detention of persons take place and even of the "underlying causes of general or specific conditions conducive to mistreatment",[11] as the European Committee for the Prevention of Torture (CPT) has aptly pointed out. The purpose of the investigative activities of the committee, however - and that is the main difference between a preventive and a repressive procedure - is not to establish and denounce past abuses, but to draw attention to them in order to prevent future occurrences. In other words: If the eyes of the committee look into the past, this is only done to discover indicators and early signs pointing to possible abuses in the future.

The non-judicial and preventive nature allows for quite a *flexible application of international standards*. If the task is prevention, understood as the working of the environment and surroundings of detention, recommended measures may go well beyond established human rights norms. The legally non-binding recommendations need not be founded on strict legal reasoning, but can also constitute quite pragmatical proposals. The described flexibility allows for the committee to take a step by step-approach in its recommendation

[11]First General Report of the CPT, CE Doc. CPT (91), para. 46, reprinted in 12 *HRLJ* (1991) p. 206.

policy, according to the particular circumstances in a given country. Thus, the rigid application of international norms to countries with very different social and economic backgrounds can be avoided.[12]

Closely linked to the preventive character of the system of visits are the principles of *co-operation* and *confidentiality*. The principle of co-operation is two-fold. Its first aspect is the co-operation between the committee and the states. Based on this principle a constructive dialogue has to be established between the states' authorities and the committee which could assist the states in the implementation of its recommendations and, if necessary, of long-term structural changes. In order to build up confidence and a constructive spirit all information gathered, the reports of the committee and the consultations shall remain strictly confidential. Only two exceptions from this duty of confidentiality are allowed. The committee can publish a report on the request of a state, and it can make a public statement, if the state fails to co-operate or refuses to improve the situation. The latter exception used as a sanction, is only allowed once a state has not acted in the spirit of co-operation.

The second aspect of co-operation concerns the community of states. The states have to ensure that the visiting mechanism has a sound financial basis for the proper fulfilment of its far-reaching functions. On the other hand, this principle can also find its concretization in special programmes of the advisory services and of development co-operation supporting the building up of a legal and penal infrastructure and assisting the required long-term structural changes.

[12]See W. Kälin, "Prävention durch ein internationales Besuchsrecht: Ein universelles Modell für den Kampf gegen die Folter", in R. Herzog, ed., Zentrum und Peripherie, Festschrift für Richard Bäumlin (Bern 1992) p. 289.

2.4 The European Convention for the Prevention of Torture

The European Convention for the Prevention of Torture and Inhuman and Degrading Treatment and Punishment (ECPT), adopted in 1987, entered into force on 1 February 1989.[13] Subsequently, the Committee for the Prevention of Torture (CPT) was established. The European Convention is thus the first international instrument which transforms the idea of a preventive system into the international law of human rights.

While an in-depth analysis of the CPT's activities will not be undertaken here, some of the characteristics of the work of the CPT are mentioned.[14] Up to the end of March 1993, the CPT carried out 18 periodic and two *ad hoc* (both to Turkey) visits, seven reports have been published on the request of the states concerned.[15] In December 1992 it made its first public statement under Article 10 paragraph 2 of the Convention on Turkey.[16] It has drawn up its Rules of Procedures and has subsequently amended them on several occasions in the light of its experiences and has published two general reports[17] in which it gives a very clear account of its activities.

The materials so far published show the quite dynamic approach of the European Committee. It has tried to establish an on-going, con-

---

[13]For the text see CE Doc. H (87) 4; as to the background and content see, e.g., Cassese, loc.cit. n. 4; K. Ginther, "The European Convention for the Prevention of Torture and Inhuman or Degrading Treatment or Punishment", 2 *European Journal of International Law* (1991) p. 123; M. Nowak, "Die Europäische Konvention zur Verhütung von Folter", *EuGRZ* (1988) p. 537; The implementation of the European Convention for the Prevention of Torture, Acts of the Strasbourg Seminar on 7/8 November 1988, 10 *HRLJ* (1989) p. 131; G. Kaiser, "Die Europäische Antifolterkonvention als Bestandteil des internationalen Strafverfahrens- und Strafvollzugsrecht", 108 *Schweizerische Zeitschrift für Strafrecht* (1991) no. 2, p. 213.

[14]A first in-depth analysis of the practice to the ECPT is to be found in M. Evans and R. Morgan, "The European Convention for the Prevention of Torture: Operational Practice", 41 *ICLQ* (July 1992) p. 590.

[15]Austria, the United Kingdom, Denmark, Sweden, Malta, France, Switzerland.

[16]Public Statement on Turkey, CE Doc. CPT/Inf (93) 1.

[17]First General Report of the CPT, CE-Doc.CPT (91) 3; Second General Report of the CPT, CE Doc. CPT (92) 3.

structive dialogue with the state authorities in order to improve the conditions and circumstances within which persons are deprived of their liberty. This has led to very critical assessments, even with regard to countries such as Austria and the United Kingdom, and to suggestions[18] which go well beyond the standards and the case law set by the international human rights treaties and the monitoring bodies. This case law is regarded merely as a "point of departure or reference".[19] The suggestions do not only concern legal matters, but often very practical measures and also long-term structural changes. Particular importance is attached to the existence of basic legal safeguards as effective means to prevent torture, e.g., the right of a detained person to inform a third party, the right of access to legal counsel and the right to be examined by a doctor of one's own choice.[20] Consistent with this approach, the first public statement - the only sanction possible under the Convention -, recently made on Turkey, in which the CPT concluded "that the practice of torture and other forms of severe ill-treatment of persons in police custody remains widespread in Turkey",[21] was mainly due to "the continuing failure of the Turkish authorities to improve the situation in the light of its [the CPT's] recommendations concerning the strengthening of legal safeguards against torture and other forms of ill-treatment".[22] The experience with the European Convention is very encouraging, it has lived up to its expectations of serving as a model for the universal level.

---

[18]The CPT distinguishes between "recommendations", which are provided for in the Convention, on the one hand, and "comments" and "requests for information", on the other. It seems that this distinction is made according to the importance of the matter.

[19]First General Report of the CPT, CE Doc. CPT (91) 3, para. 5.

[20]Second General Report of the CPT, CE Doc. CPT (92) 3, para. 36 et seq.

[21]CE Doc. CPT/Inf. (93) 1 para. 21.

[22]Ibid., para. 2.

2.5 The Draft Optional Protocol to the UN Convention against Torture

In recognition of the seemingly unsurmountable difficulties which the realisation of regional conventions outside Europe would encounter, the original approach to create a universal system of visits regained force. In December 1990 a high level seminar of experts, organised by several NGOs, elaborated a modified version of the original draft Protocol in the light of the developments both at the universal and the regional level.[23] This draft was submitted in 1991 to the Commission on Human Rights[24] which one year later set up an open-ended intersessional working group in order to elaborate a draft optional protocol.[25] In October 1992, this working group met in Geneva under the chairmanship of Mrs. Elizabeth Odio Benito, Costa Rica's Minister of Justice[26]. The deliberations focussed on the main features without already going into drafting details and turned out to be very constructive. The working group recognized "in principle the importance of regular visits"[27] to places of detention and agreed that "such a mechanism should be based on the principles of co-operation ..., confidentiality, independence, impartiality, universality and effectiveness".[28] The main features of the draft are those outlined above (see *supra* 2.3). As the body to carry out the visits a Sub-Committee is envisaged whose members are elected by the Committee against Torture (as to the relationship between the two committees see *infra* 4.2). The mandate of the Working Group was extended by the Commission on Human Rights in 1993.[29]

---

[23]SCAT, ACT, ICJ, CEPTA, Draft Optional Protocol to the Convention against Torture and Other Cruel, Inhuman or Degrading Treatment of Punishment, Colloquium of Experts on a System of Visits to Places of Detention for the Prevention of Torture, Geneva December 1990.

[24]UN Doc. E/CN.4/1991/66.

[25]Comm-Res. 1992/43.

[26]Report of the Working Group, UN Doc. E/CN.4/1993/28.

[27]Ibid., para. 22.

[28]Ibid.

[29]Comm-Res. 1993/34.

3. PREVENTIVE ELEMENTS IN OTHER INTERNATIONAL MECHANISMS

3.1 Preventive duties under international law

It is well-established that under international law there is a duty upon states to prevent violations of human rights.[30] In this regard the judgment of the Inter-American Court of Human Rights in *Velásquez Rodríguez* v. *Honduras*[31] provides for a very clear and strong expression of this preventive duty. The Court had found, *inter alia*, a violation of the right to human treatment (Art. 5 American Convention on Human Rights) by the practice of forced disappearance in Honduras. Referring to the state's "legal duty to take reasonable steps to prevent human rights violations"[32] the Court stated:

> "This duty to prevent includes all those means of a legal, political, administrative and cultural nature that promote the protection of human rights and ensure that any violations are considered and treated as illegal acts, which, as such, may lead to the punishment of those responsible and the obligation to indemnify the victims for damages. It is not possible to make a detailed list of all such measures, since they vary with the law and the conditions of each State Party."[33]

While this international duty to prevent violations concerns the whole range of human rights, it is most clearly and explicitly expressed with regard to gross violations of human rights.[34] Torture belongs to these, and in the field of torture, apart from the above-mentioned purely

---

[30]See T. van Boven, "Prevention of Human Rights Violations", in A. Eide and J. Helgesen, eds., *The Future of Human Rights in a Changing World, Essays in Honour of Torkel Opsahl* (Oslo 1991) p. 191.

[31]Judgment of 29 July 1988, Inter-American Court of Human Rights, series C: Decisions and Judgments no. 4; reprinted in 9 *HRLJ* (1988) p. 212.

[32]Ibid., para. 174.

[33]Ibid., para. 175.

[34]See T. Van Boven, loc.cit. n. 30, p. 193.

preventive mechanisms, several preventive elements can be found in various international instruments.

3.2 UN Convention against Torture

The main thrust of the UN Convention against Torture (CAT)[35] is directed at the repression of torture by means of international criminal law. Yet, it also contains provisions explicitly aimed at the prevention of torture. The basic obligation of the states parties is "to take effective legislative, administrative, judicial or other measures to prevent acts of torture in any territory under its jurisdiction" (Art. 2)[36] and several other provisions provide for specific measures to be undertaken. Thus, all acts of torture have to be offences under domestic criminal law (Art. 4), education and information regarding the prohibition of torture have to be included in the training of law enforcement officials (Art. 11), and the interrogation rules, instructions, methods and practices have to be kept under systematic review "with a view to preventing any cases of torture" (Art. 11). Articles 12 and 13 provide for a prompt and impartial investigation in any case where torture is alleged, and Article 15 declares any statement made as a result of torture inadmissible as evidence in court.

The UN Committee against Torture is entrusted with the task of monitoring the implementation of the Convention by means of the

---

[35]United Nations Convention against Torture and Other Cruel, Inhuman or Degrading Treatment or Punishment, GA Res. 39/46; for the text see HRLJ (1984) p. 350; for the background see M. Nowak, "Die UNO-Konvention gegen die Folter vom 10. Dezember 1984", EuGRZ (1985) p. 105; M.E. Tardu, "The United Nations Convention against Torture and Other Cruel, Inhuman or Degrading Treatment or Punishment", 56 *Nordic Journal of International Law* (1987) p. 303; J.H. Burgers and H. Danelius, The United Nations Convention against Torture (Dordrecht/Boston/London 1988); A. Byrnes, "The Committee against Torture", in P. Alston, ed., *The United Nations and Human Rights* (Oxford 1992) p. 509.

[36]Cf., A. Boulesbaa, "The Nature of the Obligations Incurred by States under Article 2 of the UN Convention against Torture", 12 *HRQ* (1990) p. 52.

reporting, enquiry, inter-state and individual complaints procedures.[37] Of these procedures the reporting system under Article 19 of the Convention is of a particular preventive nature.[38]

3.3 International Covenant on Civil and Political Rights

Preventive elements are also to be found in the International Covenant on Civil and Political Rights (CCPR).[39] In its recently up-dated General Comment on Article 7 of the Covenant,[40] which contains the prohibition of torture, the Human Rights Committee (HRC) has stressed that for the implementation of this right it is not sufficient to prohibit torture, but that states parties have a duty to take legislative and other measures to prevent and punish torture.

Furthermore, a number of particularly preventive duties arise from the obligation under Article 7, which correspond partly to those set forth in the CAT, but go even further: Measures of information and training have to be undertaken, the interrogation rules must be reviewed systematically, incommunicado detention shall be prohibited, detained persons shall only be kept in officially recognized places of detention, registers have to be kept, the time and place of interrogations shall be recorded and prompt and regular access shall be given to physicians, lawyers and family members.[41]

In addition, the HRC states that Article 7 is complemented by the positive requirements of Article 10(1) of the Covenant, which

---

[37]M. Nowak, "The Implementation Functions of the UN Committee against Torture", in M. Nowak, D. Steurer and H. Tretter, eds., *Fortschritt im Geist der Menschenrechte, Festschrift für Felix Ermacora*, (Kehl/Strasbourg/Arlington 1988) p. 493.

[38]See the contribution of V. Dimitrijević in the present volume.

[39]GA-Res. 2200 A (XXI), see M. Nowak, *UNO-Pakt über bürgerliche und politische Rechte und Fakultativprotokoll - CCPR-Kommentar* (Kehl/Straßburg/Arlington 1989); D. McGoldrick, The Human Rights Committee (Oxford 1991), with further references.

[40]GenC 20/44, CCPR/C/Rev.1/Add.3, A(47/40, annex VI).

[41]Nowak, op.cit. n. 39, p. 142 et seq.

stipulates the right of detained and imprisoned persons to be treated with humanity and dignity. Article 10 is of special importance for the prevention of torture, as it establishes a relationship between the rights of personal liberty and personal integrity, a relationship we have already mentioned as being of vital importance.[42]

Concerning the implementation procedure, the preventive character of the reporting system under Article 40 CCPR has to be stressed again.[43]

3.4 Special Rapporteur on Torture

In 1985 the Commission on Human Rights appointed a Special Rapporteur on Torture as one of its thematic Rapporteurs.[44] The mandate of the Special Rapporteur is to examine questions relevant to torture and to report on the occurrence and extent of its practice. He shall seek and receive credible and reliable information and respond effectively to that information. From 1985 to 1993 the Dutch expert Peter Kooijmans served as Special Rapporteur. Following his appointment as the Netherlands' Minister for Foreign Affairs, the British expert Nigel Rodley was nominated in March 1993.

Several of the activities of the Special Rapporteur have a preventive character. This is especially true for the urgent appeals procedure which is characterized by its rapid response character. The Special Rapporteur launches an urgent appeal whenever he receives information that a person has been arrested and fear is expressed that this person may be subjected to torture. These urgent appeals in which he requests the government concerned to guarantee the detained person's physical and mental integrity are of a purely humanitarian nature.[45] In 1992 a total of 79 urgent appeals were sent to 31 govern-

---

[42]Ibid., p. 192.

[43]See the contribution of V. Dimitrijević in the present volume.

[44]Comm-Res. 1985/33.

[45]Report of the Special Rapporteur on Torture, UN Doc. E/CN.4/1992/17, para. 20.

ments.[46] In this procedure the linkage between the deprivation of liberty and the risk of torture is clearly shown. While it is difficult to assess the efficiency of this preventive procedure the Special Rapporteur referred to it as "an excellent instrument"[47] to serve the purpose of reminding governments that they are obliged to take all necessary steps to prevent the occurrence of torture. On the other hand, it has to be observed that several governments approached by the Special Rapporteur have not provided (satisfactory) information.[48]

Further, the Special Rapporteur has paid visits to some countries upon governmental invitation. In principle, a visit to countries could serve two purposes, a more preventive and an investigative purpose. According to the latter, a visit could be used to investigate and clarify certain allegations if the government in question repudiates them. However, to date, no government has reacted positively to such a proposal by the Special Rapporteur.[49] The preventive purpose of a visit to a certain country is to hold consultations with the respective government and NGOs in order to discover which measures should be taken to achieve improvements. The Special Rapporteur himself sees his visits more as pertaining to the category of advisory services than as an investigative mission.[50] Although the Commission on Human Rights has expressly encouraged governments to invite its Special Rapporteurs to visit their countries,[51] only very few invitations have actually been extended to the Special Rapporteur on Torture.

---

[46]Report of the Special Rapporteur on Torture, UN Doc. E/CN.4/1993/26, para. 20.

[47]Report of the Special Rapporteur on Torture, UN Doc. E/CN.4/1991/17, para. 11.

[48]Report of the Special Rapporteur on Torture, UN Doc. E/CN.4/1993/26, para. 21 et seq.

[49]Report of the Special Rapporteur on Torture, UN Doc. E/CN.4/1992/17, para. 11.

[50]Report of the Special Rapporteur on Torture, UN Doc. E/CN.4/1993/26, para. 16.

[51]See, e.g., Comm-Res. 1992/41.

Finally, the Special Rapporteur has contributed to a better understanding of how torture can be effectively combated by analyzing the conditions leading to torture and by recommending a variety of measure at the domestic level to prevent torture. These recommendations largely correspond to those mentioned by the HRC (see *supra* 3.3). Importance is further attached to the existence of an effective *habeas corpus* procedure and guarantees of an independent judiciary.[52]

3.5 The Working Group on Arbitrary Detention

In line with the above outlined approach of establishing a close relationship between the protection of personal integrity and personal liberty, we will consider briefly the effects on the prevention of torture which the activities of the Working Group on Arbitrary Detention can have. This Working Group was set up by the UN Commission on Human Rights in 1991.[53]

It was established to investigate cases of detention imposed arbitrarily or otherwise which are inconsistent with the relevant international standards, to seek and receive information from a variety of sources, including NGOs, and to present a comprehensive report to the Commission on Human Rights.

While the elimination of arbitrary forms of detention and imprisonment would as such have a considerable impact on the occurrence of torture - and the Working Group has made a quite dynamic start - a particular working method has to be mentioned. Similar to the Special Rapporteur on Torture the Working Group has developed an "urgent action" procedure on a purely humanitarian basis. This is resorted to in cases in which there are reliable allegations that a person is being detained arbitrarily and that the continuation of the detention constitutes a serious danger to that person's health or even

---

[52] Report of the Special Rapporteur on Torture, UN Doc. E/CN.4/1992/17, para. 275 et seq.

[53] Comm-Res. 1991/42.

life.[54] In its second report the Working Group lists eleven cases in which it addressed an "urgent action" message.[55] This seems to be an efficient way of responding rapidly to situations of high risk and in order to prevent the worst from happening.

3.6 Draft Additional Protocol to the European Convention on Human Rights concerning specific rights of detained persons

Apart from the pioneering role the Council of Europe has taken with its adoption of the European Convention for the Prevention of Torture another initiative must be mentioned for the purposes of this article. The Committee of experts for the development of human rights is considering the adoption of an Additional Protocol to the European Convention on Human Rights (ECHR) recognizing certain additional rights for persons deprived of their liberty.[56] This protocol could guarantee some basic safeguards in instances of deprivation of liberty, including the right to be informed promptly of the reasons for the deprivation of liberty and the right to inform a relative or a lawyer of the arrest. Such a protocol, which will be enforced by the European Commission and Court of Human Rights, could be a major step forward if it effectively contributes to strengthening the rights of persons in police custody, particularly for the period immediately following arrest. However, from the deliberations so far held, it is difficult to avoid the impression that a quite restrictive approach is being taken. This particularly concerns the possibility of restricting these rights to an extent "necessary in a democratic society in the interest of a preliminary investigation or the prevention of crime" (Art. 2 of the draft). The drafters should keep in mind what the European Committee for the Prevention of Torture stated in its second General Report concerning the right of a detained person to inform a third party, the right of access to legal counsel and the right

---

[54]Report of the Working Group on Arbitrary Detention, UN Doc. E/CN.4/1992/20, para. 11(a).

[55]Report of the Working Group on Arbitrary Detention, UN Doc. E/CN.4/1993/24, para. 18.

[56]CE Doc. DH-DEV (92) 4.

to be examined by a doctor of one's own choice: These rights are "three basic safeguards against the ill-treatment of detained persons which should apply as from the very outset of deprivation of liberty".[57]

3.7 The Human Dimension mechanism of the CSCE

Within the framework of the CSCE, the "emergency procedure", established at the 1991 Moscow Conference on the Human Dimension[58] could have some preventive effects with regard to torture. In case of a "particularly serious threat to the fulfilment of the provisions of the CSCE human dimension" ten participating states can send a mission of rapporteurs to another CSCE state without prior consultation with the state concerned. The mandate of the mission of rapporteurs is to establish the facts, to report on them and to give advice on possible solutions. As this procedure can already be initiated upon the detection of a serious threat and without the prior consultation of the state, it could be used to intervene effectively to prevent widespread torture. The Moscow mechanism entered into force in May 1992 following the nomination of 45 experts by 15 participating States. So far, the emergency mechanism has been used once. On 5 August 1992 it was invoked by the UK with the suppport of several other Western European states with regard to Croatia and Bosnia-Herzegovina.[59]

4. COEXISTENCE AND OVERLAPPING MECHANISMS

Considering the variety of international mechanisms which can be used to combat and more specifically prevent torture, the question arises how far do they complement or overlap each other and how an edifice for the fight against torture could be built whose composing bricks fit together well. In this respect, the importance of co-operation

---

[57]Second General Report of the CPT, CE Doc. CPT (92) 3, para. 36.

[58]See the contribution of A. Bloed in the present volume.

[59]Ibid.

and exchange of information between the different mechanisms has to be stressed.

While many possibilities of overlap exist, for the purpose of this article we will deal mainly with the overlapping that exists between the preventive systems of visits and the other mechanisms containing preventive elements.

4.1 The relationship between regional and universal systems of visits

Concerning the relationship between the universal and existing regional systems the draft Optional Protocol to the UN Convention against Torture states (Art. 9(1)) that the Sub-Committee shall not visit countries which are visited by bodies established according to regional systems, but that it may enter into consultations with these, including the possibility of one of its members participating in the visit of the regional body.

4.2 The relationship between systems of visits and the ICRC

Concerning the relationship between the visiting bodies established within universal and regional treaties and the International Committee of the Red Cross (ICRC), it is provided in these treaties that they do not affect the system of visits carried out by the ICRC (Art. 17(3) ECPT, Art. 9(1) draft Optional Protocol). According to the 1949 Geneva Conventions and their Additional Protocols of 1977 the ICRC can visit places where prisoners of war or civilian detainees are held. In internal armed conflicts the ICRC has access to these places only if the state concerned so agrees. Furthermore, on the basis of Article 5 of the Statutes of the International Red Cross and Red Crescent Movement and only upon a state's consent, the ICRC also acts in cases of internal disturbances and tensions which do not yet constitute armed conflicts. In all these cases the ICRC provides recommendations for the improvement of the situation of detained persons. All its activities are strictly confidential.

4.3 The relationship between systems of visits and other human rights treaties

In concrete terms, this section deals with the relationship between the ECPT and the draft Optional Protocol, on the one hand, and the UN Convention against Torture, the Covenant on Civil and Political Rights, the European Convention on Human Rights, the American Convention on Human Rights and the African Charter on Human and Peoples' Rights, on the other.

Concerning the specific relationship between the draft Optional Protocol and the CAT, the draft Optional Protocol provides for close institutional links between the Sub-Committee and the UN Committee against Torture, which establishes the Sub-Committee by electing its members and decides on the question of making a public statement.[60] To avoid possible overlapping, when the Committee against Torture visits a country in the context of a confidential inquiry under Article 20 CAT, the Sub-Committee shall postpone its mission to such a country (Art. 8(1)).

Furthermore, the nature of the preventive systems and the other human rights treaties is fundamentally different. While the latter, as described above, also contain preventive elements, their main thrust is the repression of human rights violations, i.e., dealing with inter-state and individual communications, and in the case of the CAT, carrying out confidential inquiries. Following its seizure by individuals or states, the treaty monitoring bodies have to determine whether violations of the state's obligations have been committed. Hence, they excercise judicial or quasi-judicial functions.

In contrast, the task of the body established within a system of visits is strictly non-judicial. It has only preventive functions by giving legally non-binding recommendations and by establishing an on-going dialogue with the states. It acts in an *ex officio* capacity and is, thus, able to look in a systematic and rigorous way at situations and

---

[60]As for the convincing reasons not to entrust the UN Committee against Torture with the carrying out of visits, see Introductory Memorandum to the Draft Optional Protocol, E/CN.4/1991/66, para. 6 et seq.

circumstances in different countries. The co-operative approach of such a system is geared more towards assisting states rather than condemning them.

In this respect, the practice of the CPT, which in its report on the United Kingdom had concluded that the totality of conditions amounting to inhuman and degrading treatment,[61] was criticized as transcending the competence of the CPT by interfering with the interpretation and application of Article 3 of the European Convention on Human Rights.[62] In our opinion, such an assessment by a non-judicial body seems to be within its mandate as long as it serves primarily as a basis for recommendations for the future prevention of torture and inhuman treatment. After all, the preventive function of visits carried out by the CPT cannot be totally separated from certain investigative tasks. If the CPT is to make useful suggestions for the prevention of torture, it must have some authority to assess the *status quo*.[63]

4.4 The relationship between the system of visits and the thematic procedures of the Commission on Human Rights

As described above, two thematic procedures based on resolutions of the Commission on Human Rights, the Special Rapporteur on Torture and the Working Group on Arbitrary Detention, also have preventive functions concerning torture.

The main preventive function, namely the urgent action procedure, is to respond rapidly to emergency situations in individual cases, a task which can only be exercised by the mentioned thematic mechanisms. This short-term prevention is essentially different from the preventive functions of the body established by a treaty providing for a system of visits. Prevention for the latter means the working of the environment and, in the final consequence, the eradication of the causes leading to torture.

---

[61]CE Doc. CPT/Inf (91) 15, para. 57.

[62]Evans and Morgan, loc.cit. n. 14, p. 592.

[63]Nowak, loc.cit. n. 35, p. 114 et seq.

The second identified preventive function, i.e., the carrying out of consultation visits to countries, can overlap with the system of visits, but the different legal and institutional backgrounds of these mechanisms show that this overlap is merely theoretical. Whereas the Special Rapporteur on Torture depends on an invitation by governments, states which ratified a treaty providing for a system of visits have the legal obligation to permit visits. These visits are of a systematic and periodic nature allowing for the establishment of on-going co-operative relations between the visiting body and the state.

4.5 The relationship between the Special Rapporteur on Torture and the Working Group on Arbitrary Detention

Both thematic procedures mentioned above have established rapid response procedures, which are activated under similar circumstances, i.e., when a person is deprived of his or her liberty (in an arbitrary form) and there is a risk to the detained person's integrity. In order to avoid the duplication of action close co-operation and exchange of information between these mechanisms is required.

5. RECOMMENDATIONS

5.1 Substantive recommendations

International law and the practice of the described mechanisms provide for a wide variety of measures to be taken at the domestic level in order to effectively prevent torture. These recommendations concern essentially the basic safeguards for persons deprived of their liberty, including:

1. The prohibition of incommunicado detention;
2. The right to inform family members and/or lawyers immediately of one's arrest;
3. Access to lawyers from the very outset of detention;
4. Access to independent doctors from the very outset of detention;
5. Making the *habeas corpus* procedure a non-derogable right;
6. The systematic review of interrogation rules;

7. Training and education of law enforcement personnel;
8. A system of inspection of places of detention by independent authorities at the national level;
9. The registration of detainees;
10. The keeping detained persons only in officially recognized detention places;
11. The inadmissibility in administrative and judicial procedures of statements made as a result of torture.

5.2 Procedural recommendations

1. The institution of a system of visits at the universal level, as proposed in the draft Optional Protocol to the UN CAT, is of utmost importance as it provides for the most efficient method of preventing torture and ill-treatment during detention. The established body should have a sound financial basis for fulfilling its far-reaching functions.

2. Co-operation and exchange of information between the existing mechanism should be intensified in order to prevent duplication of activity and overlapping.

3. The activities of advisory services in the field of criminal justice and human rights should be better co-ordinated, both between universal and regional organizations and within the UN. The and the Commission on Crime Prevention and Criminal Justice in Vienna shall establish closer links with the UN Centre for Human Rights in Geneva.

4. For the effective prevention of torture the building up of a legal and penal infrastructure and long-term structural changes are required. These measures should be supported within the advisory service programme and should become the object of development co-operation programmes, in accordance with the recognized link between human rights and development. Thus, the co-operative

approach for the prevention of torture would find its concrete expression.[64]

5. The Special Rapporteur on Torture and the Working Group on Arbitrary Detention should be given sufficient financial and human resources to carry out their functions. The Working Group should consider the drawing up of country reports on the existence of arbitrary detention and safeguards for detained persons. This would strengthen the capability of the Working Group to exercise a preventive function vis-à-vis a variety of gross human rights violations.

---

[64]See, e.g., the Final Declaration of the Regional Meeting for Africa of the World Conference on Human Rights, "Tunis Declaration", UN Doc. A/CONF.157/AFRM/14-A/CONF.157/PC/57.

INTERNATIONAL MECHANISMS FOR THE MONITORING AND PROTECTION OF MINORITY RIGHTS: THEIR ADVANTAGES, DISADVANTAGES AND INTERRELATIONSHIPS

by Gudmundur Alfredsson and Danilo Türk

1. INTRODUCTION

The beginning of the "post-cold-war era" gives rise to mixed impressions concerning the future action of intergovernmental organizations in the field of minority rights. While the historical changes have brought relief to some, they have also resulted in massive human rights violations and suffering for others. More ethnic conflicts have erupted than ever before and some of them threaten international peace and security. The world situation in this era of rapid development provides both opportunities and dangers, but the international institutions have so far been unable to provide an effective and organized response to these challenges of our time.

On the one hand, the recent changes have occurred partly due to action based on human rights. The remaining minority problems would also seem to be solvable under existing human rights standards provided, however, that appropriate policies are pursued. Respect for equality and dignity, the practice of tolerance and the preservation of identities would eliminate or at least soften conflict situations, reduce other problems in such fields as social services and health, and increase the groups' productivity and other contributions to society. New mechanisms have been set up to meet these challenges, in particular those developed within the Conference on Security and Co-operation in Europe (CSCE).

Documents emerging from the CSCE are demonstrative of the new thinking. There has been a marked growth in the acknowledgement of minority issues since the Helsinki and Madrid meetings. Documents from the Copenhagen, Geneva, Paris and Vienna gatherings established a number of far-reaching minority rights provisions. These provisions, in particular the context of confidence-building and peace-keeping in which they are made, deserve active consideration in

A. Bloed et al. (eds.), Monitoring Human Rights in Europe, 169–186.

human rights standard-setting and implementation by the United Nations. And the CSCE decision, in July 1992, to establish the post of High Commissioner on National Minorities is very promising.

The new thinking is beginning to take hold at the United Nations, albeit very timidly, and the Organization is currently pondering its general approaches to the implementation of minority rights and the resolution of ethnic conflicts. Reference will be made to the 1992 adoption by the General Assembly of a new declaration on minority rights and to the report of the Secretary-General on *An Agenda for Peace*. And at its first special session in August 1992, the Commission on Human Rights adopted a resolution which, *inter alia*, absolutely condemns the concept and practice of "ethnic cleansing" in parts of the territory of the former Yugoslavia.[1]

On the other hand, innovative procedures do not *per se* provide a guarantee that international action will henceforth become more effective. At present, a qualitative change in that regard is uncertain. As before, much depends on the actual political will and wisdom of governments in making use of the procedures. Too frequently, the primary concern of governments is the potential disruption or subversion which they expect as a result of too effective minority assertion. They assume that preferential treatment, in particular any arrangements delegating political, economic and cultural functions to groups, would fuel secessionist claims threatening the national unity, political independence and territorial integrity of states. Unilateral action by states on behalf of their "own nationals" across state boundaries contributes to an unfortunate politization of minority issues and increases rather than reduces tensions. Ignorance and a lack of understanding, as well as doctrines of superiority and racism, constitute further stumbling blocks.

---

[1]Further reflection upon the term "ethnic cleansing" is called for, but many of the actual practices of "ethnic cleansing" correspond to the acts enumerated in Article II of the Convention on the Prevention and Punishment of the Crime of Genocide. On the former Yugoslavia, see the contribution by R. Wieruszewski in the present volume.

The prescription of equal enjoyment of human rights for all individuals and prohibited discrimination is not enough. Preferential treatment, as well as collective rights, are needed to overcome patterns of discrimination and to put the minority groups, as well as their members, in an equal position compared with the majority population (equality in fact). Special rights and special measures do not constitute privileges; they are rooted in the principle of equal enjoyment just as is non-discrimination. Only the communal enjoyment of these rights with minorities using native languages, running their own schools, benefitting from access to other services provided by the group for the group, and participating in the political and economic affairs of states will approximate circumstances which the majority takes for granted.[2] By denying preferential treatment, not to mention collective rights, the achievement of equality for minorities would be left in doubt.

This reluctance towards minority rights is further demonstrated in the infrequent use of implementation mechanisms for existing standards and in the rare introduction of implementation procedures specifically geared to minority rights. In addition, the relevant procedures are not always accessible to the groups concerned or, when decisions have been taken, they are blocked at the political level. Still another consequence of the reluctance is late action, most often too late for prevention purposes, and uncoordinated or haphazard political action which results in unequal treatment and which may be seen, by other minorities, as rewarding conflict.

In the light of the difficulties associated with the implementation of existing standards which would contribute to justice and help alleviate some of the conflict situations, a number of questions inevitably arise. Before coming to them, we will briefly describe the existing standards and available procedures.

---

[2]G. Alfredsson, "Minority Rights and a New World Order", in D. Gomien, ed., *Broadening the Frontiers of Human Rights. Essays in Honour of Asbjørn Eide*, (Oslo 1993), pp. 55-78, at p. 57.

2. EXISTING INTERNATIONAL STANDARDS AND IMPLEMENTATION PROCEDURES

When the General Assembly adopted the Universal Declaration in 1948, it was decided that the United Nations could not remain indifferent to the "fate of minorities".[3] In one respect, the promise has been kept. There certainly is an abundance of standards in the international human rights instruments which directly or indirectly address minority rights. And in 1992, the United Nations adopted the Declaration on the Rights of Persons belonging to National or Ethnic, Religious and Linguistic Minorities which is the first such instrument devoted solely to minority rights. It restates many of the existing rights and adds that organizations of the United Nations system have a role to play in "the full realization of the rights and principles" set forth in the Declaration. It also ties minority rights together with the "development of society as a whole and within a democratic framework based on the rule of law".

Equality and non-discrimination are prescribed in the United Nations Charter, in the Universal Declaration of Human Rights, in the International Human Rights Covenants and in a series of additional instruments, such as the Declaration on the Elimination of All Forms of Intolerance and of Discrimination Based on Religion or Belief, the Convention concerning Discrimination in respect of Employment and Occupation (ILO[4] Convention No. 111) and the regional human rights conventions. The grounds, on which discrimination is prohibited, differ from one instrument to another, but the repeated references to race, colour, language, religion, national origin, social origin, birth and other status would cover traditional minority situations.

Provisions offering special protection are contained in the Convention on the Prevention and Punishment of the Crime of Genocide, the

---

[3]General Assembly Resolution 217 C(III) of 10 December 1948. For a general overview of subsequent developments, see an article by D. Türk on "Minority Issues in the United Nations: Norms and Institutions" which will appear in a forthcoming publication of the Human Rights Programme of Harvard Law School.

[4]International Labour Organization

International Covenant on Civil and Political Rights, the International Convention on the Elimination of All Forms of Racial Discrimination, the Convention on the Rights of the Child, UNESCO's[5] Convention against Discrimination in Education, UNESCO's Declaration on Race and Racial Prejudice, and the 1992 Declaration. The special rights and special measures are mainly established for the fields of education, culture, language and religion, but they may be extended to political, economic and social affairs. For indigenous peoples, there is the Convention concerning Indigenous and Tribal Peoples in Independent Countries (ILO Convention No. 169) which, most importantly, adds land and natural resources to the protection list.[6]

Treaty-based and resolution-based implementation procedures are in place for many of these instruments within the United Nations system:

- In examining state reports under the respective conventions, the Human Rights Committee, the Committee on the Elimination of Racial Discrimination and the Committee on the Rights of the Child regularly ask questions about minority rights.

- The Human Rights Committee and the Committee on the Elimination of Racial Discrimination can receive petitions concerning minority rights, and it is to be assumed that minority complaints are considered under the 1503 procedure concerning gross and consistent patterns of violation.[7]

---

[5]United Nations Educational, Scientific and Cultural Organization

[6]In this article, we do not deal with the question of definition. In general, see O. Andrysek, *Report on the Definition of Minorities*, the Netherlands Institute of Human Rights, SIM Special no. 8, (Utrecht 1989). In 1987, the United Nations Centre for Human Rights issued a compilation of definition proposals submitted to the United Nations over a 40 year period, see UN Doc. E/CN.4/1987/WG.5/WP.1. The latest proposal was submitted by J. Deschenes in UN Doc. E/CN.4/Sub.2/1985/31 and Corr. 1; see also resolution 1985/6 by the Sub-Commission on Prevention of Discrimination and Protection of Minorities.

[7]On the case law, see G. Alfredsson and A. de Zayas, "Minority Rights: Protection by the United Nations", 14 *Human Rights Law Journal*, (1993) no. 1-2, pp. 1-9.

- Special Rapporteurs of the Commission on Human Rights have addressed minority concerns in their reports, including those on religious intolerance, Iraq, Romania and the former Yugoslavia. A new Special Rapporteur to be appointed later this year on racism, racial discrimination, xenophobia and related intolerance is likely to do the same.

- Minority rights issues are frequently brought up in the Commission and in the Sub-Commission on Prevention of Discrimination and Protection of Minorities. The debates, under various agenda items, not least those dealing with violations of human rights, serve to draw attention to problems facing minorities around the world. According to one opinion recently expressed in the Sub-Commission, violations affecting persons belonging to national, ethnic, religious or linguistic minorities account for about 2/3 of the total number of violations considered.

- Minority considerations are increasingly, albeit slowly, entering international, multilateral and bilateral technical assistance and advisory services programmes.

- And finally, the Secretary-General and heads of specialized agencies have undertaken good offices for the sake of minorities and indigenous peoples. Different ILO and UNESCO procedures can also be employed in implementation efforts for minority rights.

The 1992 Declaration is not yet accompanied by an implementation mechanism. The momentum for United Nations efforts in pursuing minority protection was enhanced by the Secretary-General when he stated, in dealing with conflicts caused by ethnic, religious or linguistic groups which claim statehood, in his report on an Agenda for Peace:

> "One requirement for solutions to these problems lies in commitment to human rights with a special sensitivity to those of minorities, whether ethnic, religious, social or linguistic. The League of Nations provided a machinery for the international protection of minorities. The General Assembly will

> soon have before it a declaration on the rights of minorities. That instrument, together with the increasingly effective machinery of the United Nations dealing with human rights, should enhance the situation of minorities as well as the stability of States."[8]

The security-oriented approach to minority rights has been a strong factor in recent resolutions of the Security Council on Iraq and the former Yugoslavia, and it is likewise a prevailing component in the standards and procedures set up by the CSCE, including those of fact-finding and mediation missions and of the High Commissioner on National Minorities.[9] It has to be kept in mind, however, that this security-oriented approach to minority rights has so far yielded more at the level of expectations than at the level of practical results.

3. EVALUATION OF EXISTING MECHANISMS

The present world situation is characterized by discrimination against most minorities and by an increasing number of ethnic conflicts, both within states and between states. This situation calls for a comprehensive approach which would take into account all the relevant human rights, political and security aspects. Thus, for example, it is already recognized that the post-conflict peace-building, one of the essential aspects of the Agenda for Peace, would necessitate action in the field of human rights, very probably much beyond the scope of international human rights activities so far developed at the international level. The situation in El Salvador is a case in point, while in the near future Cambodia, Mozambique, Somalia and Bosnia-Herzegovina will probably expand the list.

The human rights component of United Nations peace operations has so far lacked coherence. It has been developed in a haphazard

---

[8] *An Agenda for Peace: Preventive, Diplomacy, Peacemaking and Peace-Keeping* in UN Doc. A/47/277 - S/24111, 17 June 1992, para.18.

[9] On the standards and procedures of the CSCE, see the contribution by A. Bloed in the present volume.

manner which hardly promises optimum results. It is also worth noting that the input of the United Nations human rights organs to the human rights aspects of the peace-keeping operations has been insignificant. This is true for the general aspects, that is the development of methods for reconciliation, confidence-building and mediation for the purposes of prevention, peace-keeping, peace-making and peace-restoration. It is also true for the specific conflict situations which other organs have been in charge of, including the human rights components.

In his report on an Agenda for Peace, the Secretary-General makes an explicit connection between the United Nations mandates for maintaining international peace and security and promoting and protecting human rights. The mandates are and should be interlinked, but governments have been slow in recognizing the connection because preventive and restorative action by intergovernmental organizations is seen as likely to infringe further the traditional principles of sovereignty and non-interference in internal affairs of states. The procedures being set up by the CSCE, including those of fact-finding and mediation missions and of the High Commissioner on National Minorities, can likewise be characterized by the desire to gainfully use human rights in general and minority rights, in particular for preventing conflict before it arises.

The CSCE will, hopefully, mature gradually from a debating society into a framework for various practical activities. This development will require time before specific results may realistically be expected. It is important, however, to examine closely and critically and to encourage the strengthening of the CSCE mechanisms, including their institutional background, secretariat facilities, the ability to analyse various situations and to prepare well-founded proposals, etc.

In suggesting a comprehensive approach to minority problems, it is important not to allow one of the components to override the others. There could be an obvious drawback to an emphasis on the peace and security factor if the human rights of minorities were to be neglected in the process. Minorities should not be confronted with the situation that the international community will only respond to their concerns if there is a conflict. Such an approach could easily backfire and generate more conflicts than it resolves. An objective, impartial and non-selective approach to minorities, involving the application of minority standards across the board, must therefore remain a crucial part of United Nations activities in this field.

The human rights programme of the United Nations also merits critical examination. While it is clear that the success in the setting of standards represents an historical achievement, much is left to be desired with regard to implementation. The system has become diversified and not always properly co-ordinated. As far as minority rights are concerned, as stated above, the mechanisms established are somewhat insufficient in terms of both access and outcome. Recently, Amnesty International has produced a comprehensive critique of the system[10] which constitutes a valuable contribution to the discussion and should be thoroughly considered before proposals for the future are formulated. In this context, suggestions about the role of non-governmental organizations (NGOs), improved co-ordination, strengthening of the secretariat and the establishment of the post of a Special Commissioner for Human Rights deserve particular attention.

4. SUGGESTED FUTURE ACTIVITIES

Equality, non-discrimination and preferential treatment for all minority groups, building on the rule of law and on judicial or quasi-judicial avenues for redress, offer the best chances of bringing relief and justice to minorities and at the same time stability to states and peace to the international community. The continuing changes in world politics, in the interest of everyone concerned, will hopefully lead to a greater willingness to address minority issues seriously along such objective and non-selective lines.

As for suggested future activities, this chapter considers three types of situations: activities concerning situations *not* characterized by an open conflict; activities concerning situations characterized by an open

---

[10] *Facing Up to the Failures: Proposals for Improving the Protection of Human Rights by the United Nations*, December 1992, AI Index: IOR 41/16/92.

political conflict and a certain amount of violence; and activities concerning situations which may constitute a threat to international peace and security.

4.1 Activities concerning situations not characterized by an open conflict

4.1.1 Implementation of the 1992 Declaration

As to resolution-based implementation procedures for minority rights, applicable across the world map, the establishment by the Commission on Human Rights of a Special Rapporteur or a working group would be desirable. In a statement to the Commission in 1992, the then Under-Secretary-General for Human Rights, Jan Martenson, proposed the appointment of a Special Rapporteur with a fact-finding and reporting mandate. Institutional support can also be sought in General Assembly resolution 41/120 which calls for the setting up of implementation procedures whenever new human rights instruments come into being. A *working group* would have the advantage of contributing to a regional balance, and perhaps more importantly, would create a forum for minorities to air their views and grievances, thus drawing on the successful experience of the Working Group on Indigenous Populations.

While the implementation efforts would have their point of departure in the 1992 Declaration, its provisions should be supplemented by references to other instruments containing minority rights. The Commission could even establish priority areas, such as the enjoyment of equality, dignity and non-discrimination in education, the administration of justice, access to the media, and representation in government and public affairs. Special rights and special measures as set forth in existing instruments, in order to guarantee equality, must be part of the picture; it should be understood that equality in fact most often requires preferential treatment for minorities.

The mechanisms proposed in the preceding paragraphs should have a mandate beyond that of traditional implementation, that is fact-finding and reporting back to the Commission. It is important that national reconciliation, facilitation of dialogue, the building of confidence and trust, and some form of mediation or dispute resolution should be involved with a view to the prevention of violence. A Special Commissioner for Human Rights, if that post were to be established, could play an additional role. The different approaches are not mutually exclusive.

CSCE models and experience could pave the way at the United Nations. Further regional or sub-regional approaches could also be employed. Note is taken in this regard of the endorsement in principle of the idea by the Second Ministerial Session of the Council of the Baltic Sea States (CBSS) to establish a CBSS Commissioner for Human Rights and Minorities Questions.[11] As with other proposals in this book, it is necessary that co-ordination be attended to; whatever mechanisms are set up, they should work hand-in-hand with other related treaty- and resolution-based mandates. Another worthwhile recommendation would be the convening of additional regional and sub-regional consultations, as appropriate, with a view to assessing the needs for establishing region-specific mechanisms of dialogue and co-operation.

These proposals address some of the most sensitive issues on the domestic political agendas of many states. It remains to be seen whether they are willing to accept an expanded international involvement in these matters, even when objective observers would see it as in the interest of the group, the state and the international community. It should not be forgotten that all the instruments in question, including the 1992 Declaration, stipulate that the national unity of states and their territorial integrity shall not be affected by minority rights. A debate about implementation and prevention is an important beginning because, if the proposals are rejected, the situation will remain very much the same as it is today.

---

[11]Communiqué of the Second Ministerial Session of the Council of the Baltic Sea States, Helsinki, 16-17 March 1993, para. 4.

4.1.2 The treaty bodies

A large number of states have accepted some of the treaties which contain significant minority rights language, including the International Covenant on Civil and Political Rights, the International Convention on the Elimination of All Forms of Racial Discrimination, and the Convention on the Rights of the Child. The monitoring bodies set up to supervise compliance with these treaties are composed of independent experts and can therefore be expected to come up with objective and impartial observations and recommendations as to respect for minority rights, by way of consideration of both state reports and communications, as applicable. Acceptance by states and the active use of these procedures should therefore be further encouraged.

The Covenant on Civil and Political Rights and its Optional Protocol are of particular significance because the Human Rights Committee has, when dealing with communications, strengthened and even expanded the jurisprudence on minority rights. In a recent case, for example, the Committee found that economic activity, if it is an essential element in the minority culture, may fall under Article 27 of the Covenant.[12]

Other treaty bodies, such as the Committee on Economic, Social and Cultural Rights under the International Covenant on Economic, Social and Cultural Rights and the Committee on the Elimination of Discrimination against Women (CEDAW) under the Convention on the Elimination of All Forms of Discrimination against Women, could certainly pay increased attention to state reports on the respective equality and non-discrimination clauses as they affect minorities. These committees would become still more relevant if current proposals for the establishment of petition procedures under the respective conventions come into being.

[12] Views of the Human Rights Committee on communication no. 197/1985 submitted by I. Kitok, with Sweden as the State Party concerned, Doc. CCPR/C/33/D/197/1985, issued 10 August 1988, para. 9.2.

4.1.3 Advisory services and technical assistance

Minority rights components should be a constantly available feature in the advisory services and technical assistance programmes offered by the United Nations Centre for Human Rights and by other inter-governmental, multilateral or bilateral organs. This would be true for training and teaching activities, assistance in the drafting of bills of rights and other legislation, and the setting up of national infra-structures for strengthening human rights. The United Nations can certainly make a more serious effort to develop relevant expertise and to draw lessons from existing experience in order make these services meaningful for the realization of minority rights. Furthermore, when-ever appropriate, advisory services and technical assistance pro-grammes should be made available not only to governments but also to the minorities themselves.

4.1.4 Participation by the minorities themselves

Apart from the more formal procedures, public debates in inter-governmental fora about human rights standards and violations attract attention and improve compliance. One has to assume that govern-ments do not welcome and would rather avoid institutional criticism and the consequent pressure, and this embarrassment factor has been successfully employed on many occasions. Allowing groups increased access to both policy-making and implementation bodies would ensure that these debates revolve around the real issues. Such access would also serve to let off steam in tense situations, especially as national fora are often lacking, in all parts of the world, for the airing of minority grievances.

As to the implementation procedures of human rights treaties, mino-rities should be given greater access and encouragement to express their point of view when monitoring bodies scrutinize state reports and to submit complaints to the same monitoring bodies.

Facilities equivalent to the status afforded to NGOs could also be given to minorities and minority organizations at the national level. Relevant United Nations precedents, beyond umbrella organizations, include indigenous peoples who have acquired consultative status with the United Nations Economic and Social Council in their own name (the Grand Council of the Crees of Quebec and the National Aboriginal and Islander Legal Services of Australia). There is also the United Nations Voluntary Fund for Indigenous Populations which enables indigenous representatives to participate in meetings of the Working Group on Indigenous Populations.

International NGOs, which have obtained consultative status within intergovernmental organizations, can and should press for minority rights more effectively and, to that end, utilize all openings available to them. To name just two NGOs, the Minority Rights Group in London and the International Helsinki Federation for Human Rights in Vienna, as well as their national chapters, deserve credit for consistent action on minority rights.

One type of forum lends itself particularly well to minority participation. This relates to gatherings of parliamentarians, such as the International Parliamentary Union, the Consultative Assembly of the Council of Europe and the European Parliament of the European Communities. Minority representatives have spoken up at these fora, and their fair representation and active participation should be further encouraged. In cases where minorities may not have the numbers necessary for representation, special measures should be taken to secure seats for them whenever possible.

4.1.5 Evolution of further standards

The Council of Europe in 1992 adopted a Charter on Regional and Minority Languages, and the Council is now considering additional standards. These could possibly take the form of a protocol to the European Convention on Human Rights and Fundamental Freedoms. At the United Nations, it has been suggested that a convention should follow the above-mentioned Declaration. Such moves would be desirable inasmuch as they move minority rights more firmly towards objective and impartial responses at the international level and away from more political and selective treatment. Assertive general comments adopted by the human rights treaty bodies could serve the same purpose.

Drafters of human rights standards have much to learn from legislative, administrative and judicial arrangements at the national level and even from bilateral agreements. A number of states, some of them in Europe, have adopted minority rights regimes, including Finland for the Aland Islands, Denmark for the Faeroe Islands and Greenland, Germany and Poland for their respective national groups, and Italy (with Austria looking over its shoulder) for the South Tyrolians. The introduction by Spain of regional self-control has much reduced tensions between the central authorities and the Basques and Catalans.

A promising project is underway in the Sub-Commission on Prevention of Discrimination and Protection of Minorities which has appointed Asbjørn Eide as Special Rapporteur to report on constructive national arrangements for minority rights. The Rapporteur has already submitted preliminary and progress reports and the final report, with his conclusions and recommendations, is due in the summer of 1993.[13] The international community may well find worthwhile lessons in these arrangements, not least with regard to autonomy or self-government.[14]

---

[13]The most recent report is contained in UN Doc. E/CN.4/Sub.2/1992/37 and Addenda 1-2. His appointment was preceded by a working paper from C. Palley, entitled "Possible ways and means to facilitate the peaceful and constructive resolution of situations involving racial, national, religious and linguistic minorities" and contained in UN Doc. E/CN.4/Sub.2/1989/43. An expert report entitled "The Status of Minorities and Ethnic Groups in the Member States of the Council of Europe", prepared by E. Grisel and contained in Council of Europe Doc. AS/Jur (40) 7 of July 1988, presents an extensive factual and legal analysis of national undertakings. Relevant information is also available in reports submitted by the states parties to the two Covenants and the Convention on the Elimination of All Forms of Racial Discrimination.

[14]On autonomy in general, see L.B. Sohn, "The Concept of Autonomy in International Law and the Practice of the United Nations", 15 *Israel Law Review*, (1980) pp. 180-190, and H. Hannum and R.B. Lillich, "The Concept of Autonomy in International Law," 74 *AJIL*, (1980), pp. 858-889.

4.2 Activities concerning situations characterized by an open political conflict, including those which involve a certain amount of violence

As suggested above, existing or forthcoming implementation mechanisms for minority rights, whether it is a Special Rapporteur or a working group or a Special Commissioner, should be empowered to act in a preventive manner. He or she or they should have the authority to offer good offices in matters which would, according to conservative interpretations, fall within the domestic jurisdiction of states. Furthermore, in situations characterized by differences in the assessment of the relevant facts, they should be able to launch an impartial and, when necessary, international investigation and to make proposals to the government of the state and international fora concerned. They should also have the authority to use confidential or public methods of communication with the governments and minorities involved. The choice of communication would have to be made upon an evaluation of which type is most appropriate for helping in efforts to solve the conflict.

Another approach which could, in fact, represent an useful complement to the activities mentioned in the preceding paragraph would be based on the appropriate utilization of the "dormant" powers of the General Assembly as provided for in Article 14 of the United Nations Charter. This article stipulates that the Assembly may recommend measures for the peaceful adjustment of any situation, regardless of origin, which might impair the general welfare of friendly relations among states. The Assembly could take up situations involving the rights and/or status of minorities at a relatively early stage, that is before such a situation deteriorates into an open conflict. Measures recommended could relate either to procedural methods, such as negotiations, dispute settlement, etc., or to substantive policy measures necessitated by the circumstances.

The utilization of these powers would probably require a higher degree of international understanding and common interest than is currently the case. The establishment of a permanent subsidiary body of the General Assembly, empowered to take up "Article 14 type of situations", at the initiative of the Secretary-General, a state or a group of states and for the purpose of analysis and preparation of recommendations to be considered by the Assembly, might well serve as an useful method of approaching the challenges of both pre-conflict minority situations and the better utilization of existing powers of international fora. It is understood that such an evolution, if it is to lead to a realistic programme, would require political support from the major groups of member states.

4.3 Activities concerning situations which may constitute a threat to international peace and security

In situations which may constitute a threat to international peace and security the Special Rapporteur or a working group or a Special Commissioner would have to be empowered to draw the attention of the competent human rights organs and the Secretary-General to the seriousness of the situation. Although the Secretary-General would, of course, remain autonomous in his/her decision whether to invoke Article 99 of the United Nations Charter, it would have to be understood that an early warning from the Special Rapporteur/working group/Commissioner amounts to a *prima facie* case for the Secretary-General's action under Article 99. After the initiative of the Secretary-General, regular procedures of the Security Council should follow.

In this context, the experience gained from the contributions made by the Special Rapporteurs on Iraq and on the former Yugoslavia, who have appeared before the Security Council, is very important, and this experience could be used as a source of inspiration for the further development of appropriate methods of work by the Council.

5. FINAL REMARKS

Finally, and these remarks apply to all the chapters above, we would like, as do other authors in this book, to emphasize and underline the co-ordination between the different international and regional organizations involved in minority rights work. While all efforts should be made to avoid the adoption of conflicting standards, competition or overlapping responsibilities in monitoring and implementation is not necessarily a bad thing. After all, there are thousands of minority situations which need to be addressed on a continuing basis. It is important, however, that these organizations keep each other informed about their initiatives and ongoing activities and that they share the public as well as confidential information gathered for reasons of efficiency and credibility.

FUTURE PROTECTION OF ECONOMIC AND SOCIAL RIGHTS IN EUROPE

by Asbjørn Eide

1. INTRODUCTION: On the functions of international human rights protection and the obstacles confronting economic and social rights[1]

When taken seriously, international human rights law imposes obligations on states concerning their treatment of persons under their jurisdiction. These obligations set limitations and directions for domestic policy choices. International monitoring and protection of human rights should serve to influence states to abide by those limitations and directions in their domestic policy choices. This is a task of major proportions since it affects in significant ways the policy options available to the political forces within states. For reasons subsequently to be elaborated, governments are even less inclined to accept limitations and directions regarding economic and social policy than with regard to civil rights issues.

The societies in the former East European "block" are now undergoing a dramatic economic change, affecting the economic and social circumstances of their inhabitants, some for the better and others for the worse. High unemployment, unknown for decades, and a low level of social security has seriously affected the enjoyment of human rights. Western, industrialized countries are also going through a difficult period. Unemployment has been on the rise since 1973 with

---

[1]A general survey, now somewhat dated, of international protection of economic and social rights is found in A.G. Mower, Jr., *International Cooperation for Social Justice* (Westport/London 1985). On the relationship between economic and social rights see also P. Alston, "Human Rights and Basic Needs: A Critical Assessment", 12 *Revue des droits de l'homme,* (1979) pp. 19-67; P. Alston, "International Law and the Human Rights to Food", in P. Alston and K. Tomasevski, eds., *The Right to Food* (Dordrecht 1986) pp. 9-69; I. Brownlie, *The Human Rights to Food* (London 1987); A. Eide et al., eds., *Food as a Human Right* (Tokyo: United Nations University 1984); A. Eide, A. Oshaug and W.B. Eide, "Food Security and the Right to Food in International Law and Development", 1 *Transnational Law and Contemporary Problems* (1991) no. 2, pp. 415-67; K. Tomasevski, "Human Rights: The Right to Food", 70 *Iowa Law Review* (1985) pp. 1321-1328.

A. Bloed et al. (eds.), Monitoring Human Rights in Europe, 187–219.

a slight and temporary recovery in the mid-1980s, to be followed by a significant further rise to reach proportions comparable to the inter-war years.[2] Secondly, the demographic population structure in the Western countries has generated additional problems for social security and other public expenditures: the percentage of retired and disabled persons requiring support has risen steeply, while the percentage of gainfully employed persons has gone down.

Are international agencies able to monitor the processes of change in order to ensure that economic and social rights are enjoyed also during the difficult transition period in the East and the recession and adjustment period in the West?

Taking a closer look at obligations arising from the international human rights system as a whole, it can be observed that they operate on three levels. States must, on the primary level, *respect* the degree of freedom contained in human rights law for all individuals. State obligations consist, on a secondary level, of the protection of the freedom of action and the use of resources as against other, more assertive or aggressive private parties. This follows from civil and political rights but, as will later be demonstrated, this is also the most important aspect of economic and social rights. On the tertiary level, the state has the obligation to *fulfil* the conditions under which everyone can enjoy their rights. This may take two forms:

- Assistance in order to provide *opportunities* for those who do not have them under existing circumstances ("empowerment"), including employment opportunities;

- *Provisions* of resources, through educational and health services for all, through planned and co-operative social security arrangements, and through safety nets when no other possibility exists for persons whose basic needs would otherwise not be met.

---

[2]For details about the unemployment issues in different parts of the world, see International Labour Office, *World Labour Report 1993*.

It can be observed, therefore, that the obligations function as *limitations* on policy choices by requiring respect for the freedom of individuals - not only the most basic respect for life and limb, for personal liberty, for freedom of religion, conviction, information and expression, but also the freedom to form and take part in political associations to compete for political power, the freedom to choose one's own preferred work, the freedom to form and take part in trade unions and to carry out trade union activities. Governments are not entitled to pursue policies which block these freedoms.

Secondly, it can be seen that the obligations serve as directions for policy choices to be made: the state is obliged to protect the effective enjoyment of the right to life against threats from private (non-state) parties, which requires action in many fields. One direction is by way of policies related to criminal law which must be effectively enforced so that the rights and liberties of persons can be protected; another is by anti-discrimination policies protecting the effective enjoyment of free choice of work against racial or gender-based discrimination; a third direction relates to labour market policies, including the search for high (preferably full) employment and effective protection of trade union rights against employers which might seek to circumvent or block such rights. Further, the state is obliged to pursue policies aimed at ensuring the highest attainable standard of health for all, and to pursue educational policies which makes it possible for everyone to have at least primary education free of charge.

Since the state not only has to observe limits beyond which it cannot go, but also actively to pursue goals required under international human rights law, there is a delicate balance to be struck between the freedom of the individual, the obligation of the individual to do nothing that blocks the enjoyment of human rights by others, and the duties of the individual to contribute towards the solution of the common tasks required by the human rights system. The formula in the Universal Declaration of Human Rights Article 29 implicitly recognizes that duties have to be imposed in order to ensure the enjoyment of human rights.

This is why we have to recognize that human rights form a comprehensive system where the rights have to be weighed against each other.

Why is the existence of international human rights and the machineries for their protection so important, even in regard to fully democratic societies? Why could it not be left to the discretion of the democratic forces inside each state freely to determine the content and level of regulations, and the allocation of resources for economic and social purposes?

One major purpose is to lift at least the main outlines of economic and social policies above the vicissitudes of changing political alignments; in order to sustain a social contract to the benefit of everyone under the jurisdiction of a state; and to move towards an international equalization of economic and social rights enjoyment through international co-operation.

For the obligations to become real, human rights must permeate the political culture sufficiently to ensure that any government which emerges from the democratic processes of a country, whatever its political colour, complies with those obligations. When the political culture is not sufficiently influenced by human rights requirements, international protection is required in order to influence governments to keep within the political choices which are compatible with the international human rights system.

2. RECOGNITION OF ECONOMIC AND SOCIAL RIGHTS

Economic and social rights were made parts of the international system of human rights from its first inception. A major impetus to the adoption of *universal* human rights came from the United States under the Roosevelt administration during World War II. The trigger was the "Four Freedoms" address by Franklin D. Roosevelt, then President of the United States, in January 1941. One of the four freedoms which he envisaged the post-war world order would be built upon was the freedom from want.[3] The preparation of the United Nations proceeded within the U.S. administration on the basis of the ideas contained in that address. Simultaneously, the American Law Institute drafted an International Bill of Human Rights which included economic and social rights.

In his 1944 *State of the Union Message* to the U.S. Congress, Roosevelt advocated as U.S. President the adoption of an "economic Bill of Rights", saying that

> "We have come to the clear realization of the fact that true individual freedom cannot exist without economic security and independence. 'Necessitous men are not free men'. People who are hungry and out of a job are the stuff of which dictatorships are made".[4]

He proposed for inclusion many of those economic and social rights which subsequently came to be included in the Universal Declaration and later in the International Covenant on Economic and Social Rights.

During the preparation of the Universal Declaration, in 1947-1948, the United States delegation to the United Nations Human Rights Commission spoke in favour of the inclusion of economic and social rights, repeating almost verbally what Franklin Roosevelt had stated in 1944: A man in need is not a free man.

The inclusion of economic and social rights in the Universal Declaration found support both from West European states and by states of Eastern Europe. It is therefore historically wrong to claim that these rights were introduced upon the initiative of the socialist countries. Controversies were later to arise regarding the nature of the subsequent instruments, and the formulation of obligations arising

---

[3]On the Roosevelt conception of freedom from want as a source of contemporary conceptions of human rights, see further in Eide et al., loc.cit. n. 1, pp. 415-467.

[4]For details on this statement by Roosevelt, see P. Alston, "U.S. Ratification of the Covenant on Economic, Social and Cultural Rights: The Need for an Entirely New Strategy", 84 *AJIL* (1990) pp. 365-393, at p. 387.

from economic and social rights, but their inclusion in the International Bill of Human Rights were never contested during the founding years of international human rights.

The realization, particularly in the West, that the political upheavals and the emergence of totalitarian regimes in the period between the two world wars had been due to the widespread unemployment and poverty, led to a genuine interest in securing economic and social rights, not only for their own sake but for the preservation of individual freedom and democracy. It was based on a conviction that, even in periods of recession, it would not only be possible but necessary to ensure that basic economic and social rights could be enjoyed by all.

These concerns are no less important in the present time, in light of escalating unemployment and increasing poverty, particularly in Central and Eastern Europe but also in the West. It is necessary, therefore, to increase the efficiency of international mechanisms in this field and possibly to develop new ones.

The indivisibility and interdependence of civil and political rights, on the one hand, and economic, social and cultural rights, on the other, has become a fundamental tenet of the United Nations approach to human rights. But while this doctrine has frequently been reaffirmed by the various human rights organs, it has not been sufficiently reflected in practice whether at the national or international levels. Legal and political arguments have been used against these rights.

One problem is that the precise content of a number of economic, social and cultural rights, as well as the specific obligations which they imply for states parties to the International Covenant on Economic, Social and Cultural Rights, remain vague. This vagueness, when contrasted with the degree of precision with which most civil and political rights have been elaborated, has tended to encourage the relative neglect of economic and social rights. It is necessary to clarify better the scope of the right - or more precisely, of the corresponding obligations held by states.

An objection to economic rights *qua* human rights is that they are not legally enforceable. Thus, for example, it has been argued that "the implementation of these provisions [including Article 11] is a political matter, not a matter of law, and hence not a matter of rights".[5] This is hardly tenable. The adoption of laws is always a matter of politics. States have to transform their international human rights obligations into more precise domestic laws and administrative regulations. This applies both to civil, political, economic, social and cultural rights. Admittedly, some human rights already form a well-known part of domestic legal tradition in some countries and therefore do not raise much doubts as to their scope and content. In other societies those very same rights may not form part of the legal tradition and considerable transformation may be required in order to fulfil the international obligations.

It has been argued that economic rights are of a fundamentally different nature from civil and political rights in that the latter are 'negative' rights, the implementation of which is cost-free, while the former are 'positive' and costly.[6] 'Negative' means that they consist in freedom from the state, and 'positive' that they require action by the state, and therefore are costly. We cannot, however, make a neat distinction around the axis 'negative/positive' between civil and political rights, on the one hand, and economic, social and cultural, on the other.

[5]E.W. Vierdag, "The Legal Nature of the Rights Granted by the International Covenant on Economic, Social and Cultural Rights", 9 *Netherlands Yearbook of International Law* (1978) p. 103.

[6]M. Bossyut, "La distinction juridique entre les droits civils et politiques et les droits économiques, sociaux et culturels", 8 *Revue des droits de l'homme - Human Rights Journal* (1975) no. 4.

3. RIGHTS AND OBLIGATIONS

The economic and social rights listed in the International Bill of Human Rights have been elaborated and amplified in a number of universal[7] and regional[8] instruments.

They include the right to work, which gives rise to at least two major obligations on the state: to ensure that everyone can gain their living by work they freely choose and accept, and the pursuit of a policy of full and productive employment, as provided for in the International Covenant on Economic, Social and Cultural Rights (CESCR) Article 6.[9] Further included are rights in the workplace such as safe and healthy working conditions and equal pay for equal work (CESCR Art. 7);[10] the right to form and join trade unions (CESCR Art. 8);[11] the right to social security (CESCR Art. 9);[12] the right to protection of the family including protection of children and mothers (CESCR

---

[7]The "universal" instruments are those which have been adopted by the United Nations or the specialized agencies, of which the International Labour Organization (ILO) is particularly important in the field of standard-setting and monitoring.

[8]Among the regional instruments, the most important for the purpose of this paper is the European Social Charter, adopted by the Council of Europe in 1961. It will be further examined below.

[9]Relevant international instruments include the ILO's Employment Policy Convention, 1964 (No. 122), the ILO's Employment and Occupation Convention, 1958 (No. 111); International Convention on the Elimination of all Forms of Racial Discrimination, and the Convention on the Elimination of all Forms of Discrimination Against Women.

[10]Other relevant instruments include the following ILO conventions: Minimum Wage-Fixing Convention, 1970 (No. 131); Equal Remuneration Convention, 1951 (No. 100); Weekly Rest (Industry) Convention, 1921 (No. 14); Weekly Rest (Commerce and Offices) Convention, 1957 (No. 106); Holidays with Pay Convention (Revised), 1970 (No. 132); Labour Inspection Convention, 1947 (No. 81); Labour Inspection (Agriculture) Convention, 1969 (No. 129); Occupational Safety and Health Convention, 1981 (No. 155).

[11]International Covenant on Civil and Political Rights Art. 22; ILO Freedom of Association and Protection of the Right to Organise Convention, 1948 (No. 87); ILO Right to Organise and Collective Bargaining Convention, 1949 (No. 98); ILO Labour Relations (Public Service) Convention, 1978 (No. 151).

[12]Other relevant instruments include ILO Social Security (Minimum Standards) Convention, 1952 (No. 102) and other relevant subsequent ILO Conventions (Nos. 121, 128, 130 and 168).

Art. 10);[13] the right to food, clothing and housing; the right to health; and the right to education.

While economic, social and cultural rights are broadly recognized, the corresponding obligations are not. They are largely formulated as broad obligations of result rather than specific obligations of conduct.[14] This has its strengths and weaknesses. Its strength is that it allows for flexibility, making it possible for states to comply with their obligations in ways which correspond to their particular situation. The weakness is that the obligations - and their neglect - are very difficult to pinpoint.

Under the International Covenant on Economic, Social and Cultural Rights, each state party has undertaken to take steps, individually and through international assistance and co-operation, especially economic and technical, to the maximum of its available resources, to achieve progressively the rights contained in the Covenant (CESCR Art. 2).

State obligations for economic and social rights were elaborated by a group of experts, convened by the International Commission of Jurists, in Limburg (the Netherlands) in June 1986. The outcome are the so-called Limburg principles.[15] Among them we find the following:

> "7. States parties must at all times act in good faith to fulfil the obligations they have accepted under the Covenant.
>
> "8. Although the full realization of the rights recognized in the Covenant is to be attained progressively, the application of

---

[13]Other relevant instruments include: International Covenant on Civil and Political Rights Art. 23; International Convention on the Rights of the Child; International Convention on the Elimination of all Forms of Discrimination Against Women; ILO Maternity Protection Convention (Revised), 1952 (No. 102); ILO Minimum Age Convention, 1973 (No. 138).

[14]On this distinction, see G. Goodwin-Gill "Obligations of Conduct and Results", in Alston and Tomasevski, eds., op.cit. n. 1, pp. 111-118.

[15]The Limburg principles can be found in UN Doc. E/CN.4/1987/17, annex, and are reprinted in 9 *Human Rights Quarterly* (1987) no. 2.

> some rights can be made justiciable immediately while other rights can become justiciable over time."

Development essentially means the realization of human rights in all their aspects, as implicitly stated in the Declaration on the Right to Development, Article 1:

> "The individual is by virtue of the right to development entitled to participate in, contribute to and enjoy economic, social, cultural and political development in which all human rights and fundamental freedoms can be fully realized."[16]

States are under an obligation to regulate the labour market and to achieve a redistribution, transfer and allocation of resources necessary to ensure the realization of the rights contained in the Covenant. It can be done in different ways in different societies, depending on the situation prevailing there. What is important is that results are obtained in ways which ensure everyone of their rights.

A number of economic rights have been shown to be enforceable in the context of domestic law provided only that their component parts are formulated in a sufficiently precise and detailed manner. Such is the case, for example, with some of the economic rights which have been proclaimed in the International Covenant on Economic, Social and Cultural Rights and then spelled out in greater detail within the framework of the system of international labour conventions and recommendations adopted by the International Labour Organization (ILO).[17]

Several conventions take an integrated approach to the different kinds of rights, in particular the Convention on the Rights of the Child.

The major focus should be on respecting and providing space for the self-realization of economic and social rights, together with the

---

[16]Included is also the full realization of the rights of peoples to self-determination and their sovereignty over natural wealth and resources, Art. 1 para. 2.

[17]See generally N. Valticos, *Droit international de travail* (Paris 1983).

establishment of effective collective solutions to certain problems which can best be solved collectively (old age pensions, medical care).

While these are, to a large extent, obligations of result, there is a need to ensure that steps are taken in the direction leading to such results, and for that to happen it will become clear that specific steps must be taken.

According to the Limburg Principles, a state will be in violation of CESCR, *inter alia*, if

- it fails to take a step required by the Covenant;

- it fails to remove promptly obstacles which it is under a duty to remove and permit the immediate fulfilment of a right;

- it fails to implement without delay a right which is required by the Covenant to implement immediately;

- it wilfully fails to meet a generally accepted international minimum standard of achievement, which is within its power to meet;

- it applies a limitation on a right recognized in the Covenant other than in accordance with the Covenant;

- it deliberately retards or halts the progressive realization of a right, unless it is acting within a limitation permitted by the Covenant;

- it fails to submit reports as required under the Covenant.

The task is not only to determine whether violations have been committed but whether achievements are satisfactory under the prevailing conditions. For this to be possible, *indicators* are required. This issue has been thoroughly examined in the study on economic and social rights prepared by Danilo Türk in his major study for the

United Nations Sub-Commission on Prevention of Discrimination and Protection of Minorities.[18]

4. A NOTE ON INTERNATIONAL MECHANISMS IN GENERAL

At the international level we can find mechanisms for "monitoring" and "control" which are primarily political or primarily legal in their operation.[19] The dichotomy between "political" and "legal" can be applied either to the composition of the body or to the procedures used. A body is "political" if composed of representatives of states who are subject to the instructions of their governments. A body composed of independent experts is not, however, necessarily a "legal" body, unless it uses legal procedures. In practice, there are different shades of "political" versus "legal" bodies and mechanisms involved in the international protection of human rights. For economic and social rights, the emphasis has so far tended to be more on the political than the legal, but this is gradually changing.

All human rights instruments, whether declaratory or in the form of conventions, imply a duty on governments to co-operate in the realization of the rights involved. The process of transforming very general norms to more manageable and precise obligations of states, and the process of developing mechanisms of control, is primarily a task for

---

[18]His comprehensive study is found in:
D. Türk, *Realization of Economic, Social and Cultural Rights*. Progress report prepared for the United Nations Sub-Commission on Prevention of Discrimination and Protection of Minorities. UN Doc. E/CN.4/Sub.2/1990/19.

D. Türk, *Realization of Economic, Social and Cultural Rights*. Second progress report prepared for the United Nations Sub-Commission on Prevention of Discrimination and Protection of Minorities. UN Doc. E/CN.4/Sub.2/1991/17.

D. Türk, *Realization of Economic, Social and Cultural Rights*. Final report prepared for the United Nations Sub-Commission on Prevention of Discrimination and Protection of Minorities. UN Doc. E/CN.4/Sub.2/1992/16.

[19]On this distinction, see T. van Boven, "'Political' and 'Legal' Mechanisms: Their Competition and Co-existence", in A. Eide and B. Hagtvet, eds., *Human Rights in Perspective - a Global Assessment* (London 1992) pp. 36-60.

"political" machineries, whereas the examination of the compliance of states with precisely formulated commitments could be more of a legal nature.

Economic and social rights are to a large extent still in the process of being made more precise. Secondly, the impact on the realization of these rights for the economic policies of states in different stages of development is still contested. Consequently, "political" bodies have had a greater role than the more "legal" ones until now.

Reporting procedures are by their very nature somewhat more "political" in that their main focus is on the development of a dialogue which can take into account the various possibilities of states, while complaint procedures are more strictly legal.

Economic and social rights at the global level are partly dealt with by a "political" body (the Human Rights Commission) advised by its expert Sub-Commission on Prevention of Discrimination and Protection of Minorities. The Sub-Commission has over several years appointed special rapporteurs who have studied specific aspects of this category of rights.

The Commission on Human Rights has pursued a debate on a very general level about economic and social rights but has not gone into much depth. The Commission should probably be encouraged to consider the appointment of thematic rapporteurs dealing with specific economic, social and cultural rights. It should also be encouraged to draft better mechanisms to monitor the implementation of human rights. Specifically, it could explore the possibility of drafting an optional protocol to the International Covenant on Economic, Social and Cultural Rights affording individuals and groups the right to submit communications alleging non-compliance by states parties, whether by act or omission, with the provisions of the Covenant.

The main treaty body at the global level is the Committee on Economic, Social and Cultural Rights. At present, it only operates a reporting procedure.[20] The Committee has spelled out functions of reporting which may be of general relevance for other bodies also:

> "To ensure that a comprehensive review is undertaken with respect to national legislation, administrative rules and procedures and practices in an effort to ensure the fullest possible conformity with the Covenant,
>
> to ensure that the State party monitors the actual situation with respect to each of the rights on a regular basis and is thus aware of the extent to which the rights are, or are not, being enjoyed by all individuals within its territory or under its jurisdiction."

The first General Comment adopted by the Committee on Economic, Social and Cultural Rights sets out a variety of objectives, which, in the view of the Committee, should be served by reporting ...

> "2. A *first objective*, which is of particular relevance to the initial report required to be submitted within two years of the Covenant's entry into force for the State party concerned, is to ensure that a comprehensive review undertaken with respect to national legislation, administrative rules and procedures, and practices in an effort to ensure the fullest possible conformity with the Covenant ...
>
> "3. A *second objective* is to ensure that the State party monitors the actual situation with respect to each of the rights on a regular basis and is thus aware of the extent to which the various rights are, or are not, being enjoyed by all individuals within its territory or under its jurisdiction ...

---

[20]For a description and analysis of the Committee, see P. Alston, "Out of the Abyss?: The Challenges Confronting the New UN Committee on Economic, Social and Cultural Rights", 9 *Human Rights Quarterly* (1987) pp. 332-381; and P. Alston, "The Committee on Economic, Social and Cultural Rights", in P. Alston, ed., *The United Nations and Human Rights. A Critical Appraisal* (Oxford 1992) pp. 473-509.

"4. While monitoring is designed to give a detailed overview of the existing situation, the principal value of such an overview is to provide the basis for the elaboration of clearly stated and carefully targeted policies, including the establishment of priorities which reflect the provisions of the Covenant. Therefore, a *third objective* of the reporting process is to enable the Government to demonstrate that such principled policy-making has in fact been undertaken ...

"5. A *fourth objective* of the reporting process is to facilitate public scrutiny of government policies with respect to economic, social and cultural rights and to encourage the involvement of the various economic, social and cultural sectors of society in the formulation, implementation and review of the relevant policies ...

"6. A *fifth objective* is to provide a basis on which the State party itself, as well as the Committee, can effectively evaluate the extent to which progress has been made towards the realization of the obligations contained in the Covenant ...

"8. *A sixth objective* is to enable the State party itself to develop a better understanding of the problems and shortcomings encountered in efforts to realize progressively the full range of economic, social and cultural rights ...

"9. A *seventh objective* is to enable the Committee, and the States parties as a whole, to facilitate the exchange of information among States and to develop a better understanding of the common problems faced by States and a fuller appreciation of the type of measures which might be taken to promote effective realization of each of the rights contained in the Covenant ..."

The Committee on the Elimination of Racial Discrimination is very often faced with problems concerning the relationship between racial discrimination and the realization of economic, social and cultural rights. Similarly, the Committee on the Elimination of Discrimination against Women is also faced with extensive areas of discrimination faced by women with regard to their enjoyment of economic, social and cultural rights. The same applies to the Committee on the Rights of the Child, since economic, social and cultural rights of children are extensively contained in the Convention on the Rights of the Child.

The role of NGOs and interested parties other than governments in the machineries of protection is essential. In this connection, the ILO has been particularly effective. While most human rights organizations appear to be relatively unfamiliar with the ILO, it is in fact the most effective organization dealing with economic and social human rights. Much could be learned by other bodies from its experience and procedures.[21] The ILO has a special tripartite structure which makes it particularly dynamic and effective, through participation on an equal level by governments, representatives of trade union federations and by employers' associations. The latter can be seen as kinds of NGOs, albeit of a special kind. There is no doubt that their active involvement makes the ILO standard-setting, and the monitoring of its implementation, much more effective than do other institutions.

It would be desirable that active non-governmental participation be developed also outside the ILO. The body which has come furthest in this connection is the Committee on the Rights of the Child.

5. THE EUROPEAN SOCIAL CHARTER

The European Social Charter was adopted by the Council of Europe in 1961, and is the counterpart of the European Convention for the Protection of Human Rights and Fundamental Freedoms[22]. It contains in its part I a Declaration of Aims which contracting states shall pursue by all appropriate means, and in its part II a set of

---

[21]For a fuller discussion of the performance of the ILO and the lessons that can be drawn from it, see V.A. Leary, "Lessons from the Experience of the International Labour Organization", in Alston, ed., op.cit. n. 20, pp. 508-519.

[22]For more details about the European Social Charter, see D. Harris, *The European Social Charter* (Charlottesville, VA 1984). See also A. Berstein, "Economic and Social Rights: Their Inclusion in the European Convention on Human Rights: Problems of Formulation and Interpretation", 2 *Human Rights Law Journal* (1981) pp. 257-280.

articles which to a large extent correspond to the provisions in the International Covenant on Economic, Social and Cultural Rights. However, states do not have to accept *all* the articles of the Social Charter; they shall choose from a "menu" of obligations - 10 out of the 19 articles in part II or 45 out of the 72 "numbered paragraphs" of which the 19 articles consist.

The Charter protects most of the internationally recognized economic and social rights, but the right to education is not included, in contrast to the International Covenant on Economic, Social and Cultural Rights. It may be argued that the right to education is cultural rather than economic or social, but education is essential for performance in the economic field.

Contracting parties submit reports concerning the application of the provisions they have accepted. They also have to support information at appropriate intervals as requested by the Committee of Ministers on the provisions that they have not accepted.

In the latter field, parties are required to give a concise summary of current law and practice in the fields covered by the provisions that they have not accepted, and to give reasons why they have not been accepted.

States are obliged to send copies of its reports to "such of its national organizations as are members of the international organizations of employers and trade unions" and the latter are entitled to make comments on the reports by states. In practice, very few organizations have made such comments, and the lack of interest by these organizations has deprived the supervisory system of a potentially important source of information. Generally speaking, the national employers and trade union organizations appear to take little interest in the reports. Part of the explanation for this is that a large part of the provisions in the European Social Charter have been more fully developed in conventions and recommendations under the ILO, and the supervisory mechanism under the ILO is more effective than that of the European Social Charter.

National reports by the contracting parties are first examined by a "committee of independent experts". This body has seven members who are chosen in their personal capacity by the Committee of Ministers of the Council of Europe. In contrast, however, with the rules of membership concerning the European Commission of Human Rights and the European Court of Human Rights, the Parliamentary Assembly of the Council of Europe has no role to play in the election.

Nevertheless, the Committee has manifested considerable independence. It has functioned as an impartial body, whose task it is to discover what the law and practice of the contracting parties is, and to oversee its conformity with the obligations undertaken by the states under part II of the Social Charter. It has performed its task with considerable vigour, modelling its efforts closely to that of the Committee of Experts in the ILO.

The reports of the contracting parties and the conclusions of the Committee of Experts are, in accordance with Article 2, to be submitted for examination to what is called the "Sub-Committee of the Governmental Social Committee" of the Council of Europe. This is a purely governmental committee, composed of one representative of each of the contracting parties; the members are civil servants appointed by the governments and may be changed by them at any point in time.

This governmental committee shall examine the reports and the conclusions of the Committee of Independent Experts and report to the Committee of Ministers. This is where the weakness of the supervisory system appears. The governmental committee, consisting of civil servants, has taken upon itself to make its own assessment of the compliance of states with their obligations. Since it is obviously not an independent body, it tends to be rather reluctant to determine non-compliance. Consequently, it has given a more restrictive interpretation of the obligation of states and has rarely found that obligations have been violated. Admittedly, this has changed during the last few years; the practical difference between the Committee of Independent Experts and the government committee has been less apparent.

The lack of interest by the relevant trade union and employer organizations, due in part to the weakness of the system and in part to the better performance of the ILO, has had as a consequence that the European Social Charter has not fully lived up to expectations.

Due to the weaknesses experienced with the Social Charter, there is now a plan to set up a system of collective complaints, intended to increase the efficiency of the supervisory machinery which is presently based solely on the submission of governmental reports. In particular, it is hoped that a complaint system would increase the participation by employers and trade unions as well as other relevant NGOs. It is further hoped that such participation may increase interest in the supervisory system as a whole. A draft additional protocol to the European Social Charter was therefore adopted in 1992 and transmitted to the Committee of Ministers.[23] The draft is presently being studied by governments and the relevant organizations. Apparently, the organizations are generally in favour of the protocol, and it is likely to be adopted.

Complaints can, under the draft protocol, be made by international and national organizations of employers and trade unions and other

---

[23]The text prepared by the Committee on the European Social Charter is found in Council of Europe Doc. CHARTE/REL (92) 21.

international and national NGOs.[24] The complaints are examined by the Committee of Independent Experts, and submitted directly to the Committee of Ministers.[25] In contrast to the procedure for examining governmental reports, the Governmental Committee is not involved. This was the main purpose. Part of the reason is to emphasize the independence of the supervisory body; the other is to make the procedure as expeditious as possible.

---

[24]The current draft reads as follows:

Article 1

The Contracting Parties to this Protocol recognise the right of the following organizations to submit complaints alleging unsatisfactory application of the Charter:

a) international organizations of employers and workers referred to in paragraph 2 of Article 27 of the Charter,
b) other international non-governmental organizations which have consultative status with the Council of Europe and have been put on a list established for this purpose by the Governmental Committee,
c) representative national organizations of employers and workers within the jurisdiction of the Contracting Party against which they have lodged a complaint.

Article 2

1. Any Contracting State may also, when it expresses its consent to be bound by this Protocol in accordance with the provisions of Article 12, or at any moment thereafter, declare that it recognises the right of any other representative national non-governmental organization within its jurisdiction which has particular competence in the matters governed by the Charter, to lodge complaints against it.

[25]The present draft reads as follows:

Article 7

1. The Committee of Independent Experts shall draw up a report in which it shall describe the steps taken by it to examine the complaint and present its conclusions as to whether or not the Contracting Party concerned has *ensured the satisfactory* application of the provisions of the Charter referred to in the complaint.
2. The report shall be transmitted to the Committee of Ministers. It shall also be transmitted to the organization that lodged the complaint and to the Contracting Parties to the Charter, *which* shall not be at liberty to publish it.

   It shall be transmitted to the Parliamentary Assembly and be made public at the same time as the resolution referred to in Article 8 or *no later than* four months after it has been transmitted to the Committee of Ministers.

6. THE EUROPEAN COMMUNITY

While some social aims have been expressed in the Community treaties, it has been rather general and vague. The Preamble to the European Community (EC) Treaty refers in its first three paragraphs to the social perspective of the Community. Articles 2, 48-51 and 117-122 contain provisions concerning social rights and outline basic elements of a Community social policy. Further elaboration can be found in the Single European Act, such as Articles 118(a) and 118(b). The former deals with the improvement and harmonization of working conditions while the latter establishes requirements for a "social dialogue" between "management" and "labour" on a Community level.

Economic co-operation and integration should go hand in hand with co-operation and integration in the social field. In its 1974 Social Action Programme, the European Council stated that social policy measures are as important as economic and monetary policy measures, and focused in the Programme on three main points: (a) increase of employment; (b) improvement of working and living conditions; (c) increased participation of employees and employers in the Community decision-making process.[26]

The Economic and Social Committee stated in its opinion on basic Community social rights of February 1989:

> "These basic social rights are also part and parcel of the rights inherent in a people's Europe and encompass, more generally, the shared values of European society. They relate to the various aspects of the lives of all Europeans (right to work; right to adequate living conditions; right to a decent retirement; access to education) [...]"[27]

In 1989, the EC Heads of State or Government adopted the Community Charter of the Fundamental Social Rights of Workers, by eleven

---

[26]Bull. EC, Suppl. 2/74.

[27]Opinion of 22 February 1989 OJ C 126/4 (22.5.1989).

votes to one (the United Kingdom voted against).[28] It is a declaration and thus contains political rather than legal obligations. The main stated purpose is, "in accordance with the national practices, notably through legislative measures or collective agreements, to guarantee the fundamental social rights in this Charter and to implement the social measures indispensable to the smooth operation of the internal market as part of a strategy of economic and social cohesion".

Examining the Charter, Andrew Clapham expresses doubts about the effectiveness of protection unless the rights operate at the same level as Community fundamental freedoms found in the EC treaty. He nevertheless finds that the Community Charter has real value by expressing a commitment towards a Community social policy. It gives a social momentum to the detailed action programme of the Community.[29]

If the new protocol to the European Social Charter providing for complaint procedures is adopted and enters into force, the Community might be prevailed upon to accede to the Social Charter.

7. THE CONFERENCE ON SECURITY AND CO-OPERATION IN EUROPE

Principle VII of the Helsinki Final Act of 1975 states: "They will promote and encourage the exercise of civil, political, economic, social, cultural and other rights and freedoms all of which derive from the inherent dignity of the human person and are essential for his free and full development."

Thus, the foundation of the Conference on Security and Co-operation in Europe (CSCE) envisages the indivisibility of the different kinds of human rights as parts of the basis of the inherent dignity of the human person. In practice, however, the CSCE has not given much

---

[28]The text is found in A. Clapham, *Human Rights and the European Community: A Critical Overview* (Baden-Baden) vol. 1, annex 2, pp. 230-236.

[29]Clapham, op.cit. n. 28, pp. 63-65.

attention in a systematic way to the implementation of economic and social rights.

During the Cold War, the issue became very controversial and formed part of the political rhetorics between the two main parties. The former socialist bloc emphasized economic and social rights as a rhetorical justification for the neglect of civil and political rights. The Western states, led by the United States, not only downplayed but almost ridiculized economic and social rights as not being proper human rights at all.

With the Cold War gone, it is to be hoped that this sterile rhetorical confrontation will have also disappeared, and that all aspects of human rights will be taken equally seriously.

However, the CSCE has a second set of problems, which concern the lack of institutions for implementation purposes. The Helsinki follow-up meeting in 1992 does envisage a somewhat more comprehensive system of institutions, including the biennial meetings of Heads of States of Government, the review conferences which will precede the meetings of the Heads of State of Government; the permanent existence of the CSCE Council, and the Committee of Senior Officials; the Chairman of Office will have a continuous task of initiatives. The mechanisms for implementation of human dimensions are rather vague and do not, as of now, indicate any particular focus on economic and social rights. One mechanism is the holding of seminars, but there has so far been none on economic and social rights apart from a seminar on education. In that case, the focus was not on economic and social rights, but on education for tolerance. It is desirable that a seminar on economic and social rights be held in the near future, with a view to developing an approach to economic and social rights within the CSCE. An Economic Forum has now been established, and it might be that economic and social rights can be taken up there. However, it is more likely that the main focus of the Economic Forum will be on economic collaboration. Efforts should be made to emphasize the need for economic and social rights within the Forum.

The focus within the CSCE has increasingly been on security, and on the dramatic political transformations that are taking place. Within the security domain, the problem of minority and ethnic conflicts have come to be one of the most prominent issues.

The emphasis on the transition to the market has led some to believe that economic and social rights can and even should be neglected, that they may be an obstacle. This, however, is due to a simplified notion of "market". The transition from the highly centralized command economy, with public ownership of production, to a system where private property holds a large share and where creativity and private entrepreneurs can unfold, is indeed to be welcomed. This, however, does not mean and should not mean an unregulated society. There is a need for educated people, which requires a right to education; there is a need for the welfare of people, which facilitates the functions of the labour market, and the building of democracy can be achieved only when economic and social rights are taken seriously. Without attention to these, tensions can arise which can lead to an impasse both in the economic transition and in the democratic development. They might give rise to a polarization within society, leading eventually to authoritarian governments, be it of a leftist or a rightist kind. In both cases, human rights will be negatively affected in the extreme.

Time has therefore come to give genuine commitment to economic and social rights within the CSCE. This is particularly important in the light of the very substantial economic assistance which is now envisaged to be given by the major industrialized market economies to the Russian Federation and other states within the former Soviet bloc.

8. ASSESSMENT OF THE MECHANISMS

The effectiveness of international mechanisms depend on several factors. At the general political level, it depends on the degree consensus regarding the rights concerned. There is near-consensus on the principle of the indivisibility of the different kinds of rights - civil and political, economic, social and cultural.

Since 1981, if not before, there has been one major exception: notwithstanding the fact that the United States was active in the early post-war years in supporting the inclusion of economic and social rights, Republican U.S. administrations have generally challenged economic and social rights as not being "proper" human rights.[30] This has weakened the possibilities of the United Nations organs to pursue with determination the implementation of economic and social rights. With the return of a Democratic administration in the United States in 1993, this may possibly change.

Even among those states who in general endorse economic and social rights as part of the human rights system, the degree of consensus on ways to implement such rights is often relatively low. The current economic depression in most industrialized Western countries, with high unemployment and a negative demographic balance, has also led to substantial reductions in traditional welfare allocations. This places monitoring bodies in a difficult position.

At the United Nations, there is a certain tension between, on the one hand, efforts to make states implement their obligations under the relevant conventions, and, on the other, to develop a world community approach by which the gap between rich and poor states will change in favour of a more equitable world economy.[31] When

---

[30]The United States policy has been examined in Alston, loc.cit. n. 4, pp. 365-393.

[31]The trends in the United Nations debate on economic and social rights have been described by P. Alston, "No Right to Complain about Being Poor: The Need for an Optional Protocol to the Economic Rights Covenant", in A. Eide and J. Helgesen, eds., *The Future of Human Rights Protection in a Changing World. Fifty Years since the Four Freedoms Address. Essays in Honour of Torkel Opsahl* (Oslo 1991) pp. 83-86.

Third World states emphasize the importance of economic and social rights, they are often less concerned with their own implementation of these rights than with changes in international economic relations. This concern, reflected during the 1970s in the demand for a New International Economic Order, is to some extent reflected in the Declaration on the Right to Development, adopted by the General Assembly in 1986, and in several of the studies prepared by the Sub-Commission.

The Committee on Economic, Social and Cultural Rights has sought to focus more specifically on the implementation by the states of their obligations under the Covenant. The Committee has in recent years been innovative and resourceful. Its effect, however, is limited due to the great differences in economic and cultural conditions among the states parties to the Covenant. It has also noted the weakness of the reporting system, and its present chairman, Philip Alston, has called for an additional protocol to allow for a complaint procedure, similar to the one now drafted for the European Social Charter.[32]

At the regional level, the attention and approach to economic and social rights depends on the values common to the set of states participating in the regional system, and to their position in the world economy. Consequently, the approaches in the Council of Europe differ substantially from those of the Organization of African Unity. The CSCE, which groups states at very different levels of economic development, has not yet found a profile with regard to economic and social rights. Political rights are much higher on the agenda, and are generally interweaved with security considerations.

Consensus can only be developed over time. The international agencies have the double task of exploring the road to consensus and promoting the implementation of rights which have been adopted but in practice often disregarded. With regard to economic and social rights this is compounded by the vagueness of the rights and particularly of the corresponding obligations of states.

---

[32]Alston, loc.cit. n. 31, pp. 79-100.

The reporting process should be used to assist states in the realization of economic and social rights. It is important to explore the ways in which the different functions and phases of the reporting process can be improved. This includes initial review, monitoring, policy formulation, public scrutiny, evaluation, identification of problems and exchange of information.

Essential would be the widest possible participation by citizens, community-based organizations and NGOs. The lack of such involvement is now widely recognized, and efforts are made both at the United Nations and in the Council of Europe to remedy this weakness. One of the main purposes of complaint procedures would be to involve such organizations more strongly. They should, however, also be encouraged to play a constructive role in developing approaches for the better realization of the rights concerned. This would be helped if state reports were widely publicized within the states parties to the Covenant so that a national dialogue could be developed.

Perfect realization of all economic and social rights is probably impossible under the difficult conditions prevailing in many societies, but it should be recognized that minimum core obligations exist and should be fully ensured. International dialogue on economic and social rights through the monitoring bodies should be developed.

9. CONCLUSIONS AND RECOMMENDATIONS

9.1 Conclusions

A growing need for international protection of economic and social rights in Europe is evident, due in part to problems arising from transitions to market-oriented economies in Central and Eastern Europe, and in the West to a long cyclic recession coinciding with changes in demographic structures of Western societies. The balance is tilting towards the non-productive part of the population. Governments facing increasing constraints are tempted to neglect their international obligations, a danger reinforced by the lack of knowledge of or concern with economic and social rights among non-governmental human rights organizations. International financial institutions have for some time been demanding adjustments which run counter to international human rights.

Far from neglecting economic and social rights, constructive approaches should be found which can ensure the enjoyment of economic and social rights under the more difficult circumstances now prevailing. While modifications may have to be made, acquired rights cannot be taken away unless satisfactory alternatives are found. Under no circumstances should the burden of transition be placed on the most vulnerable groups, but rather on those whose resource base can easily carry the transition costs. NGOs should not only contribute with information, ideas and efforts to that end, but also help in cementing the network of solidarity and collective self-help which can ease the burden of the state.

With the passing of the Cold War, the sterile ideological debate over the place of economic and social rights should have been laid to rest. Both sides relied on rhetorics rather than on genuine discourse. The indivisibility of the different sets of rights is evident in practice and is also proved by the content and application of human rights instruments, such as the Convention on the Rights of the Child.

In real life, the neglect of economic and social rights is likely to engender racism, xenophobia and lawlessness, to undermine democracy and foster authoritarian regimes, thus generating serious threats to civil and political rights.

The theoretical legalistic debate - whether economic and social rights are or can be justiciable - is largely off the mark. The significant question is how to protect these rights, which does not have to be through the use of normal courts. While many economic and social rights are or can be made justiciable and have been treated as such by courts in many countries, remedies and mechanisms for protection can also be found for those rights which are not immediately justiciable.

In practical terms, new thinking may be required on how to ensure the enjoyment of economic and social rights. The command economy of the so-called "real socialist" systems in Central and Eastern Europe failed not only because it implied substantial violations of civil and political rights, but also because it took away the sense of responsibility of individuals for their own needs. It is also recognized that the welfare state in Western Europe had become overgrown with too much state responsibility for all their inhabitants. The need to maintain a welfare society as the basis of a properly functioning welfare state was overlooked. Pushing the welfare state too far made it less resilient in times of crisis, leading to an abdication of group responsibility inherent in a welfare society. While modifications are now required, it is essential to maintain the key elements of the social contract on which modern democratic society must function.

The most important aspect of state obligations in this field is to ensure space, particularly for the most vulnerable and the most deprived, to take care of their own needs under conditions safeguarding human equality and dignity. This requires protection from more aggressive and expansive private parties. Protection requires regulation, a task from which a democratic state cannot abdicate. The state must also organize co-operation to solve the common tasks of society as a whole, including health services, education, and provisions for the disabled, the elderly and others unable to take care of their own needs.

Positive developments have taken place within the international machineries monitoring the implementation of economic and social rights. The ILO has a long record of standard-setting and procedural efficiency in applying the standards. The relatively new Committee on the Rights of the Child, having learnt from the weaknesses of the older treaty bodies, has shown considerable procedural innovation and openness to NGOs. The reconstituted Committee on Economic, Social and Cultural Rights has, with the blessing of ECOSOC, made itself wide open to involvement by NGOs in the reporting process. This can facilitate an active role by the NGOs in the national follow-up of the recommendations made on each state report by the Committee in the form of concluding observations and comments. The Committee on Economic, Social and Cultural Rights is now far ahead of the Human Rights Committee. The involvement of NGOs and the role of the Committee itself would be further strengthened should the proposed optional protocol to the Covenant be adopted, providing for the submission of complaints alleging the violation of economic, social and cultural rights.

Changes made in 1991 to the European Social Charter has made its reporting process more open to NGO involvement. More promising, the 1992 draft Protocol to the European Social Charter on a collective complaint procedure would, if adopted, revitalize that Charter, by involving more actively the main social partners, trade unions and employers' organizations, and other relevant NGOs. It would no longer be blocked by a Government Committee which would water down the efforts made by the independent experts.

In sum, the problem is no longer the lack of procedures. The greatest weakness in the protection of economic and social rights is the absence of competent non-governmental human rights organizations making use of the new opportunities.

The weakness of the CSCE in the field of economic and social rights is not surprising in view of its historical function during the Cold War. The awareness is growing, however, that the stability and indeed the security of the whole of Europe - and that of the United States and Canada - depends on healthy social and economic developments in Central and Eastern Europe, including Russia and other states of the former USSR. Considerable aid is now being promised. The interrelationship between the evolution of co-operative security and social development is readily apparent. The more successful the evolution of a common, all-European security is (including the United States and Canada), the less do states have to spend on military expenditures, releasing resources for social concerns.

The Marshall aid to Western Europe after World War II was essential to the development of stable democratic societies where welfare played an important role; it is equally essential that protection of economic and social rights are made an integral part of economic cooperation with Central and Eastern Europe. With the new U.S. administration there is reason to hope that this will be recognized, in the same way as it was at the time of the Roosevelt and Truman administrations. The CSCE may in the future have a considerable role with regard to economic and social rights, notwithstanding its past neglect.

9.2 Recommendations

Under the Covenant on Economic, Social and Cultural Rights Article 2, state parties are required to "take steps" for the progressive realization of rights contained in the Covenant. It should be a standing rule for the Committee to include, in its concluding observations regarding each state report, an indication of which specific steps should next be taken by the state concerned. When the next periodic report is presented by that state, it should also report on what has been done to implement the specific steps suggested by the Committee.

NGOs, which should have access to the report of the state party well before it is examined, should provide the Committee with proposals for the next steps to be taken, and should also keep track of the implementation of the recommended steps by the state.

An optional protocol to the Covenant on Economic, Social and Cultural Rights should be adopted to provide for submission of complaints alleging violations of the Covenant.

The draft Protocol to the European Social Charter providing for a collective complaint procedure should be adopted and quickly accepted in order to breathe life into the Council of Europe's protection of economic and social rights.

The CSCE should urgently initiate a discourse on how the economic transition can take a direction which ensures economic and social rights for all, and how technical and economic co-operation can be arranged to promote that goal. The CSCE should set up its own monitoring mechanism to ensure that the economic and social rights, particularly of those most deprived and vulnerable, are being improved by the economic and social development policies pursued.

A degree of human rights should conditionality be introduced into the economic and social schemes of co-operation among the CSCE countries. All states participating in such co-operation should be required to report to relevant human rights monitoring bodies on their efforts to implement economic and social rights, the progress made and the obstacles encountered. Open and properly analysed presentation of the obstacles facilitates structured approaches to economic co-operation by focussing on assistance to overcome the obstacles reported.

The secretariats, both at the United Nations, the Council of Europe and the (presently very weak) secretariat of the CSCE should be further developed by the recruitment of persons with professional expertise in economic, social and cultural rights.

The impact at the national level of the reporting procedure should be strengthened. One step to that end is to make use of a system of indicators as suggested in the study by Danilo Türk, including indicators of both the process and of the current status of affairs, revealing in particular which are the most deprived groups and the effects of steps taken to improve the realization of their economic and social rights.

Most importantly, non-governmental human rights organizations should take their commitment to the whole system of human rights seriously. Few of them, if any, deny the relevance of economic and social rights; most of them, however, have failed to demonstrate any genuine commitment, involvement and creativity. By their neglect they have reinforced the view that economic and social rights are not really human rights.

They need to develop not only their commitment but also expertise, which may require recruitment from professions other than the law which appear to be the most influential leaders of human rights NGOs. Human rights organizations should not play down their valuable and competent work in regard to civil and political rights, but their professional competence in that field should be supplemented by competence in the often much more complex arena of economic and social rights. Interdisciplinary cross-fertilization between several professions, in particular economists and lawyers, may be required. This may not be easy because economists tend to have a rather utilitarian approach and have tended to play down or even to look with contempt at the notion of fundamental rights of the individual human being.

Since economic and social rights affect a wide range of groups whose concerns are articulated by many different national NGOs, it is essential to co-ordinate at the national level the input of NGOs to the international protection system.

The involvement by a wide range of national NGOs drawn from different fields (trade unions, organizations for the disabled, the elderly, the unemployed, and others) would also make the international economic and social rights and the system of protection better known at the national level.

The flow of information concerning the international protection of human rights should be strengthened. One very practical step which should be taken by the secretariats of the agencies and treaty-bodies concerned (and if not, by relevant international NGOs) should be to produce a separate publication for each state report examined. The publication should contain (a) the state report itself, (b) submissions made by NGOs in connection with that report, (c) summary records of the meetings devoted to that report by the body examining it, containing the views of experts and the replies to questions given by representatives of the state concerned, and (d) the concluding observations, or comments, made by the monitoring body to that report. This publication should quickly be made available to the state concerned and to relevant national NGOs, for the latter to inform the media and to use it in their further dialogue with the government on how to improve the situation and how to follow-up the commitments made by state representatives and the recommendations and comments made by the monitoring body.

INTERNATIONAL MONITORING MECHANISMS IN SITUATIONS OF ARMED CONFLICT

by Allan Rosas

1. HUMANITARIAN LAW APPLICABLE IN ARMED CONFLICTS

War has always been circumscribed by rules and rituals. The law of war (*ius in bello*) has occupied a prominent place in the "modern" inter-state system of public international law. During the present century, the role of humanitarian and human rights considerations has been on the increase. Since the 1960s, it has been fashionable to speak about international humanitarian law applicable in armed conflicts.[1] The backbone of this body of law is provided by the four Geneva Conventions of 1949 and their two Additional Protocols of 1977.[2]

The law of war has traditionally been a markedly inter-state body of law, where checks and balances have been provided by the common interests of belligerent states rather than by international community considerations and international mechanisms of monitoring and supervision.[3] With the formation of the International Committee of the Red Cross (ICRC) in 1863, the foundation of a semi-official and

---

[1]A. Rosas, "The Frontiers of International Humanitarian Law", 24 *Journal of Peace Research* (1987) p. 219.

[2]Convention (I) for the Amelioration of the Condition of Wounded and Sick Armed Forces in the Field, Convention (II) for the Amelioration of the Condition of Wounded, Sick and Shipwrecked Members of Armed Forces at Sea, Convention (III) relative to the Treatment of Prisoners of War, Convention (IV) relative to the Protection of Civilian Persons in Time of War 1949, 75 UNTS pp. 31, 85, 135, 287; Protocol Additional to the Geneva Conventions of 12 August 1949, and relating to the Protection of Victims of International Armed Conflicts (Protocol I), Protocol Additional to the Geneva Conventions of 12 August 1949, and relating to the Protection of Victims of Non-International Armed Conflicts (Protocol II) 1977, 1125 UNTS pp. 3, 609.

[3]The impact of military and political interests on the application of the law of war is discussed in A. Rosas, *The Legal Status of Prisoners of War: A Study in International Humanitarian Law Applicable in Armed Conflicts* (Helsinki 1976) p. 134 et seq.

A. Bloed et al. (eds.), Monitoring Human Rights in Europe, 221–246.

semi-international monitoring mechanism was created. The ICRC started to work for the amelioration of the conditions of wounded and sick combatants and later extended its activities to include work in favour of prisoners of war.[4] The first international convention to mention the role of the organization was the Prisoners-of-War Convention of 1929.[5] In the 1949 Geneva Conventions and their Additional Protocol I of 1977, several provisions refer to the ICRC and give it the status of a protecting and partly monitoring body with respect to international (normally inter-state) armed conflicts.[6]

In particular, the delegates of the ICRC, under Article 126, paragraph 4, of Convention III of 1949, have the same right as representatives of Protecting Powers "to go to all places where prisoners of war may be" and to be able to interview prisoners of war without witnesses.[7] Moreover, the ICRC may act as a substitute for Protecting Powers and also has a general mandate to carry out various humanitarian functions "in order to ensure protection and assistance to the victims of conflicts".[8] Also national Red Cross and Red Crescent societies are given a certain role as providers of assistance and protection to victims of armed conflicts.[9]

The confidentiality normally surrounding the work of the Red Cross movement, notably the ICRC, means that the concrete findings emanating from visits and missions are not generally available to the international community at large, let alone to the general public. This

---

[4]Rosas, op.cit. n. 3, p. 463.

[5]Art. 88 Convention (III) relative to the Treatment of Prisoners of War 1929, 118 LNTS p. 343.

[6]See, e.g., ICRC, *Commentary on the Additional Protocols of 8 June 1977 to the Geneva Conventions of 12 August 1949* (Geneva 1987) p. 936 et seq.; D. Weissbrodt, "The Role of International Organizations in the Implementation of Human Rights and Humanitarian Law in Situations of Armed Conflict", 21 *Vanderbilt Journal of Transnational Law* (1988) p. 313 at p. 346 et seq.

[7]See Rosas, op.cit. n. 3, p. 464 et seq.

[8]See, in particular, Art. 81(1) of Additional Protocol I of 1977.

[9]A. Rosas, "Notes on the Legal Status of National Red Cross Societies", in C. Swiniarski, ed., *Studies and Essays on International Humanitarian Law and Red Cross Principles in Honour of Jean Pictet* (Geneva-The Hague 1984) p. 959 at p. 960 et seq.

does not necessarily prevent the ICRC from issuing public statements and appeals in cases of obvious breaches of humanitarian law,[10] nor from making public its confidential reports to governments if the latter have published excerpts from the reports only. Sometimes ICRC reports or excerpts of reports have been leaked to the press.[11]

The 1949 Conventions moreover grant detainees an individual right of complaint in certain circumstances.[12] According to Convention III, prisoners of war have the right to make requests to the Detaining Power and to put forward complaints to the Protecting Power. Convention IV contains similar provisions and in a general provision (Art. 30) also mentions specifically the ICRC and national Red Cross and Red Crescent societies as addressees of applications.[13]

The institution of Protecting Powers mentioned above refers to third states, which have been assigned the duty of safeguarding the interests of the belligerent states. According to Article 5, paragraph 1, of Additional Protocol I of 1977 it is the duty of the parties to a conflict "to secure the supervision and implementation of the Conventions and of this Protocol by the application of the system of Protecting Powers". Moreover, the 1949 Geneva Conventions provide for the possibility of a conciliation procedure also involving the Protecting

---

[10]See, e.g., the ICRC appeals issued in relation to the Iran-Iraq war, ICRC, *Annual Report* 1984 p. 60, in relation to the War in the Gulf, 31 *International Review of the Red Cross* (1991) p. 22, and concerning the armed conflicts in former Yugoslavia, ibid. p. 398. See also Y. Sandoz, "The ICRC's Responsibilities in Connection with the Middle East Conflict", 31 *International Review of the Red Cross* (1991) p. 211.

[11]On such an incident during the Algerian War (1954-1962) see Rosas, op.cit. n. 3, p. 151.

[12]R. Wieruszewski, "Application of International Humanitarian Law and Human Rights Law: Individual Complaints", in F. Kalshoven and Y. Sandoz, eds., *Implementation of International Humanitarian Law* (Dordrecht-Boston-London 1989) p. 441 at p. 447.

[13]Arts. 50(3), 78, 98(1) and 108(3) Convention III; Arts. 30, 52(1), 101 Convention IV. Special representatives should also be elected to represent prisoners of war (Arts. 79-81 Convention III, Arts. 102-104 Convention IV). See also Rosas, op.cit. n. 3, p. 458.

Powers, if there is disagreement between the belligerent states as to the application or interpretation of the Conventions.[14]

However, after the Second World War the institution of Protecting Powers has normally not been used at all. It has, at best, played a marginal role as a monitoring and supervisory mechanism.[15] Independently of the system of Protecting Powers, third states have under common Article 1 of the 1949 Conventions, and Article 1, paragraph 1, of Additional Protocol I, an obligation "to ensure respect" for these instruments "in all circumstances", and according to Article 89 of Additional Protocol I also an obligation, in situations of serious violations of the Conventions and the Protocol, "to act, jointly or individually, in co-operation with the United Nations and in conformity with the United Nations Charter".[16] The legal and practical relevance of these obligations remain uncertain, however.

In this context reference should also be made to the concepts of state and individual responsibility for breaches of humanitarian law. Article 91 of Additional Protocol I affirms that states which violate the Conventions or the Protocol shall be liable to pay compensation and shall be responsible for all acts committed by persons forming part of their armed forces.[17]

---

[14]Art. 11 of Conventions I-III and Art. 12 of Convention IV.

[15]According to ICRC, op.cit. n. 6, p. 77, the institution of Protecting Powers has only been used four times (Suez 1956, Goa 1961, India and Pakistan 1971-1972, Falklands-Malvinas 1982), and even then excluding some of the humanitarian functions incumbent upon Protecting Powers under the 1949 Conventions. See also C.M. Cerna, "Human Rights in Armed Conflict: Implementation of International Humanitarian Law Norms by Regional Intergovernmental Human Rights Bodies", in Kalshoven and Sandoz, op.cit. n. 12, p. 31 at pp. 36-37; H. Coulibaly, "Le rôle des puissances protectrices au regard du droit diplomatique, du droit de Genève et du droit de La Haye", in ibid., p. 69 at p. 76; F. Kalshoven, "Prohibitions or Restrictions on the Use of Methods and Means of Warfare", in I.F. Dekker and H.H.G. Post, eds., *The Gulf War of 1980-1988: The Iran-Iraq War in International Legal Perspective* (Dordrecht-Boston-London 1992) p. 97 at p. 109.

[16]See the contribution by L. Boisson de Chazournes in the present volume.

[17]See also Arts. 51/52/131/148 of the 1949 Conventions, and G. Niyungeko, "The Implementation of International Humanitarian Law and the Principle of State Sovereignty", 31 *International Review of the Red Cross* (1991) p. 105 at p. 131.

With regard to the question of individual responsibility, the Conventions and the Protocol contain elaborate rules on the repression of "grave breaches" as well as other breaches.[18] There is a duty "to search for persons alleged to have committed ... grave breaches" and to bring such persons, regardless of their nationality, before national courts. In accordance with the principle *aut dedere aut iudicare*, the High Contracting Party may alternatively extradite such persons to another High Contracting Party. Especially in so far as this obligation applies to third states, which are not parties to the armed conflict, it has become almost a dead letter.[19] At the time of writing, however, discussions are taking place on the establishment of an international tribunal for the prosecution of persons responsible for serious violations of international humanitarian law in the territory of the former Yugoslavia, possibly to lead to the establishment of a more permanent international criminal tribunal (see *infra*).

While the above discussion has focused on international armed conflicts, the humanitarian law applicable in armed conflicts nowadays addresses situations of non-international armed conflicts as well.[20] For understandable reasons it has not been possible to devise for internal conflicts the same international mechanisms that are in place for international conflicts. But Article 3, paragraph 2, common to the Geneva Conventions of 1949 expressly refers to the right of "an impartial humanitarian body, such as the International Committee of the Red Cross" to "offer its services to the Parties to the conflict". Additional Protocol II of 1977 (Art. 18) also refers to relief actions

---

[18]See, in particular, Arts. 49-54/50-53/129-131/146-148 of the Conventions and Arts. 85-88 of the Protocol, and J.J.E. Schutte, "The System of Repression of Breaches of Additional Protocol I", in A.J.M Delissen and G.J. Tanja, eds., *Humanitarian Law of Armed Conflict: Challenges Ahead (Essays in Honour of Frits Kalshoven)* (Dordrecht-Boston-London 1991) p. 177.

[19]C. van den Wyngaert, "The Suppression of War Crimes under Additional Protocol I", in Delissen and Tanja, op.cit. n. 18, p. 197 at pp. 202-205.

[20]See, e.g., T. Meron, *Human Rights in Internal Strife: Their International Protection* (Cambridge 1987) *passim*. For a discussion on the applicability of humanitarian principles in internal armed conflicts before the 1949 Geneva Convention see L. Hannikainen, R. Hanski and A. Rosas, *Implementing Humanitarian Law Applicable in Armed Conflicts: The Case of Finland* (Dordrecht-Boston-London 1992) p. 27 et seq.

for the civilian population but, while referring to national relief societies and national Red Cross and Red Crescent organizations, avoids mentioning the ICRC.[21]

In this context it should be noted that common Article 3 apparently has a lower threshold of application than Additional Protocol II of 1977, the latter instrument being applicable in internal armed conflicts of a certain intensity (civil wars) only.[22] Despite these shortcomings in treaty law, the ICRC has been able to carry out humanitarian activities, including certain monitoring functions, in a number of non-international armed conflicts as well as situations of internal disturbances and tensions which fall short of armed conflicts.[23]

The dichotomy between international and non-international armed conflicts, underscored by the existence of two separate Additional Protocols of 1977, poses an ever increasing problem of application and enforcement. The most common type of armed conflict has become the "mixed" conflict, involving internal as well as international dimensions. The armed conflicts going on in the territories of the former Soviet Union and Yugoslavia offer sordid illustration. During the preparations of the 1974-1977 Geneva Diplomatic Conference, it was suggested to opt for common rules applicable in all armed con-

---

[21]For political reasons, it was not possible at the 1974-1977 Geneva Diplomatic Conference to include express references to the ICRC, see, e.g., M. Bothe et al., *New Rules for Victims of Armed Conflicts: Commentary on the Two 1977 Protocols Additional to the Geneva Conventions of 1949* (The Hague-Boston-London 1982) p. 694.

[22]A. Rosas, "Human Rights at Risk in Situations of Internal Violence and Public Emergency: Towards Common Minimum Standards", in A. Eide and J. Helgesen, eds., *The Future of Human Rights Protection in a Changing World: Fifty Years Since the Four Freedoms Address (Essays in Honour of Torkel Opsahl)* (Oslo 1991) p. 165 at p. 169.

[23]ICRC, *Protection of Victims of Non-International Armed Conflicts* (Report V submitted to the Conference of Government Experts on the Reaffirmation and Development of International Humanitarian Law Applicable in Armed Conflicts, Geneva 1971) p. 73 et seq.; J. Moreillon, *Le Comité International de la Croix-Rouge et la Protection des Détenus Politiques* (Genève 1973) *passim*; Meron, op.cit. n. 20, *passim*.

flicts,[24] but this idea, unfortunately, proved politically premature. We shall come back to this question at the end of this paper.

2. HUMANITARIAN FACT-FINDING

In addition to the provisions contained in the 1949 Geneva Conventions on Protecting Powers and their possible role in conciliation procedures, the Conventions provide for the possibility of an enquiry procedure concerning alleged violations of the Conventions.[25] An enquiry shall be instituted at the request of a party to the conflict. However, the manner of the enquiry, including the possible choice of an umpire, must be agreed between the interested parties.[26] This procedure has apparently never been used.[27] The ICRC has in some instances been asked by one of the parties to a conflict to investigate allegations of breaches but consent from the other party has been lacking. The ICRC has also been hesitant to become actively involved

---

[24]Norway was particularly active in advancing the idea of a single Protocol, see ICRC, *Conference of Government Experts on the Reaffirmation and Development of International Humanitarian Law Applicable in Armed Conflicts: Report on the Work of the Conference* (Geneva 1971) p. 35 (para. 111); ibid., *Second Session* (Geneva 1972) Vol. I p. 63 (paras 2.12.-214.), Vol. II p. 36 (proposal submitted by the experts of Egypt and Norway, CE/COM II/17).

[25]Arts. 52/53/132/149 of the 1949 Conventions. For a commentary to this common provision see, e.g., ICRC, *Commentary to Geneva Convention I for the Amelioration of the Condition of the Wounded and Sick in Armed Forces in the Field* (Geneva 1952) p. 374 et seq. The provision draws upon Art. 30 of the Convention for the Amelioration of the Condition of the Wounded and Sick in Armies in the Field 1929, 118 LNTS p. 303.

[26]Niyungeko, loc.cit. n. 17, p. 118.

[27]Bothe et al., op.cit. n. 21, p. 539; ICRC, op.cit. n. 6, p. 1040; S. Ihraï, "Les mécanismes d'établissement des faits dans les Conventions de Genève de 1949 et dans le Protocol I de 1977", in Kalshoven and Sandoz, op.cit. n. 12, p. 154. During the preparations for the 1949 Convention, the ICRC proposed a more automatic institution of enquiry, ICRC, op.cit. n. 25, pp. 375-377.

in enquiry procedures, fearing that its impartiality may be jeopardized.[28]

This is not to say that the ICRC cannot perform a certain (normally confidential) fact-finding role within the context of its humanitarian assistance and protection activities. Moreover, Geneva Conventions III and IV provide for specific enquiries to be carried out by the Detaining Power in cases of prisoners of war or civilian detainees killed or injured in special circumstances.[29]

The inefficacy of the procedures in the 1949 Conventions for Protecting Powers, conciliation and enquiry led some states which took part in the 1974-1977 Geneva Diplomatic Conference to propose the establishment of a permanent International Enquiry Commission to investigate into alleged violations of the Conventions, Additional Protocol I as well as other rules relating to the conduct of international armed conflicts.[30] After lengthy discussions it proved possible to provide for such a commission, finally designated the International Fact-Finding Commission, in Article 90 of Additional Protocol I.[31] The price that had to be paid for this novelty, which

---

[28]J. Pictet, *Humanitarian Law and the Protection of War Victims* (Leyden-Geneva 1975) p. 73; ICRC, "Action by the International Committee of the Red Cross in the Event of Breaches of International Humanitarian Law", 21 *International Review of the Red Cross* (1981) p. 76 at p. 80; B.G. Ramcharan, "Introduction", in idem, ed., *International Law and Fact-Finding in the Field of Human Rights* (The Hague-Boston-London 1982) p. 1 at pp. 21-22.

[29]Art. 121 Convention III and Art. 131 Convention IV. A report on the enquiry should be forwarded to the Protecting Power (but as was noted above, the institution of Protecting Powers has become almost a dead letter).

[30]See Doc. CDDH/I/241 and Add. 1 (Denmark, New Zealand, Norway, Sweden) and CDDH/I/267 (Pakistan), *Official Records of the Diplomatic Conference on the Reaffirmation and Development of International Humanitarian Law Applicable in Armed Conflicts*, Geneva (1974-1977), Vol. III (Bern 1978) pp. 338, 340.

[31]For comments see, e.g., E. Kussbach, "Commission Internationale d'Etablissement des Faits en droit international humanitaire", 20 *Revue de droit pénal militaire et de droit de la guerre* (1981) p. 91; Bothe et al., op.cit. n. 21, p. 538 et seq.; ICRC, op.cit. n. 6, p. 1039 et seq.; Ihraï, loc.cit. n. 27, pp. 162-164; J.A. Roach, "The International Fact-Finding Commission: Article 90 of Protocol I additional to the 1949 Geneva Conventions", 31 *International Review of the Red Cross* (1991) p. 167; S. Vite, *La Commission Internationale d'Etablissement des Faits* (Mémoire présenté à l'Université de Genève 1993, mimeo).

many states viewed with suspicion, if not animosity, was that the applicability of Article 90, as a "miniature convention", was made dependent on separate acts of state consent.

The system established by Article 90 is roughly the following: The International Fact-Finding Commission shall be established when not less than 20 High Contracting Parties have agreed to accept the competence of the Commission by issuing a special declaration in accordance with paragraph 2 of Article 90. The twentieth declaration of this nature was made in 1990 and the fifteen members of the Commission were elected by the relevant High Contracting Parties in June 1991. The Commission held its first meeting in March 1992.[32] It has met subsequently to adopt its Rules of Procedure. As of 31 December 1992, 33 states had accepted the competence of the Commission.[33] No formal request for an enquiry has been made so far.

The Commission will be automatically competent to conduct enquiries only when both the requesting state and the state against which the allegation has been made have issued declarations recognizing, *ipso facto* and without special agreement, the competence of the Commission. On the other hand, the requesting state does not have to be a party to an armed conflict but can be any High Contracting Party which has recognized the Commission's competence.[34] There is thus an element of *actio popularis*, reminiscent of the systems of inter-state complaints, recognized under some international human rights con-

---

[32]ICRC, *Bulletin* April 1992 (No. 195) p. 4. The present author is a member of the Commission.

[33]In chronological order: Sweden, Finland, Norway, Switzerland, Denmark, Austria, Italy, Belgium, Iceland, the Netherlands, New Zealand, Malta, Spain, Liechtenstein, Algeria, the Russian Federation, Belarus, the Ukraine, Uruguay, Canada, the Federal Republic of Germany, Chile, Hungary, Togo, Quatar, the United Arab Emirates, Slovenia, Croatia, the Seychelles, Bolivia, Australia, Poland, Bosnia-Herzegovina.

[34]Bothe et al., op.cit. n. 21, p. 543; ICRC, op.cit. n. 6, p. 1044; Roach, loc.cit. n. 31, pp. 168, 176; Vite, op.cit. n. 31, p. 32.

ventions.[35] In this context, it will be recalled that all High Contracting Parties are under an obligation "to ensure respect" for the Geneva Conventions and the Protocol. On the other hand, unlike the system contained in the initial proposal for what later became Article 90,[36] Article 90 does not recognize a right for the Commission to undertake an enquiry on its own initiative.

A further condition for the automatic competence of the Commission is that it is asked to enquire into "any facts alleged to be a grave breach as defined in the Conventions and this Protocol or other serious violation of the Conventions or of this Protocol" (Art. 90, para. 2(c)(i)). There must thus be a *prima facie* case for at least a "serious violation", which is not required under the above-mentioned enquiry procedures provided for by the 1949 Geneva Conventions.[37]

The requirement of previous declarations of acceptance does not apply if the parties to an international armed conflict agree otherwise. This is spelled out in Article 90, paragraph 2(d), according to which the Commission can institute an enquiry also "in other situations", but then "only with the consent of the other Party or Parties concerned". Thus, the consent of both parties is needed; on the other hand, these parties do not have to be High Contracting Parties to Additional Protocol I.[38] Moreover, the reference to the "other Party or Parties concerned" should be interpreted to mean only those parties alleged to have committed a serious violation and/or on whose territory the violation is alleged to have taken place and not necessarily all parties to a (multilateral) armed conflict.[39]

---

[35]For instance, Art. 24 of the European Convention for the Protection of Human Rights and Fundamental Freedoms (ECHR) 1950, 213 UNTS p. 221; Art. 41 International Covenant on Civil and Political Rights, 999 UNTS p. 171. For further examples see, e.g., A. Rosas, "Human Rights Obligations: A Finnish Perspective", in Z. Kedzia et al., eds., Perspectives of an All-European System of Human Rights Protection, 1 *All-European Human Rights Yearbook* (1991) p. 235 at pp. 241-243.

[36]A proposal put forward by Sweden and some other countries, see *supra* n. 30.

[37]Art. 90(2)(e) of Additional Protocol I makes it clear that the enquiry procedure of the 1949 Conventions shall apply to any alleged violations of the Protocol as well.

[38]ICRC, op.cit. n. 6, p. 1046.

[39]Vite, op.cit. n. 31, p. 29.

The wording of Article 90, paragraph 2(d), where this reference to "other situations" is preceded by the delimitation to serious violations only, does not preclude an interpretation, according to which the Commission could enquiry into any violations, provided that both parties agree.[40] In any case, the Commission would seem to be able (but would then not be obliged) to accept an enquiry mandate agreed between the parties to the conflict on the basis of the provisions on enquiry procedures contained in the 1949 Conventions.

Could the Commission instigate enquiries also in non-international armed conflicts, given the consent of all the parties to the conflict? As the Commission is established under Article 90 of Additional Protocol I and no mention is made to it in Additional Protocol II, enquiries or other activities possibly undertaken by the Commission would, strictly speaking, constitute extra-conventional activities.

But it should be recalled, on the other hand, that the distinction between international and internal conflicts is not an easy one in situations such as the on-going armed conflicts in some parts of the former Soviet Union and Yugoslavia. In conflicts of a "mixed" nature, the competence of the Commission must at least extend to facts alleged to be serious violations of the Conventions and Additional Protocol I. Moreover, the possibility of *ad hoc* agreements on the competence of the Commission under paragraph 2(d) seems to apply to entities other than states as well (the provision does not speak of High Contracting Parties but of "Parties concerned").[41] This perspective could be of special relevance in the context of "mixed" conflicts.

Article 90, paragraph 2(c)(ii), states that the Commission shall be competent not only to enquire into facts alleged to be serious viola-

---

[40]*Contra* Bothe et al., op.cit. n. 21, pp. 543-544, who appear to rely on the fact that the essence of para. 2(d) was originally contained in para. 2(a) and that the transfer to sub-para. (d) was said not to involve a substantial change but an improvement in drafting. See also ICRC, op.cit. n. 6, p. 1046, where it is also assumed that enquiries into grave breaches or other serious violations only can be undertaken.

[41]Vite, op.cit. n. 31, p. 28. Compare also the wording of paragraph 2(d), which speaks of "the other Party or Parties concerned", with the wording of paragraph 5(c), which provides that the Commission shall not report its findings publicly, "unless all the Parties to the conflict have requested the Commission to do so".

tions of the Conventions or Additional Protocol I, but also to "facilitate, through its good offices, the restoration of an attitude of respect for the Conventions and this Protocol". The meaning of this provision, which was inserted mainly on the basis of a Japanese proposal,[42] is far from clear. Does it presuppose that the Commission has already instituted, or completed, an enquiry? There is no such explicit requirement in the wording of Article 90; the main initiator of the proposal (Japan) emphasized that good offices could have a preventive role.[43]

Could the Commission offer its good offices on its own initiative? This is not excluded by the wording of Article 90 and could also be based on some other provisions of the Conventions and the Protocol[44] (although the parties to the conflict are not, under this sub-paragraph alone, legally obliged to enter into a process of mediation or conciliation). Moreover, the Commission may offer its good offices even if there has been no finding of grave breaches or other serious violations.[45] The reference to good offices in sub-paragraph 2(c)(ii) should also be read in conjunction with sub-paragraph 5(a), according to which the Commission, on the basis of an enquiry, "shall submit to the Parties a report on the findings of fact of the Chamber, with such recommendations as it may deem appropriate".

As will be seen from this quotation, enquiries, unless otherwise agreed between the parties concerned, shall be undertaken by a Chamber consisting of seven members. The Chamber may also carry out investigations *in loco*. The report of the Commission shall not be made public, unless all the parties to the conflict have requested the Commission to publish the report. This can be seen as a serious shortcoming, since publicity could be one of the few tools available

---

[42]CDDH/I/316, *Official Records* (see *supra* n. 30) Vol. III p. 342.

[43]CDDH/I/SR. 57, *Official Records* (see *supra* n. 30) Vol. IX p. 216 (paras. 49-50).

[44]Vite, op.cit. n. 31, pp. 53-55. Cf., Roach, loc.cit. n. 31, p. 176, who states that it would not seem to be within the competence of the Commission "for its President to exercise this power independently of any request for an enquiry". Does this restriction apply to the right of initiative of the President alone?

[45]Roach, loc.cit. n. 31, pp. 175-176.

to give effect to the findings and recommendations of the Commission.

There is some uncertainty as to what type of findings and conclusions the Commission would be able to make. It is a fact-finding body, not a conciliation commission, let alone an arbitration tribunal or international court.[46] On the other hand, the Commission is empowered to enquire into any facts alleged to be serious violations. Already in order to assert its own competence, some legal evaluation is needed. Moreover, the right to include "such recommendations as it may deem appropriate" in the report as well as its competence to "facilitate, through its good offices, the restoration of an attitude of respect" for the Convention and the Protocol, may give the Commission a mediatory role.[47]

The International Humanitarian Fact-Finding Commission is thus in place and could be used to clarify the allegations of breaches which surround many on-going armed conflicts. The still limited number of states which have accepted the competence of the Commission, and the political hesitancy of states to accept third-party involvement generally and in situations of armed conflicts in particular, may not augur for widespread use of the Commission's services. However, the Commission should have a role to play in present and future armed conflicts. This could be furthered by a flexible interpretation of the Commission's right of initiative and its role in providing good offices.

In this context, it should also be noted that Article 89 of Additional Protocol I provides that in situations of serious violations of the Conventions and the Protocol, "the High Contracting Parties undertake to act, jointly or individually, in co-operation with the United Nations and in conformity with the United Nations Charter". This reference to the United Nations (UN) might inspire the organization to call upon parties to armed conflicts to make use of the International Humanitarian Fact-Finding Commission. And refusal to comply with

---

[46]This is also emphasized by Bothe et al., op.cit. n. 21, p. 544; ICRC,. op.cit. n. 6, p. 1045; Ihraï, loc.cit. n. 27, p. 163.

[47]"This may be interpreted as a first step towards mediation", ICRC, op.cit. n. 6, p. 1050.

such a request might be considered by the UN in considering the need for further action, including, at least in theory, determination that a situation constitutes a "threat to the peace" within the meaning of Article 39 of the Charter.[48]

3. MONITORING BY INTERGOVERNMENTAL ORGANIZATIONS

The above-mentioned reference in Article 89 of Additional Protocol I of 1977 to the UN recognizes, at least implicitly, that the world organization may play a role in monitoring state behaviour and securing compliance with humanitarian law and human rights in situations of armed conflict. At the Geneva Diplomatic Conference 1974-1977, it was proposed to give the UN an even more visible role in this respect. According to a Norwegian amendment, and a draft text submitted by a Working Group, the UN could have designated a body to undertake the functions of a Protecting Power in case the discharge of the functions of a Protecting Power had not been assumed according to the normal procedure to be followed.[49] This idea, which was not actively supported by the UN itself, did not carry the day, however.[50]

This does not mean that the UN cannot perform a certain monitoring role in accordance with its general mandate, based on the Charter. Since the 1960s and 1970s, UN fact-finding missions, including visits

---

[48]H. Kelsen, *The Law of the United Nations* (New York 1951) p. 728 mentions as examples of behaviour which could lead to the determination of a "threat to the peace" non-compliance with recommendations made by the Security Council or the General Assembly concerning the peaceful settlement of disputes. Determination of the existence of a threat to the peace (or breach of the peace or act of aggression), of course, enables the Security Council to resort to binding enforcement measures under Chapter VII of the Charter.

[49]CDDH/I/83 (Norway), *Official Records* (see *supra* n. 30) Vol. III p. 35; Working Group proposal CDDH/I/235 Rev. 1 p. 3. See also Bothe et al., op.cit. n. 21, pp. 69-70.

[50]The Working Group draft was rejected by 32 votes to 27, with 16 abstentions, CDDH/I/SR. 27, *Official Records* (see *supra* n. 30) Vol. VIII p. 253 at p. 264.

on-the-spot, have been undertaken in the field of human rights.[51] The institutions of Working Groups, Special Rapporteurs, Special Representatives and Independent Experts established by the UN Commission on Human Rights have become an increasingly important tool for monitoring human rights problems.[52]

The missions of the UN Special Rapporteur on the situation in the former Yugoslavia attest to the fact that these missions may extend to situations of armed conflict as well.[53] The situation in the former Yugoslavia also led the Commission, for the first time in its history, to convene, in August 1992, a special emergency session.[54] A second special session was held in December 1992. There is now a growing awareness that the Commission and its Special Rapporteurs and Representatives should act with vigilance in urgent situations.[55]

As the examples of Cambodia, El Salvador, Somalia and the former Yugoslavia demonstrate, there may also be a more or less permanent UN mission, including peacekeeping and police forces, to monitor activities and provide assistance and protection. The UN then can become involved in various humanitarian assistance activities, including assisting in bringing about exchanges and releases of military prisoners and civilian detainees, helping enclaved towns and villages

---

[51]B.G. Ramcharan, "The Experience of the United Nations", in idem, ed., op.cit. n. 28, p. 176.

[52]P. Parker and D. Weissbrodt, *The U.N. Commission on Human Rights, Its Sub-Commission, and Related Procedures: An Orientation Manual Prepared for the Minnesota Advocates for Human Rights and the International Service for Human Rights* (Minneapolis 1993) pp. 8-10.

[53]See R. Wieruszewski's contribution in the present volume.

[54]The Commission had been empowered to convene special sessions by resolution 1990/48 adopted by the UN Economic and Social Council (ECOSOC).

[55]R. Cohen, *Human Rights and Humanitarian Emergencies: New Roles for U.N. Human Rights Bodies* (Paper prepared for the Refugee Policy Group, Washington 1992) pp. 1, 8-10.

to get aid, and so on.[56] Such activities, of course, may also fulfil a monitoring role.[57]

In some instances, the UN have also specifically investigated alleged breaches of humanitarian law and the law of war. For instance, the UN Secretary-General in 1983 dispatched a mission to inspect civilian losses in the war between Iran and Iraq and in 1984 appointed a group of experts to visit prisoner-of-war camps in the two countries.[58] The Secretary-General has also carried out investigations concerning the possible use, in contravention of the 1925 Geneva Gas Protocol,[59] of chemical or bacteriological weapons. This he has been explicitly authorized to do under General Assembly and Security Council resolutions.[60] A recent example is provided by the ad hoc Commission of Experts which was appointed by the Secretary-General to investigate violations of humanitarian law in the former Yugoslavia.[61]

---

[56]Exceptionally, the UN has itself become involved in active fighting involving the taking of military prisoners. In the armed conflict and peace-keeping operation in the Congo, military prisoners taken by the UN and the armed forces of the Katanga secessionist government were visited by the ICRC, Rosas, op.cit. n. 3, pp. 152-155.

[57]On the activities of the UN Observer Mission in El Salvador (ONUSAL) and other UN bodies see A. Rosas and K. Vainio, "El Salvador", in B.-A. Andreassen and T. Swinehart, eds., *Human Rights in Developing Countries: Yearbook 1991* (Oslo 1992) p. 98, *passim.*

[58]UN Docs. S/15834 (1983) and S/16962 (1985). See also Kalshoven, loc.cit. n. 15, p. 111; T. Opsahl, "Blant titusener av Irak-Irankrigens ofre, 3 *Mennesker og Rettigheter* (Nordic Journal on Human Rights) (1985) no. 2 p. 2; Wieruszewski, loc.cit. n. 12, p. 453.

[59]Protocol for the Prohibition of the Use in War of Asphyxiating, Poisonous or Other Gases, and of Bacteriological Methods of Warfare 1925, 94 LNTS p. 65.

[60]UN General Assembly Resolutions 35/144 C of 12 December 1980, 37/98 D of 13 December 1982, 42/37 C of 30 November 1987, 44/115 B of 15 December 1989; Security Council Resolution 620 of 26 August 1988. See also G. Cottereu, "The Geneva Protocol on Chemical and Biological Methods of Warfare (1925) and Related Procedures", in S. Sur, ed., *Verification of Current Disarmament and Arms Limitation Agreements: Ways, Means and Practices* (Dartmouth 1991) p. 45 et seq.; Kalshoven, loc.cit. n. 15, pp. 112-113.

[61]See UN Security Council Resolutions 771 and 780 (1992) and the Interim Report of the Commission of Experts, UN Doc. S/25274 (1993), Annex I.

These activities, of course, may also lead the Security Council or the General Assembly[62] to denounce breaches and, as far as the Security Council is concerned, even to resort to binding enforcement measures. The Security Council has in recent resolutions relating to Iraq, Yugoslavia, Libya and Somalia confirmed that the use of Article 39 and Chapter VII of the Charter does not presuppose the immediate threat of an inter-state war but can come into play also when serious human rights and humanitarian considerations are at stake.[63] In Resolution 808 (1993), adopted on 22 February, the Security Council expressed its grave alarm at continuing reports of widespread violations of international humanitarian law occurring within the territory of the former Yugoslavia and determined that "this situation constitutes a threat to international peace and security". Moreover, there is a tendency to give a broad interpretation to the right and duty of the Security Council, under Article 39, "to maintain or restore international peace and security", as shown by the decision, made in Resolution 808 (1993), to start the preparations for the establishment of an international tribunal for the prosecution of persons responsible for serious violations of international humanitarian law committed in the territory of the former Yugoslavia.

Also regional organizations may carry out monitoring and fact-finding missions not only in peacetime but also to further the respect for human rights and humanitarian principles in situations of armed conflict.[64] For instance, the Inter-American Commission on Human Rights has carried out various missions and visits to American states plagued by internal conflicts.[65] European examples are provided by the Conference on Security and Co-operation in Europe (CSCE) and

---

[62]On the use by the UN General Assembly of the Geneva Conventions and the Additional Protocols during the period 1977-1986 see Weissbrodt, loc.cit. n. 6, p. 325 et seq.

[63]See, in particular, Resolutions 688 (1991; Iraq), 748 (1992; Libya), 771 (1992; Yugoslavia) and 794 (1992; Somalia). See also the contribution by L. Boisson de Chazournes in the present volume.

[64]Cerna, loc.cit n. 15, pp. 49-50, 58.

[65]Such visits may also extend to prisoners detained for reasons related to the armed conflict, Rosas, op.cit. n. 3, p. 217 (concerning the Dominican civil strife in 1965).

other organizations such as the European Community. The CSCE human dimension missions, which have included missions to Croatia, deserve special mention here.[66]

Sometimes an international observer mission may be specifically designed to observe the application of humanitarian standards in armed conflict. An example is provided by an International Observer Team, consisting of nationals of some European states as well as representatives of the UN and the Organization of African Unity (OAU), which was invited by the Nigerian Central Government in 1968 to observe the conduct of Nigerian troops in the Nigerian civil war 1967-1970.[67]

While it goes beyond the framework of this paper to discuss the specific role of non-governmental organizations (NGOs) as monitoring bodies in the context of armed conflicts, two aspects could be briefly mentioned here. First of all, the "global village" implies that international NGOs, such as Amnesty International, the Watch organizations, the International Commission of Jurists and the International Helsinki Federation for Human Rights, are increasingly both alert and able to have a presence in situations of armed conflict, too. Secondly, their awareness of the need to respect not only human rights law but also the humanitarian law applicable in armed conflicts has been on the increase.[68]

The missions and enquiries considered above are normally either of an extra-conventional character, or they relate to more general human rights or human dimension mandates which have not been specifically designed for monitoring respect for humanitarian law applicable in armed conflicts. Apart from such procedures, some human rights conventions provide for special treaty bodies entrusted with the task of monitoring observance, including the application of the convention in

---

[66]See A. Bloed's contribution in the present volume. The European Community, too, has sent investigative missions to the former Yugoslavia, see, e.g., UN Doc. S/25240, Annex I.

[67]The findings of the International Observer Team were made public, Rosas, op.cit. n. 3, p. 198.

[68]Weissbrodt, loc.cit. n. 6, pp. 318 et seq., 331 et seq., 360 et seq.

question in situations of war and other public emergency. It is to some of these treaty regimes that we shall now turn.

4. PUBLIC EMERGENCY REGIMES

Some of the major human rights conventions contain special clauses allowing derogations in times of war or other public emergency threatening the life of the nation. The main provisions in this regard are Article 4 of the International Covenant on Civil and Political Rights of 1966 (CCPR), Article 15 of the European Convention for the Protection of Human Rights and Fundamental Freedoms (ECHR) of 1950, Article 30 of the European Social Charter of 1961[69] and Article 27 of the American Convention on Human Rights.[70] The meaning and interpretation of these provisions as well as the (all too often quite grim) practice surrounding emergency regimes imposed in various countries have by now received considerable attention in the literature and cannot be analysed in greater detail within the framework of this short paper.[71]

What is important to stress in this context is, first of all, that the human rights treaties are, in principle, applicable in situations of armed conflict as well. Both international wars and non-international armed conflicts are included in the definition of public emergency.[72] To be sure, derogations may be possible during an armed conflict, but they need some justification and a minimum core of rights must always be upheld.[73] While there is some uncertainty as to the relevance of the specifics of human rights law in combat situations,

---

[69]529 UNTS p. 89.

[70]1144 UNTS p. 123.

[71]Recent contributions include J. Oraá, *Human Rights in States of Emergency in International Law* (Oxford 1992); S. Stavros, "The Right to a Fair Trial in Emergency Situations", 41 *ICLQ* (1992) p. 343; A. Rosas, "Emergency Regimes: A Comparison", in D. Gomien, ed., *Broadening the Frontiers of Human Rights: Essays in Honour of Asbjørn Eide* (Oslo 1993) p. 165.

[72]See Rosas, loc.cit. n. 71, pp. 170-171, 174, with references.

[73]For a table listing the non-derogable rights of five binding treaties and four soft law instruments see ibid., pp. 190-191.

European case-law confirms that military control of foreign territory constitutes jurisdiction within the meaning of Article 1 of the ECHR and entails the responsibility of the sending state.[74]

Secondly, these human rights treaties do not contain any specific monitoring mechanisms for public emergencies but all monitoring, whether in time of peace or in time of war, takes place within the framework of the same institutional structure. Thus, for instance, the European Commission and Court of Human Rights, acting under the ECHR, the Committee of Independent Experts and the Governmental Committee, acting under the European Social Charter, and the European Committee for the Prevention of Torture, acting under the European Torture Convention of 1987,[75] are competent to perform their functions in relation to situations of public emergencies as well. It should be noted, on the other hand, that the body of law the observance of which they are monitoring may, in theory at least, include international humanitarian law applicable in armed conflicts.[76]

This is not to say that there may be no special arrangements prompted by emergency situations. For instance, the Human Rights Committee acting under the CCPR may, in addition to the normal periodic national reports, request special reports "whenever the Committee so requests" (Art. 40 CCPR). There is a new tendency in the work of the Committee to ask for such reports in emergency or

---

[74]Cyprus *v.* Turkey, Applications No. 6780/74 and No. 6950/75, 18 *Yearbook of the European Convention on Human Rights* (1975) p. 82 at pp. 116-118 (the Commission spoke of "actual authority and responsibility"); Application No. 8077/77, 13 Decisions and Reports (1979) p. 85 at pp. 148-150.

[75]European Convention for the Prevention of Torture and Inhuman and Degrading Treatment and Punishment 1987, 27 *ILM* (1988) p. 1152. See also the contribution of M. Nowak and W. Suntinger in the present volume.

[76]This follows from the requirement, e.g., in Art. 4 of the CCPR and Art. 15 of the ECHR that the measures of derogation are not only strictly required by the exigencies of the situation but are also not inconsistent with the State Party's "other obligations under international law" (these other obligations may include humanitarian law treaties), see, e.g., P. van Dijk and G.J.H. van Hoof, *Theory and Practice of the European Convention on Human Rights*, second edition (Deventer-Boston 1990) p. 555; R. Ergec, *Les droits de l'homme à l'épreuve des circonstances exceptionnelles. Etude sur l'article 15 de la Convention européenne des droits de l'homme* (Brussels 1987) p. 223 et seq.

other special situations.[77] The Freedom of Association Committee of the Governing Body of the International Labour Organization (ILO) has adopted a special procedure for urgent cases, including cases arising out of a continuing state of emergency.[78] By contrast, monitoring functions which are fully applicable under normal circumstances, may be curtailed in an emergency situation. Thus, the European Committee for the Prevention of Torture may see its right to carry out a visit restricted (but not abolished) "in exceptional circumstances".[79] And according to Article 17, paragraph 3, of this Convention the Committee shall not visit places which representatives or delegates of protecting powers or the ICRC "effectively visit on a regular basis" by virtue of the 1949 Geneva Conventions and their Additional Protocols of 1977. During armed conflicts, a certain priority is thus given to visits carried out by the ICRC.

Outside the framework of treaty law, the human dimension of the CSCE has developed a special procedure for situations posing "a particularly serious threat to the fulfilment of the provisions of the CSCE human dimension".[80] In such a situation, exemplified by the

---

[77]This method has been applied with respect to Iraq (1991), Yugoslavia (1991, 1992), Bosnia-Herzegovina (1992) and Croatia (1992), see V. Dimitrijević's contribution in the present volume. See also Cohen, op.cit. n. 55, p. 11. It should be noted in this context that the international humanitarian law applicable in armed conflicts does not contain a similar reporting system. This has been considered a shortcoming, K. Drzewicki, "National Legislation as a Measure for Implementation of International Humanitarian Law", in Kalshoven and Sandoz, op.cit. n. 12, p. 109 at p. 113 et seq.

[78]V. Leary, "Lessons from the Experience of the International Labour Organisation", in P. Alston, ed., *The United Nations and Human Rights: A Critical Appraisal* (Oxford 1992) p. 604.

[79]Art. 9 of the European Convention for the Prevention of Torture and Inhuman or Degrading Treatment or Punishment (ECPT). More specifically, the reservation against a visit made by the competent authorities of the High Contracting Party "may only be made on grounds of national defence, public safety, serious disorder in places where persons are deprived of their liberty, the medical condition of a person or that an urgent interrogation relating to a serious crime is in progress". This limitation clause thus does not presuppose the proclamation of a public emergency. See also L. Hannikainen, "International Monitoring of Respect for Human Rights Norms during Public Emergencies in Europe", in Kędzia et al., op. cit. n. 35, p. 117 at p. 120, and the contribution of M. Nowak and W. Suntinger in the present volume.

[80]Paras. 10-12 of the Document adopted by the Moscow Meeting of the Conference on the Human Dimension of the CSCE 1991, 30 ILM (1991) p. 1671.

situation in the former Yugoslavia,[81] a participating state may, with the support of at least nine other states, engage a special rapporteur procedure.[82]

In this context reference may also be made to the activities of the Special Rapporteur on States of Emergencies, appointed by the UN Sub-Commission on Prevention of Discrimination and Protection of Minorities.[83] In trying to obtain information about the possible existence of public emergencies, the Special Rapporteur also plays a certain monitoring role. Situations of public emergencies can, of course, also be considered in the Sub-Commission itself.[84]

5. CONCLUSIONS AND RECOMMENDATIONS

What this paper has brought out is that there is an abundance of international mechanisms which are able, *de facto* or *de jure*, to monitor compliance with humanitarian and human rights standards in situations of armed conflict.[85] Some of these mechanisms, notably the new International Humanitarian Fact-Finding Commission, have a mandate limited to armed conflicts or certain types of armed conflicts and the humanitarian law applicable in such conflict situations. Others are either convention-based bodies monitoring human rights primarily applicable in peacetime or involve mechanisms of an extra-conventional character (e.g., the political organs and the human rights rapporteurs of the UN), which enables them to move around more freely, unfettered by legal thresholds of applicability. There are mechanisms both of a universal, regional and sub-regional character.

---

[81]See *supra* at n. 66.

[82]See also Arie Bloed's contribution in the present volume.

[83]See the fifth annual report and list of states which have proclaimed, extended or terminated a state of emergency since 1 January 1985, presented by Mr. Leandro Despouy, Special Rapporteur appointed pursuant to Economic and Social Council Resolution 1985/37, UN Doc. E/CN.4/Sub.2/1992/23 (6 July 1992).

[84]An account of discussions on the Moscow *putsch* of 19 August 1991 in the Sub-Commission is given by Rosas, loc.cit. n. 71, pp. 166-167.

[85]A table on most of the mechanisms which can play a role in situations of public emergency has been compiled by Rosas, loc.cit. n. 71, pp. 196-197.

With the exception of the European Court of Human Rights and the UN Security Council, no legally binding decisions can emanate from these bodies.

One could ask whether or not this institutional and normative jungle adds to the inefficacy of the system, seen as a whole. Should we fall back on the specific mechanisms and instruments of humanitarian law (such as the ICRC), which are designed to give assistance and protection in armed conflicts, and ask the human rights bodies and the political bodies to focus their attention on peacetime situations? This does not seem a realistic alternative. Armed conflicts are today viewed as the foremost threat not only to peace and stability but also to human rights. The international community and its many offsprings will not sit idle in the face of armed conflicts and internal strife. Their often felt inability to provide effective remedies will lead them, in a combination of guilt, anger and frustration, to step up rather than scale down various monitoring activities. After all, this is better than simply doing nothing.

Moreover, the nature of armed conflicts has changed and seems to be changing. Rare have become the traditional inter-state wars with permanent armies, front-lines and victory and defeat. Most armed conflicts are either non-international or of a mixed character, which makes the determination of the applicable rules more difficult. Many conflicts take place in a grey area between armed conflicts and disturbances and tensions. Such situations cast the applicability even of common Article 3 of the 1949 Geneva Convention in doubt.

What is in fact needed is a minimum core approach with a combination of simplicity, generality and determination. During the preparations for the 1974-1977 Geneva Diplomatic Conference, the idea came up to have common minimum rules for international and non-international armed conflicts.[86] Subsequently, also the grey area between armed conflicts and peace has received increasing attention, and, in this context, the trend towards a convergence of humanitarian

---

[86]See *supra* at n. 24.

law and human rights law has been emphasized.[87] In 1990, a Declaration of Minimum Humanitarian Standards was adopted by an expert meeting in Turku, Finland.[88] The Declaration affirms certain minimum standards which are, in principle, applicable at all times, both in times of peace and armed conflict.

This and other compilations of minimum core rules may be of help in providing clearer yardsticks for international monitoring activities in chaotic situations such as the one prevailing in Bosnia-Herzegovina and some other parts of the former Yugoslavia. To seek a single and more powerful monitoring and enforcement institution for situations of armed conflict and/or tensions and disturbances is not a realistic goal, however. For the foreseeable future, we may have to rely on more or less the present myriad of bodies and mechanisms. It goes without saying that improvements may be possible, and that there is a need for co-ordination and avoidance of unnecessary duplication.

In this regard, the following recommendations can be put forward:

- Concerning substantive law, there should be more emphasis on minimum humanitarian and human rights standards applicable in all situations, irrespective of the legal nature of the conflict.

- The ICRC, with its well-established status and expertise in providing assistance and protection to victims of armed conflicts, should be supported and respected by all parties concerned.

- States should be encouraged to make use of the fact-finding and good offices procedures of the new International Humanitarian

---

[87]See, e.g., Rosas, loc.cit. n. 1; idem, loc.cit. n. 22; P.H. Kooijmans, "In the Shadowland between Civil War and Civil Strife: Some Reflections on the Standard-Setting Process", in Delissen and Tanja, op.cit. n. 18, p. 225.

[88]Published as UN doc. E/CN.4/Sub.2/1991/55, and in *Declaration of Minimum Humanitarian Standards* (Turku 1991); 85 *American Journal of International Law* (1991) p. 377; 31 *International Review of the Red Cross* (1991) p. 328. The groundwork for the Turku Declaration was laid by Theodor Meron, see, e.g., T. Meron, "Towards a Humanitarian Declaration on Internal Strife", 78 *American Journal of International Law* (1984) p. 859.

Fact-Finding Commission; the Commission itself could adopt an active role and invoke its rights of initiative.

- The UN Commission on Human Rights should continue to develop a permanent emergency readiness, involving special sessions outside the regular annual sessions, more effective use of special bodies and rapporteurs and close co-operation with other UN organs; the UN human rights activities, including the Centre for Human Rights, must be given adequate resources and support to cope with urgent situations.

- Human rights treaty bodies should be alerted to monitor closely emergency situations and problems; full support should be provided to the Special Rapporteur of the UN Sub-Commission to obtain fresh information about new states of emergency or *de facto* emergencies.

- As emphasized also in many other contributions to this volume, there should be more co-ordination and exchange of information between the various humanitarian and human rights organs and bodies, including the regional organizations, in dealing with particular situations of armed conflict and public emergency, such as the situation in the former Yugoslavia.[89]

The implementation of these and other similar recommendations could significantly enhance the efficacy of the international monitoring of armed conflicts and situations of disturbances and tensions. But it takes a considerable dose of optimism to conclude that such improvements would suffice. We have not reached the stage when principles of decency will be respected simply because it is the decent thing to do. An effective legal system cannot do away with the notions of sanctions and punishment.

The current plans to establish an international tribunal for the prosecution of persons responsible for serious violations of international

---

[89]An interesting precedent is the preference given in the ECPT to the ICRC, see *supra* at n. 79.

humanitarian law committed in the territory of the former Yugoslavia deserve our support.[90] This tribunal should be seen as a step leading to the establishment of a permanent international criminal court.[91]

Another development which merits our attention relates to the powers of enforcement and sanction vested in the UN Security Council, which have now surfaced after a rather long beauty sleep. To prevent bloodshed and suffering, and implement basic humanitarian standards, armed force may have to be used. International monitoring mechanisms are toothless without the backing of collective force.

Thomas Hobbes observed that "Covenants, without the sword, are but words, and of no strength to secure a man at all".[92]

Unfortunately, he still has a point. If this is so, let it be the collective sword rather than unilateral measures.

---

[90]See *supra* at n. 63.

[91]The International Law Commission is presently working on a draft statute for such a court. See also Recommendation 1189 (1992) on the establishment of an international court to judge war crimes, adopted by the Parliamentary Assembly of the Council of Europe on 1 July 1992, and the contribution by Nicholas Howen in the present volume.

[92] T. Hobbes, *Leviathan, or the Matter, Form and Power of a Commonwealth Ecclesiastical and Civil*. Edited, with an Introduction by C.B. Macpherson (London 1968; first published London 1651) Ch. 17 p. 223.

THE COLLECTIVE RESPONSIBILITY OF STATES TO ENSURE RESPECT FOR HUMANITARIAN PRINCIPLES

by Laurence Boisson de Chazournes

1. INTRODUCTION

To speak of the social or political responsibility of the international community to ensure respect for humanitarian principles[1] is not as heretical as it might have seemed a few decades ago. Nor should it be when one speaks of this collective responsibility in a legal perspective, that is the duty of each state to ensure respect for humanitarian principles in relation to each other.

The international legal system has gradually accepted that some obligations such as those deriving from "the principles and rules concerning the basic rights of the human person, including protection from slavery and racial discrimination"[2] are "by their very nature ... the concern of all States. In view of the importance of the rights involved, all States can be held to have a legal interest in their protection; they are obligations *erga omnes*".[3]

Third states[4] can find a legal basis for their right to ensure respect of humanitarian principles in the notion of obligations *erga omnes*. This principle would be strengthened if the right of third states to conduct an *actio popularis* was accompanied by an obligation to ensure respect for humanitarian principles. This would give a deeper and more action-oriented meaning to the collective responsibility of states.

---

[1]The expression "humanitarian principles" is used to mean both human rights law and international humanitarian law.

[2]*Barcelona Traction Light and Power Company* (Belgium *v*. Spain) (Merits), I.C.J Reports 1970, para. 34, p. 32.

[3]*Barcelona Traction Light and Power Company*, ibid., para. 33, p. 32.

[4]For practical reasons, we shall use the term "third states" to refer to states that have not violated humanitarian principles. When we speak of collective responsibility, we mean responsibility assumed by all states.

A. Bloed et al. (eds.), *Monitoring Human Rights in Europe*, 247–260.

Even if the obligation to ensure respect for humanitarian principles appears to have some ground in the international legal system,[5] defining its legal parameters is a rather difficult task.[6] This is due, in great part, to the lack of precision of how, in fact, it should be implemented. Should it be considered, for example, that states parties to human rights treaties are obliged to bring, under the inter-state procedures provided for by the treaties, claims in response to infringements committed by other states parties?[7] However, an analysis of state practice demonstrates the reluctance of third states to consider themselves under a duty to allege the international responsibility of a state violating human rights.[8] This situation would explain the paucity of inter-state claims brought under treaty-based mechanisms.

2. THE OBLIGATION TO ENSURE RESPECT FOR INTERNATIONAL HUMANITARIAN LAW

Given the rather theoretical nature of the notion of collective responsibility, it is worth considering how this principle has found application in international humanitarian law. In effect, the obligation to ensure respect for humanitarian principles has received its clearest

---

[5]Resolution on the Protection of Human Rights and the Principle of Non-intervention in Internal Affairs of States adopted by the Institute of International Law, *Yearbook*, Vol. 63, Part II (Paris 1990) p. 338 at p. 345.

[6]M.T. Kamminga, *Inter-State Accountability for Violations of Human Rights* (Philadelphia 1992) pp. 183-190.

[7]This was the position taken by the Consultative Assembly of the Council of Europe as regards the European Convention on Human Rights when in 1967 it adopted a resolution on the human rights situation in Greece which, *inter alia*, expressed the view that "in an important and serious case of this kind, the contracting Parties to the Convention have a duty to act under article 24 of the Convention and that, if they do not act as requested, the mechanism of collective guarantee of human rights set up by the Convention runs the risk of becoming meaningless" (Res. 346 (1967), *Yearbook of the European Convention on Human Rights* (1967) p. 96). Denmark, Norway, Sweden and the Netherlands filed an application under Article 24 of the Convention which referred expressly to the Consultative Assembly's resolution (*Yearbook of the European Convention on Human Rights* (1967) p. 586); see Kamminga, op.cit. n. 6, p. 185.

[8]See the contribution of V. Dimitrijević in the present volume.

formulation in common Article 1 of the four Geneva Conventions of 12 August 1949 and its Additional Protocol I of 1977.[9] Common Article 1 provides: "The High Contracting Parties undertake to respect and to ensure respect for ... in all circumstances."

The International Court of Justice recognized the importance of the obligation defined in common Article 1, finding its origins in the field of general international law.[10] International Conferences have also given credence to this obligation [11].

Common Article 1 establishes legal grounds for action against a state violating humanitarian law which are applicable in international armed conflicts, internal armed conflicts and all other situations covered by common Article 3 to the four 1949 Geneva conventions. It also emphasizes the non-reciprocal nature and absolute character of this fundamental obligation, which obliges states, whether or not parties to conflicts, to react to violations of international humanitarian

---

[9]Convention (I) for the Amelioration of the Condition of Wounded and Sick Armed Forces in the Field, Convention (II) for the Amelioration of the Condition of Wounded, Sick and Shipwrecked Members of Armed Forces at Sea, Convention (III) relative to the Treatment of Prisoners of War, Convention (IV) relative to the Protection of Civilian Persons in Time of War 1949, 75 UNTS pp. 31, 85, 135, 287; Protocol Additional to the Geneva Conventions of 12 August 1949, and relating to the Protection of Victims of International Armed Conflicts (Protocol I), Protocol Additional to the Geneva Conventions of 12 August 1949, and relating to the Protection of Victims of Non-International Armed Conflicts (Protocol II) 1977, 1125 UNTS pp. 3, 609.

[10]*Military and Paramilitary Activities in and Against Nicaragua* (Nicaragua *v.* United States of America), Merits, Judgment, ICJ Rep. (1986), para. 220, p. 114.

[11]Resolution XXIII adopted by the Conference on Human Rights held in Teheran in 1968 provided, *inter alia*, "that States parties to the Red Cross Geneva Conventions sometimes fail to appreciate their responsibility to take steps to ensure the respect of these humanitarian rules in all circumstances by other states, even if they are not themselves directly involved in an armed conflict", *Final Act of the International Conference on Human Rights*, United Nations, A/CONF.32/41, p. 18. The same approach was adopted by the states participating in the CSCE Helsinki Summit, *Helsinki 1992 Document*, p. 57.

law regardless of the circumstances, so as to ensure respect for the aforementioned principles.[12]

The Geneva Conventions and their Additional Protocol I offer states the means by which to enforce this obligation. This could, for example, include convening meetings of the High Contracting Parties, resorting to the Protecting Powers institution and its substitutes, enforcement of the repression of grave breaches system, in particular those calling for the greatest measure of mutual assistance in criminal matters, or resorting to the International Fact-Finding Commission recently established under Article 90 of Protocol I.[13]

The obligation to ensure respect for humanitarian principles can also be implemented through other channels such as diplomatic action or public denunciation. It can also find application through the principle of universality of jurisdiction which implies that states should try or extradite alleged criminals.

Furthermore, common Article 1 can find concrete meaning within the framework of the United Nations. As such, actions so conducted give tangible meaning to Article 89 of Additional Protocol I to the Conventions, which reads as follows:

---

[12]J. Pictet, under the direction of the ICRC, *Commentaires des Conventions de Genève*, International Committee of the Red Cross, 4 vols. (Geneva 1952-1956); Y. Sandoz et al., eds., *Commentary on the Additional Protocols of 8 June 1977 to the Geneva Conventions of 12 August 1949* (Geneva 1987) pp. 33-38; L. Condorelli and L. Boisson de Chazournes, "Quelques remarques à propos de l'obligation de 'respecter et faire respecter' le droit international humanitaire 'en toutes circonstances'", in Ch. Swinarski, ed., *Studies and Essays in International Humanitarian Law and Red Cross Principles in Honour of JEAN PICTET* (Geneva -The Hague 1984) pp. 17-35; *Respect of Human Rights in Time of Armed Conflict*, Report of the Secretary-General, A/7720 (UN), 20 November 1969, p. 33, para. 82.

[13]Any state which made a declaration recognizing the competence of the International Fact-Finding Commission under Article 90 of Protocol I, be it or not a victim of violations of humanitarian principles, would be able to request the Commission to institute an inquiry "into any facts alleged to be a grave breach as defined in the Conventions and this Protocol or other serious violation of the Conventions or of this Protocol" and "facilitate, through its good offices, the restoration of an attitude of respect for the Conventions and this Protocol" (Article 90, para. 2(c)), provided that the state against whom the allegation is made has made a similar declaration or accepts the *ad hoc* competence of the Commission; see the contribution of A. Rosas in the present volume.

> "In situations of serious violations of the Conventions or of this Protocol, the High Contracting Parties undertake to act, jointly or individually, in co-operation with the United Nations and in conformity with the United Nations Charter."

This Article provides that in certain circumstances ("in situations of serious violations"), the parties have a more stringent obligation to ensure respect for humanitarian principles: they have expressly committed themselves to act in co-operation with the United Nations to remedy such violations.

3. THE IMPLEMENTATION OF THE OBLIGATION TO ENSURE RESPECT OF HUMANITARIAN PRINCIPLES WITHIN THE FRAMEWORK OF THE UNITED NATIONS

The United Nations General Assembly, the Security Council and the Commission on Human Rights have on various occasions condemned violations of humanitarian principles.[14] Among the means that have been used to confront such violations are calls to respect humanitarian principles; good-offices; the sending of observer missions[15] and peace-keeping operations[16] (whose mandate has included, *inter alia*, the promotion of humanitarian principles). The collective denunciations of abusive violations and the institutional actions which can be undertaken to monitor the promotion of humanitarian prin-

---

[14]B.G. Ramcharan, *The International Law and Practice of Early-Warning and Preventive Diplomacy: The Emerging Global Watch* (Dordrecht-Boston-London 1991) pp. 89-100. More specifically, on the practice of the Security Council, see T. van Boven, "The Security Council: The New Frontier", *International Commission of Jurists, The Review* (1992) p. 12 at p. 23; B.G. Ramcharan, "The Security Council: Maturing of International Protection of Human Rights", ibid., p. 24 at p. 37.

[15]S.C. Res. 693 of 20 May 1991 establishing the United Nations Observer Mission in El Salvador (ONUSAL) to monitor all agreements concluded by the two parties, which includes components on the respect of humanitarian principles.

[16]S.C. Res. 745 of 28 February 1992 on the establishment of a United Nations Transitional Authority in Cambodia (UNTAC) which has as part of its mandate the protection of humanitarian principles.

ciples give substance to the implementation of collective responsibility of states to ensure respect for humanitarian principles.

The Security Council has also recently given a new dimension to this obligation, which could prove to be fruitful. In Resolution 681 (1990) of 20 December 1990, the Security Council, which was

> "gravely concerned at the dangerous deterioration of the situation of all the Palestinian territories occupied by Israel since 1967, including Jerusalem, and at the violence and rising tension in Israel ..."

called upon

> "5. ... the High Contracting Parties to the said Convention[17] to ensure respect by Israel, the occupying Power, for its obligations under the Convention in accordance with article 1 thereof;"

and requested

> "6. ... the Secretary-General, in co-operation with the International Committee of the Red-Cross, to develop further the idea, expressed in his report, of convening a meeting of the High Contracting Parties to the said Convention to discuss possible measures that might be taken by them under the Convention and, for this purpose, to invite the Parties to submit their views on how the idea could contribute to the goals of the Convention, as well as on relevant matters, and to report thereon to the Council."

The Security Council, referring to common Article 1, asked each contracting party to contribute meaningfully to the meeting of the states parties of the fourth Geneva Convention. The Security Council thus found, within the meaning of common Article 1, explicit grounds

---

[17] I.e., the Geneva Convention (IV) relative to the Protection of Civilian Persons in Time of War, of 12 August 1949.

for the collective responsibility of states to ensure that international humanitarian law is respected.[18]

During the Iraq-Kuwait conflict the Security Council, acting expressly under Chapter VII of the Charter of the United Nations, included stringent requests for respect for humanitarian law in its decisions[19] and also dealt with Iraq's responsibility for violations of humanitarian principles. In its cease-fire resolution,[20] the Security Council confirmed that Iraq was "liable under international law for any direct loss, damage, ... or injury to foreign Governments, nationals and corporations, as a result of Iraq's unlawful invasion and occupation of Kuwait". Claims for compensation of violations of humanitarian principles can clearly be brought before the Commission under this basis established by the Security Council[21] to deal with the relevant claims. This mechanism offers yet another promising dimension to the obligation to ensure respect for humanitarian principles, identifying a means of practical implementation of the consequences deriving from state responsibility for humanitarian violations.

The Security Council has also taken another step by determining that large-scale and gross violations of humanitarian principles constitute threats to, or breaches of, the peace as qualified by Article 39 of the Charter of the United Nations[22] and decided to take specific actions

---

[18]See also *Report submitted to the Security Council by the Secretary-General in accordance with Resolution 681* (1990), S/22472, 9 April 1991.

[19]S.C. Res. 666 of 13 September 1990, S.C. Res. 670 of 25 September 1990, S.C. Res. 674 of 29 October 1990, S.C. Res. 686 of 2 March 1991 and S.C. Res. 687 of 3 April 1991. See C. Bourloyannis, "The Security Council of the United Nations and the Implementation of International Humanitarian Law", *Denver Journal of International Law and Policy* (1992) p. 348 at p. 350.

[20]S.C. Res. 687 of 8 April 1991.

[21]S.C. Res. 692 of 2 May 1991.

[22]On the material scope of application of Article 39 of the Charter of the United Nations which encompasses threats to, and breaches of, the peace other than aggression, see H. Kelsen, *The Law of the United Nations* (London 1950) p. 438 and p. 736; see S.C. Res. 232 (1966) of 16 december 1966 in which the Security Council considered the racist regime of Southern Rhodesia as a threat to international peace and security.

under Chapter VII to confront such threats to, or breaches of, the peace.

Considering the action to be taken against the massive violations of humanitarian principles in Bosnia-Herzegovina, the Security Council, acting on the basis of Chapter VII, decided that violations of international humanitarian law constituted a breach of the peace under Article 39 of the Charter of the United Nations[23] and determined that a wide range of measures should be taken in order to restore international peace. As with Resolution 688 of 5 April 1991 condemning "the repression of the Iraqi civilian population in many parts of Iraq, including most recently in Kurdish populated areas, the consequences of which threaten international peace and security in the region", the Security Council enlarged its interpretation of Article 39 and found consistent patterns of gross violations of internationally recognized humanitarian principles to be threats to, or breaches of, the peace. It reiterated its interpretation with the adoption of Resolution 794 of 3 December 1992 "determining that the magnitude of the human tragedy caused by the conflict in Somalia, further exacerbated by the obstacles being created to the distribution of humanitarian assistance, constitutes a threat to international peace and security".

Under Chapter VII the Security Council may indicate provisional measures, apply economic sanctions and all other peaceful means that may be necessary to maintain international peace and security. As a last resort, when all peaceful means have failed, it may decide to have recourse to military measures. In so doing, the Security Council may direct measures to put an end to the violation of humanitarian principles or, at a minimum, to diminish the suffering of victims.[24]

---

[23]S.C. Res. 771 of 13 August 1992.

[24]It should be noted that while analysing how common Article 1 finds application within Chapter VII, we are focusing on the *ius in bello* to see how the obligation to ensure respect for humanitarian principles can benefit from implementation within this institutional pattern. Thus, the questions which arise in respect of the *ius ad bellum* are not considered although the application of fundamental principles such as the inadmissibility of the acquisition of territory by war or the right to self-defence also have their part in ensuring respect for humanitarian principles.

Obviously, the Council must take into account the circumstances of the breach of the peace involved. Humanitarian principles have value *per se* and should not be considered only when security issues which endanger international peace and security are at stake. The fundamental nature of humanitarian principles would have to be considered by the Security Council when it decides on the measures to be taken.

Gross violations of humanitarian principles are matters of international concern and not "matters which are essentially within the domestic jurisdiction". In addition, it should be stressed that measures taken under Chapter VII to remedy violations of humanitarian principles should not be considered as a breach of the principle of non-intervention in the internal affairs of states. These measures would, in fact, benefit from the exception stated in Article 2, paragraph 7, of the United Nations Charter, which states that the principle of non-intervention in domestic affairs "shall not prejudice the application of enforcement measures under Chapter VII".

In view of this, humanitarian assistance decided by the Security Council under Chapter VII would not conflict with the domestic jurisdiction principle.[25] But the provision of humanitarian assistance decided under Chapter VII must meet certain requirements:[26] it

---

[25]The "novelty" of the question of organizing an international humanitarian operation and the political context which prevailed in the aftermath of the Gulf War, have to be taken into account if one wants to give an explanation of the content of Resolution 688 of 5 April 1991, and more specifically of its inconsistencies as regards Article 2, paragraph 7 of the Charter. For a political and legal interpretation of Resolution 688, see P. Malanczuk, "The Kurdish Crisis and Allied Intervention in the aftermath of the Second Gulf War", *European Journal of International Law* (1991) p. 114 at p. 132.

[26]S.C. Res. 688 of 5 April 1988; S.C. Res. 794 of 3 December 1992.

should be provided to people who are in need, in conformity with the principle of non-discrimination.[27]

Recently, the Security Council has authorized states "to use all necessary means"[28] to apply its decisions. It should, however, maintain control over the way these decisions are implemented. Absence of control by the Security Council presents the risk that states are given a blank cheque and might abuse and exceed their powers, especially if they were to take military action.[29,30] On the other hand, the absence of control by the Security Council could leave states without any pressing incentives to implement the measures and actions decided by this organ. In this context, it is regrettable that the collective security mechanisms provided for under Articles 43 to 49 of Chapter VII of the Charter of the United Nations have not yet been functioning as originally envisaged.

If the Security Council were to decide to send peace-keeping forces, it should first define their mandate, and extend it if necessary, so as to render effective the respect for humanitarian principles. Ideally, the peace-keeping forces should be in charge of guaranteeing, if necessary with recourse to armed force, the smooth administration of all humanitarian aid activities conducted by organizations such as the United Nations High Commissioner for Refugees (UNHCR), the United Nations Children's Fund (UNICEF), the International

---

[27]These criteria are similar to those prescribed by general international law which require that, to preclude intervention in the internal affairs of a state, "an essential feature of truly humanitarian aid is that it is given 'without discrimination' of any kind" and is "limited to the purposes hallowed in the practice of the Red Cross, namely 'to prevent and alleviate human suffering', and 'to protect life and health and to ensure respect for the human being'", *Military and Paramilitary Activities in and Against Nicaragua*, *supra* n. 9, p. 125, para. 243.

[28]Para. 2 of S.C. Res. 678 of 29 November 1990 (Gulf War); Para. 10 of S.C. Res. 794 of 3 December 1992 (Operation "Restore Hope" in Somalia).

[29]For a critical appraisal of the military operations conducted during the Gulf War, see R. Zacklin, *Les Nations Unies et la crise du Golfe, Les aspects juridiques de la crise et de la guerre du Golfe* (Paris 1991) pp. 68-70.

[30]It should be stressed that "any use of force, individual or collective, even when consistent with the Charter, is subject to the rules of international law applicable in armed conflict, in particular those codified in the Conventions and the Protocol", Sandoz et al., eds., op.cit. n. 11, p. 1035.

Committee of the Red Cross (ICRC) and non-governmental organizations (NGOs). The United Nations forces should also be in charge of, for example, the protection of civilians, access to detainee camps and the establishment of safe zones under international protection.

The restoration of international peace can be encouraged by the relationships referred to in Chapter VIII of the Charter which incorporates regional arrangements and agencies into the UN scheme. These relationships have been interpreted largely in terms of military operations and peace-keeping forces. Recent trends in international practice have shown that the Security Council has become involved in new types of collective security issues, such as gross violations of humanitarian principles. The cessation of these acts could benefit greatly from combined actions conducted both at the universal and at the regional level.[31] At the European level, initiatives conducted by the Conference on Security and Co-operation in Europe (CSCE),[32] the European Community or the Council of Europe could provide means by which to ensure the cessation of violation of humanitarian principles. This would offer new perspectives in interpreting Chapter VIII which would thus enlarge relationships between the United Nations and regional arrangements and agencies to include operational actions (other than military operations) to ensure respect for humanitarian principles.

In order to prevent the recurrence of gross violations of humanitarian principles, action should be taken to strengthen and solidify the restoration of peace. In this context, promotion of the respect of humanitarian principles is a necessary component of all actions

---

[31]Note the emphasis placed by the Secretary-General on the role of regional arrangements and institutions within the framework of maintaining and restoring peace in *An Agenda for Peace, Preventive Diplomacy, Peacemaking and Peace-keeping*, United Nations, 1992, p. 35 at p. 38.

[32]Considering the CSCE as a regional arrangement under the meaning of Chapter VIII of the Charter of the United Nations, the states participating at the CSCE Helsinki meeting declared that the CSCE would closely collaborate with the United Nations, particularly as regards the prevention and settlement of conflicts, *Helsinki Summit Declaration*, para. 25. See A. Bloed, "The CSCE: A New International Security Organization in Europe?", in H. Fischer, ed., *CSCE in Transition* (Publications of Bochum University 1993).

undertaken to sustain peace after the settlement of a conflict. It should be considered as a "post-conflict *peace-building*" measure as qualified by the Secretary-General, Boutros Boutros-Ghali, in his *Agenda for Peace*.[33] Post-conflict promotional actions could also benefit from joint and complementary efforts between the United Nations and regional arrangements and organizations.

4. CONCLUSIONS AND RECOMMENDATIONS

From the above, the following conclusions and recommendations may be made:

1. Common Article 1 of the four Geneva Conventions of 12 August 1949 and their Additional Protocol I provide that states are under a general obligation to ensure respect for humanitarian principles. In implementing this obligation, states should utilize all the means they are legally entitled to use, be they diplomatic, treaty-based or institutional.

2. Recent trends have consolidated the United Nations Charter as a legal and institutional framework for prescribing action to ensure respect for humanitarian principles.[34] This development has, without any doubt, strengthened the identification and enforcement of the duty to ensure respect for humanitarian principles. One must not overlook the richness of the resources of *all* of the United Nations Charter. This offers states new perspectives in their role as guarantors of the principle of respect for humanitarian principles.

3. All the United Nations organs should fulfil their mandates to remedy grave violations of humanitarian principles. In this respect, it should be stressed that Articles 10 to 14 provide the General Assembly with a wide range of functions and powers which can be used to ensure the redress of violations of humanitarian principles.

4. Actions undertaken under Chapter VII to ensure respect for humanitarian principles should be considered as a means of last resort, that is when no other action by the Security Council or other competent United Nations organ would prove to be effective in such grave and urgent situations.

5. The Security Council should not be selective in qualifying gross violations of humanitarian principles as threats to, or breaches of, the peace. There is a risk of a double standard ensuing. In this respect the veto power and the voting procedure could play a role against a potential double standard, but there is absolutely no guarantee of consistency. Because of this risk of selectivity it is very important that external checks and balances are also developed within the constitutional order of the United Nations system. They could be of a political nature such as the establishment by the General Assembly of a Committee which would provide opinions on the validity of the decisions of the Security Council.[35] The International Court of Justice could also be requested by the General Assembly to give an advisory opinion on the legitimacy of a decision of the Security Council.[36]

6. Joint and complementary efforts should be encouraged between the United Nations and regional arrangements and organizations with the purpose of improving the effectiveness of the implementation of collective responsibility to ensure respect of humani-

---

[35]See B. Conforti, "Non-Coercive Sanctions in the United Nations Charter: Some Lessons from the Gulf War", *European Journal of International Law* (1991) p. 112 at p. 113.

[36]Art. 96, para. 1, of the Charter of the United Nations.

tarian principles. Operational actions and "post-conflict *peace-building*" measures should be conducted on this basis.

7. The obligation to ensure respect for humanitarian principles should not be interpreted too narrowly, that is in the sense of providing only *urgent* humanitarian assistance. If such was the case, it could become an easy alibi for states wishing not to wholly assume their collective responsibility. There would be the great risk that humanitarian assistance would become a pawn of political interests, impossible of any meaningful implementation, in particular as regards the guarantee of access to victims and safety for people providing aid. The obligation to ensure respect for humanitarian principles should be interpreted in a broad sense, so as to include the search for a peaceful resolution of a conflict based on the respect for fundamental human rights. The promotion of respect for humanitarian principles as a "post-conflict *peace-building*" measure to consolidate peace and prevent any recurrence of gross violations of humanitarian principles should also be part of this process.

8. However, long before actions to ensure respect for humanitarian principles are taken, basic anticipatory measures should first be taken. Problems such as the continuous deterioration of terms of trade, debt crises and the arms trade must be faced head-on and resolved. This approach would be far more effective than simple remedial measures taken *post facto* because they would, in effect, prevent the very emergence of threats to, or breaches of, the peace. Such preventive measures would also facilitate and promote the implementation of the objectives set out in Articles 55 and 56 of the Charter of the United Nations, that is "the creation of conditions of stability and well-being which are necessary for peaceful and friendly relations among nations based on respect for the principle of equal rights and self-determination of peoples".

FROM NUREMBERG TO THE BALKANS: THE INTERNATIONAL WAR CRIMES TRIBUNAL FOR THE FORMER YUGOSLAVIA

by Nicholas Howen

1. SIGNIFICANCE OF A WAR CRIMES TRIBUNAL FOR THE BALKANS

For the first time since the Nuremberg and Tokyo war crimes tribunals more than 40 years ago, the world is poised to create a court to try war criminals. On 22 February 1993 the United Nations (UN) Security Council decided in principle to set up an *ad hoc* international tribunal (the Tribunal) to try serious violations of humanitarian law committed during the conflicts in the former Yugoslavia since 1991.[1] The Security Council asked UN Secretary-General Dr. Boutros-Ghali to make recommendations about how to set up the Tribunal.[2]

The creation of this *ad hoc* international Tribunal embodies the principle clarified at the Nuremberg and Tokyo war crimes tribunals, reaffirmed in UN General Assembly resolutions[3] and embodied in

[1]See Security Council Resolution 808 (1993). This war crimes tribunal is only one of many initiatives taken by the UN and other intergovernmental organizations in an attempt to deal with gross human rights violations in the former Yugoslavia. For an overview of the effectiveness of these initiatives, see the contribution by R. Wieruszewski in the present volume.

[2]At the time of writing (April 1993) these recommendations had not yet been submitted. Some of the issues addressed in this paper respond directly to concrete proposals submitted to the Security Council by France, Italy, the USA, the Conference on Security and Co-operation in Europe (CSCE) and the Organization of Islamic Conference (OIC). See French proposal - UN Doc. S/25266, 10 February 1993; Italian proposal - UN Doc. S/25300, 17 February 1993; USA proposal - UN Doc. S/25575, 12 April 1993; OIC proposal - UN Doc. A/47/920 and S/25512, 5 April 1993. For the CSCE proposal see, Corell, Türk and Thune, *Proposal for an International War Crimes Tribunal for the Former Yugoslavia under the CSCE Moscow Dimension Mechanism to Bosnia-Herzegovina and Croatia* (CSCE, 9 February 1993).

[3]See, e.g., UN General Assembly (hereafter UNGA), Resolution 95 (1), 11 December 1946 which affirmed the principles of international law recognized by the Nuremberg Charter; UNGA Resolution 96 (1), 11 December 1946 re genocide.

A. Bloed et al. (eds.), Monitoring Human Rights in Europe, 261–283.

several UN conventions,[4] that individuals are criminally responsible for any act which constitutes a crime under international law, even if internal law does not criminalize the same act or even authorizes it. These international crimes, which shock the conscience of humankind, include crimes against humanity, war crimes, torture, genocide, slavery and apartheid.

In practice, international criminal law has been enforced, if at all, only indirectly by states exercising universal jurisdiction; viz., exercising their duty either to prosecute suspected perpetrators found on their territory or to extradite them to a country which will prosecute.[5] Direct enforcement by the international community has been more theoretical than real because of the lack of political will to create a permanent international criminal court. Nuremberg, Tokyo and now the Balkans, are rare expressions of the responsibility of the international community to reassert the rule of law and minimum standards of humane conduct.[6]

The purpose of this paper is to examine some of the practices and safeguards which should be followed if this Tribunal is to be just, fair and effective, if it is to learn from the mistakes of Nuremberg[7] and take account of the radical development of human rights principles since the Second World War.

---

[4]See UN Convention on the Prevention and Punishment of the Crime of Genocide, Art. 1; UN International Convention on the Suppression and Punishment of the Crime of Apartheid, Art. 1.

[5]See M.C. Bassiouni, "Characteristics of International Criminal Law Conventions", in M.C. Bassiouni, ed., *International Criminal Law*, vol. I (New York 1986) pp. 1-9.

[6]Regarding collective responsibility see also the contribution of L. Boisson de Chazournes in the present volume.

[7]For the latest in a number of personal accounts by people involved in the Nuremberg trials, see T. Taylor, *The Anatomy of the Nuremberg Trials: A Personal Memoir* (New York 1992). Many of the legal controversies at Nuremberg are echoed in the current debates about how the tribunal for the former Yugoslavia should be set up.

2. WHY SEEK JUSTICE AT ALL?: IMPUNITY AND HUMAN RIGHTS VIOLATIONS

Human rights violators should be brought to justice because impunity - literally the exemption from punishment - is one of the main contributing factors to continuing patterns of human rights violations.[8] Holding people personally accountable for acts which violate basic rules of minimum civilized conduct is as essential in war as in peacetime.[9] Proper investigations into individual and collective responsibility for abuses helps to provide a full account of the truth to victims, their families and society. Furthermore, seeing that justice is done in individual cases is not only important for victims and their families, it also sends a clear message to military and civilian authorities that violations of basic human rights will not be tolerated. Sweeping aside the question of responsibility only leads to renewed cycles of violence and impunity, sometimes immediately; sometimes the wounds erupt many years after life has apparently returned to normal.

The creation of an international Tribunal will not remove the continuing obligation of all relevant authorities in the former Yugoslavia, whether or not recognized governments, to investigate allegations of human rights and humanitarian law abuses and to bring violators to justice. The evidence must be collected quickly before it is destroyed, to be used in trials at either the national or international level. Some human rights violations will not fall within the jurisdiction of the international Tribunal. For example, the Tribunal will only be able to try crimes which were committed after a certain date in 1991 (still to be decided, but probably either 1 January or 25 June 1991) so any crime committed before that date will have to be dealt with by national courts. In other cases the international Tribunal may be

---

[8]See Amnesty International, "Oral Statement under Agenda Item 10", *Statements to the 43rd session of the UN Sub-Commission on Prevention of Discrimination and Protection of Minorities*, AI Index: IOR 41/06/91 (September 1991).

[9]See also F.J., Hampson, *The Case for a War Crimes Tribunal*, The David Davies Memorial Institute of International Studies, Occasional Paper No. 3 (London, February 1993).

authorized to transfer a case back to the national courts for trial (see *infra* 8.).

Many of the human rights mechanisms described elsewhere in this book monitor broad patterns of human rights violations,[10] only address the responsibility of states and rely on political pressure to encourage governments to change their practices.[11] In contrast, bringing human rights violators to justice is intensely individualized: it focuses on the responsibility of individuals for past acts committed against individual victims and relies on judicial sanctions.[12] Bringing violators to justice is one form of redress for specific past abuses yet, as described above, it also contributes to the prevention of future human rights violations. It compliments other human rights strategies.

3. JUSTICE, FAIRNESS AND EFFECTIVENESS

The international Tribunal will only be the first step in breaking the cycle of impunity in the former Yugoslavia if it is taken seriously by governments and the UN.

Will this Tribunal actually prosecute and convict those it finds responsible for gross human rights violations in the former Yugoslavia? There is a real danger of it being no more than a token political gesture. Governments and the UN will be discredited if the Tribunal is not given the wide powers, resources and political backing it must have if it is to have any chance of bringing perpetrators to justice in very difficult circumstances.

Will this Tribunal be fair? Lingering doubts about the trials will always remain and the UN will violate its own detailed human rights standards unless the Tribunal scrupulously complies with guarantees

---

[10]For example, see the contribution of V. Dimitrijević in the present volume.

[11]Regarding the CSCE see the contribution of A. Bloed in the present volume; regarding torture the one of M. Nowak and W. Suntinger.

[12]Individual complaint procedures also focus on violations against individual victims, but determine state and not individual responsibility. See the contribution by R. Müllerson in the present volume.

for fair trial and treatment of detainees. Indeed, the Tribunal will hopefully be a model by aiming for the highest human rights standards. It would be tragic, for example, if the death penalty could be imposed, at a time when more and more countries are abolishing this form of punishment and when more states are ratifying the UN and the Council of Europe Protocols aimed at stopping executions and abolishing the death penalty.[13]

Justice must be impartial by being equally fair and equally rigorous, irrespective of what official position the accused holds, Serb, Croat or Muslim. Partial justice would thoroughly discredit the judicial process. This Tribunal may not be victor's justice, but will it be disinterested justice?

Justice has many faces. There must be justice for the victims and their families who have suffered personal horrors; for the accused who must be treated fairly and equally; for the Serb, Croat, Muslim and other communities in the former Yugoslavia; and for the international community which must reassert the rule of law and the primacy of human rights. Different aspects of justice demand different powers and safeguards, some of which are explained in this paper.[14]

4. *AD HOC* OR PERMANENT TRIBUNAL?

The establishment of an *ad hoc*, or *temporary*, international war crimes tribunal for the former Yugoslavia should not be confused with

---

[13]UN Second Optional Protocol to the International Covenant on Civil and Political Rights aiming at abolition of the death penalty, which had been ratified or acceded to by 15 states as at 26 February 1993, and Protocol No. 6 to the European Convention on Human Rights, which had been ratified or acceded to by 18 states as at 26 February 1993.

[14]For a more detailed explanation of the reasoning underlying many of the recommendations made in this paper, see Amnesty International, *Memorandum to the United Nations: The Question of Justice and Fairness in the International War Crimes Tribunal for the Former Yugoslavia*, AI Index: EUR 48/02/93 (April 1993).

quite separate attempts over the last 70 years to set up a *permanent* international criminal court.[15]

There have been many false starts this century in an attempt to establish a permanent international criminal court. The *Treaty of Versailles* after the First World War contemplated an international tribunal to try German war criminals but political enthusiasm quickly waned and the tribunal was never established. After the Second World War there was great optimism that the Nuremberg and Tokyo tribunals would be the impetus to create a permanent institution. The UN established an International Law Commission which was asked to draft a code of offences against the peace and security of mankind as well as a statute for an international criminal court. The Cold War, however, stifled progress and the 1953 draft statute for a permanent court produced by the International Law Commission has languished in the UN General Assembly ever since. At least two international conventions, on apartheid and genocide, provide for the establishment of an international criminal jurisdiction which have come to nothing.

The end of the Cold War and the atrocities in the former Yugoslavia may have again breathed life into this area of the International Law Commission's work.[16] The 1992 UN General Assembly mandated the International Law Commission to draft a new statute for a permanent court and to report to its 1993 session. Such a court would probably cover a broad range of offences such as drug-trafficking and air-hijacking, as well as war crimes and crimes against humanity.

Meanwhile, calls to set up an *ad hoc* war crimes tribunal for the former Yugoslavia rapidly increased in the wake of the vivid portrayal by the media of the atrocities, the failure of attempts to end the war

---

[15]For an historical overview of efforts to establish a permanent criminal court, as well as the latest proposal from one of the leading proponents of such an institution, see M.C. Bassiouni, "Draft Statute International Criminal Tribunal", 9 *Nouvelles Etudes Pénales* (1992).

[16]For the most recent International Law Commission proposal for a permanent international criminal court, see "Report of the Working Group on the Question of an International Criminal Jurisdiction", in *Report of the International Law Commission on the work of its forty-fourth session 4 May-24 July 1992*, UN Doc. A/47/10, (New York 1992), Annex, paras. 393-556.

and pressure from some governments and human rights organizations.[17]

Security Council resolutions in 1992 repeatedly warned that individuals in the former Yugoslavia are personally and criminally responsible for their acts which breach international humanitarian law. The first practical step was taken when the Security Council sought to systematize the collection of evidence of abuses.[18] Calls for the creation of an *ad hoc* tribunal came from many international bodies including the UN General Assembly, the Organization of Islamic Conference (OIC), the Conference on Security and Co-operation in Europe (CSCE)[19] and many states including Australia, Austria, Canada, Indonesia, Iran, Malaysia, Senegal and the USA. Some countries even named individuals who they considered should be brought before such a court. The pressure ultimately led to the historic Security Council decision on 22 February to establish the Tribunal.

There are at least two problems with an *ad hoc* approach. Firstly, experience at the national level has shown that *ad hoc* judicial tribunals are too often created and manipulated to serve short term political goals. They often lack real independence and impartiality and fail the basic tests of justice and fairness. This, together with the fact that initiatives to deal with human rights violations in the former Yugoslavia are already politicized, makes it imperative that from the

---

[17]Following the 1991 Gulf War and the occupation of Kuwait there were similar calls for the establishment of an international tribunal to try Iraqis of war crimes, which came to nothing.

[18]In August the Security Council called on governments and humanitarian organizations to submit to it substantiated information about violations of humanitarian law in the former Yugoslavia [Resolution 771 (1992), 13 August 1992]. In October the Security Council established a five-member impartial Commission of Experts, which has been collecting and analysing evidence of grave breaches of the 1949 Geneva Conventions and other violations of humanitarian law in the former Yugoslavia [Resolution 780 (1992), 6 October 1992].

[19]Partly in response to the conflicts in the Balkans, the Parliamentary Assembly of the Council of Europe added its voice in support of a permanent international criminal court and urged the International Law Commission to come to a decision within twelve months, see Parliamentary Assembly Recommendation 1189 (1992), 1 July 1992.

very beginning this Tribunal has real power to bring people to justice and strictly conforms to international human rights standards.

Secondly, by creating this *ad hoc* tribunal only for the former Yugoslavia, the Security Council is guilty of double standards in selectively enforcing universal human rights and humanitarian law. Universal principles must be implemented in all countries throughout the world. The UN should, therefore, expressly recognize that this Tribunal is only the first step in establishing a permanent, international criminal court competent to try gross violations of human rights and humanitarian law wherever they occur. It should be noted that while the *ad hoc* Tribunal should be a model of high standards, on some issues different solutions will be more appropriate for a permanent institution.

5. CREATION OF TRIBUNAL AND JUDICIAL INDEPENDENCE

If the Tribunal is to be free from political manipulation, the way it is set up and allowed to operate must guarantee that judges, prosecutors and investigators are free to act independently, for as many years as it takes to bring people to justice.

The CSCE proposal[20] recommends setting up the Tribunal by treaty, possibly limited to participating states of the CSCE. A treaty, however, seems more appropriate for a permanent court. Negotiating a treaty would take too long and the Tribunal would face enormous difficulties imposing its authority within any country in the former Yugoslavia which did not become a state party.

It seems likely that the Security Council, as the only UN body able to bind states, will set up the Tribunal by a resolution using its power under Chapter VII of the UN Charter "to maintain or restore international peace and security". While a Chapter VII resolution would be a quick and effective method, the Tribunal could be

---

[20] *Supra*, n. 2.

dissolved by the Security Council for political reasons as swiftly as it is created, perhaps after the conclusion of any peace settlement. The Security Council should therefore expressly recognize that the Tribunal will continue to operate as long as is necessary to bring to justice gross violators of human rights and humanitarian law in the conflicts in the former Yugoslavia.

In this highly politicized environment, it will be particularly vital to ensure that the Tribunal is able to carry out its work without any direct or indirect interference by states and that judges (as well as prosecutors and investigators) are acknowledged as being independent, impartial and suitably qualified.[21] The main function of the Tribunal will be to assess complex and confusing facts, so judges should have proven competence as criminal law judges or criminal law lawyers.

If states are to appoint judges, the process should not be controlled by a small group of states. To enhance the Tribunal's legitimacy and ensure a broad cross-section of different legal systems and regional experience, both the Security Council and the General Assembly should be involved in the selection process, along the lines used for appointing judges to the International Court of Justice. However, rather than involving the Permanent Court of Arbitration, it would be more appropriate for candidates to be nominated by the International Court of Justice.[22]

---

[21]To help guarantee judicial independence, the Tribunal could also be required to comply with the UN Basic Principles on the Independence of the Judiciary, endorsed by the UNGA, Resolution 40/32, 29 November 1985.

[22]In a departure from the traditional practice of states appointing international judges, the French proposal (*supra*, n. 2, paras. 170-175) recommends that the judges be appointed by the International Court of Justice and the highest human rights bodies in Europe, the Americas and Africa, viz., the European Court of Human Rights, the Inter-American Court of Human Rights and the African Commission on Human and Peoples' Rights (there is no international human rights body in Asia). This method would help to depoliticize the appointment process, but may not give the same legitimacy and authority which judges might enjoy if appointed jointly by the General Assembly and Security Council.

6. ENSURING THE TRIBUNAL HAS POWERS TO EFFECTIVELY PROSECUTE AND CONVICT

6.1 What crimes should be punishable?

The Tribunal should be able to punish a broad range of existing[23] crimes under international law if it is going to be able to cover all gross abuses committed in the former Yugoslavia.[24] The Tribunal should at least be able to punish the following crimes under international law:[25]

6.1.1 War crimes and other violations of the laws or customs of war

'War crimes' is a very broad and confusing term. Today it generally refers to acts committed in an international war which amount to "grave breaches" of the 1949 Geneva Conventions (and 1977 Additional Protocol I), though it can also mean violations of other customary rules of war which have grown up over the centuries. The term covers a very wide range of acts, including wilful killing, torture or inhuman treatment, wilfully causing great suffering or serious injury to body or health, taking civilian hostages, deportation or forced transfer of civilians, indiscriminate attacks on civilians and depriving prisoners of war of a fair trial.

---

[23]There is a well-established rule that no one can be found guilty of an act which was not a crime under international or national law at the time the act was committed (Art. 15, UN International Covenant on Civil and Political Rights and Art. 7, European Convention on Human Rights). This will not be violated if the Tribunal draws on crimes which are sufficiently well-defined in international treaties or customary international law.

[24]Because of its specific mandate, Amnesty International's starting point is to ask whether the Tribunal is able to try acts which violate people's rights not to be deliberately and arbitrarily killed, or arbitrarily detained, and to be free from torture and from cruel, inhuman or degrading treatment or punishment and "disappearance", as well as the right of political prisoners to receive a fair trial.

[25]Although international law should be the primary source of crimes, there is no reason why the Tribunal should not also draw on domestic criminal law in force at the time the acts were committed to support and strengthen the international jurisdiction. See Amnesty International, op.cit. n. 14, section 5.1.

There are less detailed rules for civil wars and other non-international conflicts which may be needed because it is not at all clear in law whether the conflicts in the former Yugoslavia are international or internal.[26]

6.1.2 Crimes against humanity

This category of crimes was written into the Nuremberg Charter[27] as a way of trying Nazis for atrocities against German citizens, such as Jews and Gypsies (Roma/Sinti), because a war crime can only be committed against the soldiers or civilians of an opposing party. It is a vigorous and useful category of crime which has developed considerably since the Nuremberg tribunal.[28] In particular, it is no longer necessary to show that a crime against humanity was committed in execution of or in connection with a crime against peace or a war crime.[29] Crimes against humanity could be committed in peacetime or in war, whether a civil war or international war. This would help to avoid a debilitating controversy at the trials about whether the conflicts in the former Yugoslavia are international or non-international conflicts.

---

[26]The five-member UN Commission of Experts, *supra* n. 18, headed by Prof. Kalshoven, neatly dealt with the problem by concluding that "the character and complexity of the armed conflicts concerned, combined with the web of agreements on humanitarian issues the parties have concluded among themselves" justifies applying rules on international armed conflict to all the conflicts, see *Interim Report of the Commission of Experts Established Pursuant to Security Council Resolution 780 (1992)*, UN Doc. S/25274, 10 February 1993, para. 45. The USA proposal, *supra*, n. 2, deems the conflicts to be of an international character while the Italian and OIC proposals, *idem*, do not address this problem and the French proposal, *idem*, avoids the problem by listing acts which would be punishable by the Tribunal without reference to international treaties or international customary law.

[27]Art. 6(c), *Annexed Charter of the International Military Tribunal* (Nuremberg). The Charter, together with the London Agreement of 8 August 1945 signed by France, the UK, the USA and the USSR, formed the jurisdictional basis for the Nuremberg trials.

[28]For the historical development, see M.C. Bassiouni, "Crimes Against Humanity", in M.C. Bassiouni, ed., *International Criminal Law*, vol. III (New York, 1987), pp. 51-71.

[29]This was a limitation set out in the Nuremberg Charter.

Crimes against humanity are now generally considered to include[30] murder, torture (including rape), other inhumane acts, slavery, servitude or forced labour, deportation or forcible transfer, arbitrary imprisonment, enforced disappearances[31] and persecutions on political, racial or religious grounds, if these acts are conducted on a mass or systematic scale, as well as genocide[32] and apartheid.[33] Crimes against humanity would cover many of the gross abuses committed by the military and civilian authorities in the former Yugoslavia against civilians under their administrative control, sometimes in the course of the forcible expulsion of thousands of people.

6.1.3 Torture

For many years torture has been recognized as an international crime and it has been defined in the UN Convention against Torture and Other Cruel, Inhuman or Degrading Treatment or Punishment.

[30]Cf., crimes against humanity as defined by the International Law Commission, Art. 21, 1991 Draft Code of Crimes Against the Peace and Security of Mankind, in *Report of the International Law Commission on the Work of its Forth-third Session, 29 April - 19 July 1991*, UN Doc. A/46/10, para. 176.

[31]The preamble to the UN Declaration on the Protection of All Persons from Enforced Disappearance, adopted by UNGA Resolution 47/133, 18 December 1992, recognizes the systematic practice of enforced disappearance to be in the nature of a crime against humanity.

[32]Genocide is included as a crime against humanity in the UN Convention on the Non-Applicability of Statutory Limitations to War Crimes and Crimes against Humanity, adopted by UNGA 26 November 1968.

[33]Art. 1, International Convention on the Suppression and Punishment of the Crime of Apartheid.

Because of the scale of allegations of rape, forced prostitution and sexual abuse,[34] these should be separate indictable crimes.

6.1.4 Genocide

It is not clear whether any of the atrocities committed in the former Yugoslavia amount to genocide, and the Tribunal should have the opportunity of making a ruling on this issue.[35] Genocide, as defined in the UN Convention on the Prevention and Punishment of the Crime of Genocide, is committed when members of a national, ethnic, racial or religious group are killed or injured or their children are taken away, or births in the group are prevented, with the intention of completely or partly destroying the group, or when physical conditions of living are imposed on the group with the same intention.

6.2 Impartial justice

In some cases it has been reported that military or civilian authorities have directly ordered abuses in the former Yugoslavia to be carried out, or their policies have directly led to crimes being committed. In many cases military forces know they are free to use whatever

---

[34]See Amnesty International, *Bosnia-Herzegovina: Rape and Sexual Abuse by Armed Forces*, AI Index: EUR 63/01/93 (January 1993); *European Community Investigative Mission into the Treatment of Muslim Women in the Former Yugoslavia*, Report to European Community Foreign Ministers (January 1993); "Report of Team of Experts on their Mission to Investigate Allegations of Rape in the Territory of the Former Yugoslavia from 12 to 23 January 1993", in *Report on the Situation of Human Rights in the Territory of the Former Yugoslavia Submitted by Mr. Tadeusz Mazowiecki, Special Rapporteur of the Commission on Human Rights*, UN Doc. E/CN.4/1993/50, 10 February 1993.

[35]The International Court of Justice recently ordered provisional measures calling on the Federal Republic of Yugoslavia to do all it can to prevent genocide in Bosnia-Herzegovina, including ensuring that forces within the country which it may support do not commit such acts. Being a provisional order, however, the court made no final findings of fact or law. See Bosnia-Herzegovina *v.* Yugoslavia (Serbia and Montenegro), ICJ, Order, 8 April 1993.

methods they wish to achieve political goals and leaders have failed to use their power to stop violence against civilians.[36]

Impartial justice will not be done - nor seen to be done - unless both leaders and subordinates are prosecuted, regardless of whether they are heads of state or infantry privates, civilians or members of military, paramilitary, irregular forces or police forces, Serb, Croat or Muslim. Those who have committed, ordered or tolerated gross human rights violations should be brought to justice.

6.3 Giving investigators strong enough powers

In the absence of an international police force with enforceable powers, one of the most difficult problems will be how to collect evidence, arrest suspects and bring them to court. Investigators and prosecutors will need wide powers to act quickly and effectively, including summoning witnesses for questioning and carrying out thorough investigations within the former Yugoslavia, including the power to search and seize evidence. They will need unrestricted access across borders and the freedom to travel anywhere in the territory of the former Yugoslavia.

These powers of investigation and arrest will need to have political backing. The Security Council should take the steps necessary to ensure that all governments, particularly those in the former Yugoslavia, and other parties to the conflicts, are obliged actively to co-operate, including helping to investigate cases, arresting suspects and handing them over to the Tribunal. The Security Council can build on the obligations states already have under international law

---

[36]See, e.g., Amnesty International, *Bosnia-Herzegovina: Rana u duši - A Wound to the Soul*, AI Index: EUR 63/03/93 (January 1993) and *Bosnia-Herzegovina: Gross Abuses of Basic Human Rights*, AI Index: EUR 63/01/92 (October 1992).

to prosecute or extradite persons suspected of having committed crimes under international law.[37]

6.4 Overriding unfair or fraudulent national trials

National authorities have the primary obligation to bring violators to justice. If such trials are fair and just, there is no reason to disturb the verdict. However, recent trials in the former Yugoslavia may not have been either just or fair. If a person has been convicted at the national level in a trial which was manifestly unfair or which was a sham, perhaps in an attempt to avoid justice, the person should be retried by the international Tribunal.[38] The conviction and punishment imposed by the national court would have no effect. Conversely, to prevent political show trials, national authorities should be prohibited from retrying a person who has been convicted or acquitted by the international Tribunal.

6.5 Powers are useless without resources

All of the Tribunal's powers will be of little use unless it has enough money and staff. It will need hundreds of people and one governmental proposal estimated the cost at US $16 million per year. But this amount should be put in perspective. UNPROFOR (the United Nations Protection Force), the peace-keeping force in the former Yugoslavia, has over 23,000 personnel and costs more than US $46 million *every month*. If the Tribunal is starved of resources, governments will have turned the whole process into an ineffective political gesture.

---

[37]See in particular the 1973 UN General Assembly's Principles of international co-operation in the detection, arrest, extradition and punishment of persons guilty of war crimes and crimes against humanity, UNGA Resolution 3074 (XXVIII), 3 December 1973.

[38]The rule against double jeopardy, embodied in Art. 14(7), International Covenant on Civil and Political Rights, does not prohibit the trial in different jurisdictions of the same person in relation to the same facts. It therefore does not prevent the Tribunal from trying a person who has been already convicted or acquitted by a national court.

At this stage no one knows how many cases should be investigated and how many will be brought to trial. While the Tribunal could begin as a relatively modest exercise, it must be flexible and able to increase staff and resources rapidly if necessary. An arbitrary, maximum limit to the number of judges, investigators and prosecutors should not be fixed.

7. OBJECTIVE JUSTICE

The role of a court is objectively to determine individual guilt or innocence. With anything less the court will start to look like a forum for political show trials.

7.1 Trials *in absentia*

It has been suggested, for example, that the Tribunal should be allowed to hold trials *in absentia* - without the presence of the accused - if he or she cannot be arrested. Trials *in absentia* were the exception at Nuremberg, but here, where the difficulties of bringing the accused before the court are far greater, the risk is that this will become the norm. The creation of this Tribunal is already politicized and trials *in absentia* would be more like political show trials.[39] Anything which prejudices the objective determination of guilt or innocence must be avoided and given the likely complexity of the cases, the reliability of the verdict will always be in doubt if the accused is not present to challenge the prosecution case. To ensure the truth starts to be uncovered and evidence preserved, the Tribunal

---

[39]The International Law Commission has recommended against trials *in absentia* in any permanent international criminal court, see International Law Commission, op.cit. n. 16, para. 504. Trials *in absentia* would seem to be excluded by the unambiguous words of Art. 14(3)(d), International Covenant on Civil and Political Rights, which guarantees the right of an accused "to be tried in his presence", although the UN Human Rights Committee considers that trials *in absentia* are justified in exceptional circumstances. Art. 6(3)(c), European Convention on Human Rights is not as clear as the International Covenant on Civil and Political Rights (CCPR), as it only guarantees the right of an accused "to defend himself in person".

could still hold a preliminary hearing if the accused wilfully refuses to appear, provided it does not determine individual responsibility.

7.2 Membership of "criminal" organizations

There is also a suggestion that a defendant will be deemed to have committed specific criminal acts merely by being a member of an organization that had as its object the commission of these crimes. For example, if defendant X joined a para-military group which intended to kill and terrorize particular civilians, he or she would be held guilty of those killings merely by having joined the group. There is no place for such collective guilt in criminal law. Membership of the organization may be evidence towards proving that the accused participated in the crimes, but it does not prove guilt. The prosecution must still prove that the individual committed the crimes in a particular place at a particular time with the necessary criminal intent.

It would be equally unfortunate if the Tribunal's statute included past membership of any organization declared by the Tribunal to be "criminal" as a separate offence. If the organization was not "criminal" under national or international law at the time an accused joined, such a declaration after the fact, with criminal consequences, would amount to a retroactive application of the law.

What is not prohibited by criminal law principles is the indictment, as a separate criminal act, of anyone who has set up or helped to set up a formal or informal group of people for the purpose of committing crimes punishable by the Tribunal. The prosecution would still have to establish, however, that the individual accused participated in the creation of the group with the necessary intent to create a group with such aims.

8. FAIRNESS: PROTECTING THE ACCUSED

Even if the Tribunal prosecutes and convicts violators, it will be seen as a political exercise unless the accused receives a fair trial. It would be unthinkable for a UN court to fall below guarantees for fair trial and treatment of detainees approved by the UN General Assembly. Some of these standards have been the result of 40 years of progress in human rights since Nuremberg.

At the very least, the statute of the Tribunal should incorporate by reference, and require all organs of the Tribunal to observe, Articles 9, 10, 14 and 15(1) of the International Covenant on Civil and Political Rights, the UN Body of Principles for the Protection of All Persons Under Any Form of Detention or Imprisonment (the Body of Principles),[40] and the UN Standard Minimum Rules for the Treatment of Prisoners (the Standard Minimum Rules).[41] These safeguards apply from the moment the accused is arrested until the conviction or acquittal is finally confirmed.

Although the Body of Principles and Standard Minimum Rules are not in the form of treaties, they represent an international consensus on minimum standards for the treatment of anyone detained or imprisoned, including those awaiting trial and those imprisoned under sentence. They will be particularly important in regulating aspects of detention on which there is a wide divergence of national practice, such as limiting incommunicado detention by ensuring regular access to family, doctors and lawyers.

Because it may be difficult to ensure that defence lawyers with the necessary expertise are quickly available in this unique, international court, a separate public defender's office should be set up, independent of other Tribunal organs. It should provide free legal aid for those who cannot pay and should set up branch offices in the former Yugoslavia.

---

[40]Adopted by UNGA Resolution 43/173, 9 December 1988, without a vote.

[41]Adopted by the First UN Congress on the Prevention of Crime and the Treatment of Offenders, 1955, approved by the Resolutions 663 C (XXIV) 31 July 1957 and 2076 (LXII) 13 May 1977 of the UN Economic and Social Council (ECOSOC). In 1984 UNGA endorsed the ECOSOC Procedures for the Effective Implementation of the Standards Minimum Rules for the Treatment of Prisoners, in Resolution 39/118, 14 December 1984.

Because of the primary role of national courts, the Tribunal should be able to transfer cases down to national courts. But the Tribunal should not transfer a case to a national court unless it is satisfied that the trial at the national level will be just and effective, comply with all human rights guarantees, and be carried out by a court which is manifestly independent and impartial and which cannot impose the death penalty. The accused should have a right to appeal against a decision to transfer to the national court.

9. JUSTICE FOR THE VICTIM: COMPENSATION, RESTITUTION AND REHABILITATION

Justice includes justice for the victims and their families. They have a vital interest in finding out the truth about human rights violations they have suffered, in seeing that justice is done and getting compensation for their suffering. Victims could, for example, be represented at the trial by a lawyer, provided that the right of the accused to a fair trial is not prejudiced.[42]

The court should have the power to order a convicted person to pay compensation or return property if the victim has suffered because of the crime. But this will not be sufficient and the Security Council should also indicate what mechanism will be established to protect the rights of victims to receive compensation, restitution and rehabilitation, including the establishment of a separate international commission to process claims against individuals, as well as claims against states. After the 1991 Gulf War, for example, the UN set up an international commission and fund to process compensation claims

[42]This right of participation by victims is guaranteed by para. 6(b), UN Declaration of Basic Principles of Justice for Victims of Crime and Abuse of Power (the UN Declaration on Victims), adopted by UNGA, Resolution 40/34, 29 November 1985.

against Iraq for injury suffered by individuals during the occupation of Kuwait.[43]

10. PROTECTING VICTIMS, FAMILIES AND WITNESSES

The hostility between national groups in the former Yugoslavia has been so intense that the Tribunal will need wide powers to protect victims, their families and witnesses from reprisals - a danger which can remain long after the verdict. Furthermore, witnesses could suffer considerable mental anguish by having repeatedly to relive horrific events before investigators, prosecutors and judges. The UN Declaration on Victims[44] emphasizes that "victims should be treated with compassion and respect for their dignity" (para. 4). It also provides in para. 6(d) that the judicial system should take:

> " ... measures to minimize inconvenience to victims, protect their privacy, when necessary, and ensure their safety, as well as that of their families and witnesses on their behalf, from intimidation and retaliation".

In exceptional circumstances, the Tribunal should be able to exclude the press and suppress the names of witnesses, or even hide the identity of witnesses from the accused. In all cases the interests of the witness to be protected must be balanced against the right of the accused to hear all the prosecution evidence and to cross-examine witnesses.

The Tribunal will have to provide real support and care for victims and witnesses involved in the judicial process. For example, if children testify in court, psychologists should advise on ways in which the

---

[43]Pursuant to Security Council Resolution 687 (1991), paras. 16 and 18. In the context of the Yugoslav conflicts, the Commission on Human Rights and the General Assembly have reaffirmed that states are to be held accountable for violations of human rights which their agents commit upon the territory of another state, see UN Commission on Human Rights Resolution 1992/s-1/1, 14 August 1992 and UNGA Resolution 47/147, 18 December 1992, para. 10.

[44]*Supra*, n. 42.

potential psychological damage of the investigatory and court process could be minimized. A special unit could be set up to deal with all the protection issues which arise at each stage of the proceedings.

There have been consistent reports of widespread and sometime systematic rape, sexual abuse and forced prostitution in the conflicts in the former Yugoslavia. Collecting evidence has been very difficult. Some women try to obliterate the experience from their memory, others feel degraded and ashamed or fear they will suffer social stigma if they reveal what happened to them. The trauma and stress has been exacerbated by women being repeatedly pressured to talk to journalists or fact-finding missions.[45]

The Tribunal's extraordinary powers to protect victims from reprisals and unnecessary mental distress will be particularly necessary in cases of violence against women. How will the Tribunal deal with a female rape victim who may be willing to testify against an accused, but only if her husband and community do not find out what happened to her? In such a case the court might be justified in keeping her identity a secret. If prosecutions are to be successful while minimizing the trauma, the Tribunal will also need investigators, prosecutors and judges, including women, with specific knowledge of the cultural and religious mores and experience in collecting such evidence.

11. SUMMARY OF RECOMMENDATIONS

A number of practices and safeguards have been suggested in this paper which could help to make the *ad hoc* international war crimes tribunal for the former Yugoslavia more just, fair and effective. These recommendations are summarized in the following 15 principles which governments and the UN should abide by in the creation and operation of the Tribunal:

1. It must be *independent* from political manipulation by one or more states and free to complete its work, however long it takes.

---

[45]See generally reports cited, *supra*, n. 34.

2. It must be *global* in its establishment, composition and operation.

3. It must be *competent*, with appropriately qualified judges, prosecutors, investigators and expert advisers.

4. It must have *jurisdiction* over a broad enough range of crimes to cover all relevant gross violations of human rights and humanitarian law.

5. It must be *impartial* by prosecuting perpetrators from all parties to the conflict, both leaders and subordinates.

6. It must be *empowered* to carry out thorough investigations in the former Yugoslavia with relevant authorities obliged to co-operate, arrest and hand over suspects.

7. It must be *fair* by scrupulously observing all internationally accepted guarantees for fair trial at every stage of proceedings.

8. It must *convict* those it finds responsible for gross violations of human rights and humanitarian law.

9. It must be *objective* in its determination of guilt or innocence and not hold trials *in absentia*.

10. It must *protect* victims, their families and witnesses from reprisals and unnecessary mental anguish and be able to order compensation.

11. It must *retry* anyone convicted or acquitted in a national trial which was manifestly unfair or a sham.

12. It must *not impose the death penalty*.

13. It must have enough *resources* to carry out its work properly at all stages.

14. It must be a *model* in its rigorous compliance with international human rights standards, including those developed by the UN itself.

15. It must be the *first step* in the creation of a permanent international criminal court to try gross violations of human rights and humanitarian law wherever they occur.

CASE STUDY ON THE FORMER YUGOSLAVIA: THE INTERNATIONAL MECHANISMS, THEIR EFFICIENCY AND FAILURES

by Roman Wieruszewski

1. INTRODUCTORY REMARKS

The tragic conflicts on the territory of the former Yugoslavia have involved human rights violations on an unprecedented scale in Europe after the Second World War. The events constitute a very serious test and challenge to the international systems of human rights protection. From the very beginning both regional and universal international organizations have been trying to stop the cruel atrocities and to improve the human rights situation in that region. One may ask to what extent these efforts have been successful? The answer should not leave any doubts - they have failed to stop and much less to prevent the massive and systematic violations of human rights from being conducted unabatedly. Therefore, if the effectiveness of the implementation mechanisms is to be measured by their impact on the human rights situation in a given territory, we have to assume that the international machinery for the implementation of human rights and for the prevention of violations of human rights has proved to be ineffective in the case of Yugoslavia.

The Yugoslav conflict is still far from being resolved. Therefore it is not easy to identify all the reasons for those inefficiencies. The author of this paper is in a difficult position. He is actively participating in the monitoring of the human rights situation in the former Yugoslavia, initially as an expert of the Conference on Security and Co-operation in Europe (CSCE), at present as a staff member of the United Nations (UN) Centre for Human Rights. Thus he views the crisis from the perspective of the activities of the Special Rapporteur of the Commission on Human Rights. Nevertheless, attempts to assess critically the activities of other agencies acting in the former Yugoslavia have been made.

A. Bloed et al. (eds.), Monitoring Human Rights in Europe, 285–317.

Due to the character of this paper certain important initiatives dealing with the human rights situation will not be presented. Let me mention as one example the role of local non-governmental organizations (NGOs). Also the problem of promoting freedom of expression and free press in the former Yugoslavia will not be discussed in spite of its vital importance for solving the crisis.

This paper will rather focus on the activities of the United Nations' organs and the CSCE. The role of the European Community (EC) will be touched upon and, finally, it is worth mentioning that the Council of Europe also undertakes activities offering its assistance in the process of improving the human rights situation.[1]

I assume that the gross human rights violations occurring in the former Yugoslavia are well known and that a detailed description of the atrocities is thus not necessary. World public opinion has been shocked by the practices associated with the so-called "ethnic cleansing" including mass killings, rape, torture, the forced expulsion of the population, terror, and inhuman conditions in detention facilities and camps. People have been attacked and terrorized on the grounds of their national, ethnic and religious origin. The above-mentioned abuses are taking place mainly on the territory of the Republic of Bosnia-Herzegovina. That violence did not come as a surprise. The war between the Republic of Croatia and the former Federal Republic of Yugoslavia also brought many examples of human rights violations and violations of humanitarian law.

---

[1]According to the Committee of Ministers' Resolution 93(6) of 8 March 1993 "At the request of a European non-member State, the Committee of Ministers may, after consultation of the European Court and Commission of Human Rights, appoint specially qualified persons to sit on a court or other body responsible for the control of respect for human rights set up by this State within its internal legal system." It is indeed an interesting initiative. It seems, however, that the character of human rights violations on the territory of the former Yugoslavia is not suited to that mechanism.

2. POLITICAL PERSPECTIVE[2]

The Yugoslav crisis once again proved the direct link between politics and human rights. What role should human rights play in the process of solving such conflicts and in the resulting gross human rights violations? Political bodies seem to avoid any answer to that question. Consequently, the above-mentioned failures of the international mechanisms for the protection of human rights can be largely attributed to political development.

It is worth mentioning that in spite of the war in Croatia the United Nations Security Council remained inactive for a long time. Only on 25 September 1991 did the Security Council adopt Resolution 713 in which it expressed its deep concern about the fighting in Yugoslavia and its consequences for the whole region. The Resolution states: "the continuation of this situation constitutes a threat to international peace and security." It should be noticed that the above statement according to Article 39 of the Charter of the United Nations will allow the use of provisions contained in Chapter VII of the Charter.[3] Consequently the Council, acting under Chapter VII, decided to impose "... a general and complete embargo on all deliveries of weapons and military equipment to Yugoslavia." The Security Council appealed for the peaceful settlement of disputes and expressed its full support for negotiations through the EC-sponsored Conference on Yugoslavia. By its resolution, the Security Council invited the Secretary-General to offer his assistance, in consultation with the Government of Yugoslavia and all those promoting the peace efforts.

On 8 October 1991 the Secretary-General appointed Cyrus Vance as his personal envoy to Yugoslavia. In the report issued by Vance, in this capacity, it was stated that the fighting had caused extensive humanitarian problems, including, in addition to losses of life and

---

[2]For a comprehensive analysis of the political development of the crisis in Yugoslavia see M. Weller, "The International Response to the Dissolution of the Socialist Federal Republic of Yugoslavia", 86 *AJIL* (1992) pp. 569-607.

[3]Cf., the contribution of L. Boisson de Chazournes in the present volume.

injuries, some 300,000 displaced persons. This figure later rose to 600,000.

On 18 October 1991 the Presidents of five of the six republics expressed their general agreement to continue working on a draft paper prepared by Lord Carrington, the EC envoy to Yugoslavia, concerning "Arrangements of a General Settlement". The arrangement contained elements of the proposed settlement of conflicts including commitments by the republics on the protection of human rights, referring to the Universal Declaration of Human Rights, the International Human Rights Covenants, CSCE human dimension standards, and relevant Council of Europe instruments. Human rights provisions referring to national and ethnic groups were specified and a special status was to be established for areas in which national or ethnic groups form a majority. The President of Serbia refused to consider those proposals as suitable for discussion. Nevertheless, on 4 November 1991, the Lord Carrington conference presented a draft convention for general settlement. The draft included a detailed catalogue of human and minority rights. It provided for the creation of autonomous structures, comprising legislative, executive and judicial functions, in areas where members of a national minority form a local majority.

Compliance with the provisions on human and minority rights was to be ensured by a permanent international monitoring mission, to be established on the territories of the former Yugoslav republics. The new states would be treaty-bound to give effect to the recommendations of the monitoring body. Supreme jurisdiction was to be exercised by the human rights court. The court would be composed of one member nominated by each of the former republics and an equal number plus one nominated by the Community. In addition, the draft convention made provision for a special mixed commission to deal with political problems concerning minorities. Serbia refused to accept the revised terms of the proposed agreement and the EC was unable to enforce its proposals. Since then a more active UN role has been observed.

Vance proposed the deployment of troops and police monitors in certain areas of Croatia, to be designated as "United Nations Protected Areas" (UNPAs). The areas were supposed to be demilitarized and the armed forces in them withdrawn or disbanded. The UN troops were to ensure the implementation of that plan. It also provided for UN police monitors whose task was to ensure that the local police carried out their duties without discrimination against persons of any nationality or abusing anyone's human rights. Additionally, the presence of the United Nations Protection Force (UNPROFOR) should have facilitated the voluntary return of displaced persons to their homes.

The United Nations Security Council, invoking Article 25 of the Charter of the United Nations, established UNPROFOR by Resolution 743, adopted on 21 February 1992.

On 16 December 1992, at the extraordinary ministerial meeting of the European Political Co-operation (EPC) in Brussels the EC adopted Guidelines on the Recognition of New States in Eastern Europe and in the Soviet Union. The following conditions were established:

- respect for the provisions of the Charter of the United Nations and the commitments subscribed to in the Final Act of Helsinki and in the Charter of Paris, especially with regard to the rule of law, democracy and human rights;

- guarantees for the rights of ethnic and national groups and minorities in accordance with the commitments subscribed to in the framework of the CSCE;

- respect for the inviolability of all frontiers which can only be changed by peaceful means and by common agreement;

- acceptance of all relevant commitments with regard to disarmament and nuclear non-proliferation as well as to security and regional stability;

- commitment to settle by agreement, including where appropriate by recourse to arbitration, all questions concerning state succession and regional disputes.

The Arbitration Commission received applications for recognition from Slovenia, Croatia, Macedonia and Bosnia-Herzegovina. Slovenia and Croatia were recognized in January 1992. In the case of Croatia this occurred in spite of the fact that it did not accept the provisions dealing with the "special status" of minorities. On 6 April 1992 the EC decided to recognize Bosnia-Herzegovina despite the outbreak of hostilities there and the refusal by a part of the population to accept the referendum on independence held on 1 March 1992.

In spite of the decision by the Arbitration Commission that Macedonia had satisfied the conditions for recognition, the EC member states have not recognized this country to date.

The EC and CSCE initiated a number of measures aiming to prevent the deterioration of the situation in Bosnia-Herzegovina. In spite of all those efforts, including the initiation of the CSCE mechanism for Consultation and Co-operation with Regard to Emergency Situations, the bloodshed in Bosnia-Herzegovina escalated.

Since August 1992 diplomatic efforts to resolve the Yugoslav crisis have been undertaken on the basis of the principles of the International Conference on the former Yugoslavia, adopted at its London session. On 4 January 1993 during the Geneva round-table talks, the Co-Chairmen proposed to the parties concerned - the Government of Bosnia-Herzegovina, the Bosnian Croats and the Bosnian Serbs - a comprehensive package as the basis for a fair, just and lasting peace. The package included a set of Constitutional Principles along with a map setting out the organization of the country into ten provinces, and a military agreement. All three elements of the package were inextricably linked and could not be implemented separately.[4]

---

[4]For an overview of the peace negotiations see the reports of the Secretary-General on the activities of the International Conference on the Former Yugoslavia published as Security Council Documents.

3. THE SPECIAL RAPPORTEUR OF THE COMMISSION ON HUMAN RIGHTS

3.1 Characteristics of the Special Rapporteur's mandate

On the basis of the principle adopted by the United Nations Economic and Social Council (ECOSOC) in its Resolution 1990/48[5] the UN Commission on Human Rights is able to organize, in addition to its ordinary sessions, special sessions. In a letter of 5 August 1992 the Permanent Representative of the United States to the UN in Geneva requested the convening of a special session to examine the human rights situation in the former Yugoslavia. This initiative was taken on the day after the publication of reliable information in the international press according to which one of the parties to the conflict, the Serbs in Bosnia-Herzegovina, had set up concentration camps.

The consultation immediately conducted by the UN Centre for Human Rights was successful. By the established deadline of 10 August 1992, 35 members of the Commission had positively answered the American request. In accordance with the established procedures, a special session of the Commission, the first in its history, was immediately convened and was held in Geneva from 13-14 August 1992.

On 14 August 1992, the Commission adopted by consensus Resolution 1992/S-1/1[6], which was approved on 18 August 1992, by the ECOSOC decision 1992/305 in which it:

> "12. *Requests* its Chairman to appoint a special rapporteur to investigate first-hand the human rights situation in the territory of the former Yugoslavia, in particular within Bosnia and Herzegovina, and to receive relevant, credible information on

---

[5]Resolution 1990/48 was adopted on 25 May 1990. It authorized the Commission on Human Rights to hold special emergency meetings between its regular sessions, "as long as the majority of the Member States of the Commission agree" (para. 3).

[6]UN Doc. E/CN.4/1992/84/Add.1.

the human rights situation there from Governments, individuals, intergovernmental and non-governmental organizations, on a continuing basis, and to avail himself or herself of the assistance of existing mechanisms of the Commission on Human Rights;

...

"14. *Requests* the Special Rapporteur to visit areas of interest in the former Yugoslavia, and in particular Bosnia and Herzegovina, forthwith and to report on an urgent basis to the Commission on Human Rights, providing a preliminary report no later than 28 August 1992 on the situation of human rights in the former Yugoslavia, including his or her recommendations for bringing violations to an end and preventing future violations, and requests the Secretary-General to make the report of the Special Rapporteur available to the Security Council;

"15. *Also requests* the Special Rapporteur to report his or her findings and recommendations to the members of the Commission on Human Rights periodically thereafter until its next regular session, and to report to the General Assembly at its 47th session, as well as to the Commission at its next regular session, under agenda item 12, and requests the Secretary-General to make the reports of the Special Rapporteur available to the Security Council;

"16. *Further requests* the Special Rapporteur to gather and compile systematically information on possible violations of human rights in the territory of the former Yugoslavia, including those which may constitute war crimes, and to make this information available to the Secretary-General, and notes that such information could be of possible future use in prosecuting violators of international humanitarian law;

...

> "20. *Requests* the Special Rapporteur to take into account and seek to complement the efforts being undertaken by the Conference on Security and Co-operation in Europe with respect to the crisis in the former Yugoslavia."

It would seem that the following aspects of the Special Rapporteur's mandate according to the above-quoted resolution are of particular interest: (a) a request to investigate first-hand the human rights situation, (b) a request to receive and gather relevant information on a continuing basis, (c) a suggestion that the Special Rapporteur should be assisted by existing mechanisms of the Commission on Human Rights, (d) a request that the Secretary-General should make the reports of the Special Rapporteur available to the Security Council. Tadeusz Mazowiecki was appointed as Special Rapporteur on the Former Yugoslavia.

When discussing the form of the mandate of the Special Rapporteur one additional element should be mentioned. The Commission acted under strong pressure. World public opinion has been alarmed at the atrocities committed in Bosnia-Herzegovina. For that reason the initiators of the resolution decided that the function of Special Rapporteur should be entrusted to one of the prominent European political personalities. It was quite obvious that the activities of the Special Rapporteur should raise public conscience about the dramatic human rights situation in the former Yugoslavia. He was requested to act very quickly. The first report based on information gathered during a mission was supposed to have been presented before 28 August 1992. Such an approach, however, bears certain implications, which will be discussed below.

3.2 Activities of the Special Rapporteur between two special sessions of the UN Commission on Human Rights

Human rights violations occurring in the territory of Bosnia-Herzegovina and to a certain extent in some other regions of the former Yugoslavia are massive and systematic. The very nature of these violations conditioned and in fact still influence the way the mandate entrusted to the Special Rapporteur by the UN Commission on Human Rights has been implemented. It was quite clear that the realization of the mandate should lead to concrete and immediate effects. In his memorandum addressed to the Secretary-General, Mazowiecki stated, "it is not possible to limit the mandate to the preparation of reports stating facts and expressing opinions which are submitted to UN bodies. The mandate should lead to prompt and concrete measures benefitting the populations which are suffering and whose rights are being violated."[7]

Immediately after his appointment the Special Rapporteur had to organize a mission. The results of that mission were presented in the report of the Special Rapporteur to the Commission on Human Rights of 28 August 1992.[8] It contained a number of recommendations of a different nature. Let me recall those which are of a procedural character:

> "The multiplicity of international activities aimed at bringing the conflict and human rights violations in the former Yugoslavia to an end limit the efficiency of such efforts. Consequently, there is an urgent need for concerted international action to improve the fate of victims of human rights violations. The decisions of the London Conference, in particular the creation of the Steering Committee, is a step in this direction. Better co-ordination among the various United Nations agencies and bodies would also contribute to improving the efficiency of such international efforts.
>
> "Further implementation of the mandate of the Special Rapporteur requires the appointment of staff based in the territories of the former Yugoslavia, in order to co-ordinate the monitoring of human rights violations together with the other United Nations bodies mentioned above, and the creation of an adequate professional and logistical infrastructure within the UN Centre for Human Rights. It also

---

[7]See the Memorandum concerning the implementation of the mandate of the Special Rapporteur on the situation of human rights in the territory of the former Yugoslavia, sent to the Secretary-General on 4 September 1992.

[8]UN Doc. E/CN.4/1992/S-1/9.

requires the establishment of a working relationship with other multilateral initiatives, in particular the above-mentioned Steering Committee."

In order to understand the importance of those recommendations it is necessary to describe, very briefly, the kinds of assistance which the UN Centre for Human Rights could offer the Special Rapporteur. In short, it seems like the following - a lack of everything but the willingness to help. A shortage of office space, elementary equipment (word processors), faxing equipment. A very poor system for securely storing the information received and inadequate secretarial service. At the same time the Special Rapporteur has been confronted with great expectations concerning his mandate. Immediately after his appointment the Geneva office received a great number of documents of a different nature. It became clear that without additional resources it would not be possible to carry out the Special Rapporteur's duties.

In the above-mentioned memorandum the Special Rapporteur described the functions of professional staff based in various territories of the former Yugoslavia in the following way: (a) to receive information and complaints of human rights violations, including violations which may constitute war crimes, (b) to prepare the missions of the Special Rapporteur, (c) to promote awareness, understanding and compliance with basic human rights standards, in particular through contacts with local authorities.

When planning his field activities the Special Rapporteur was aware that only by close co-operation with representatives of other UN agencies present in the former Yugoslavia, would he be in a position to implement his mandate properly. Let us not forget that the UN has a sizeable presence in the former Yugoslavia, mainly in the form of UNPROFOR and the United Nations High Commissioner for Refugees (UNHCR).[9] It was to be expected that both agencies could assist the Special Rapporteur in various ways, in particular by providing direct or indirect access to information concerning human rights

---

[9]See F.D. Gaer, "The United Nations and the Yugoslav Crisis", a paper published by the United Nations Association of the United States of America, August 1992.

violations. Both bodies were, and in fact still are, sensitive to human rights concerns and, within the limitations inherent in their respective mandates, have made important contributions to the protection of human rights in the former Yugoslavia. However, the type of action UNHCR and UNPROFOR are able to carry out is limited, because the central part of their mandates is the delivery of humanitarian assistance and peace-keeping, rather than the protection of human rights as such. While they are important sources of information, they cannot respond to the information in the same way as the Special Rapporteur without jeopardizing their primary functions. It was thus of great importance to establish a mechanism for channelling such information to the Special Rapporteur, in particular the first-hand credible information which the Special Rapporteur has been mandated to gather and compile.

Let me quote the memorandum once again:

> "Since the mandate of the Special Rapporteur covers several countries, and taking into account the magnitude of the human rights violations and the logistical difficulties resulting from the conflict and other factors, the minimum number of staff required in the field would be four. They would in principle be located in Zagreb, Split, Sarajewo and Belgrade. Given the urgency of events, at least some of the field staff should be in place by 15 September [1992]".

Instead of describing in detail the reactions to the above proposals, let me make the following observation - as of 21 March 1993 the Special Rapporteur did not have a single member of staff in place in the field. Only by the end of March did the first field officer take up his post in Zagreb.

In October 1992 the Special Rapporteur conducted his second mission. As a result he submitted reports to the Commission on Human Rights on 27 October 1992[10] to the forty-seventh session of the UN

---

[10]UN Doc. E/CN.4/1992/S-1/10.

General Assembly.[11] He was also invited to present his findings before the Security Council which constituted an interesting development.

In both his missions the Special Rapporteur took advantage of the provisions of the resolution of the Commission authorizing him to invite other Rapporteurs or Working Groups to assist him. Additionally, he requested the Special Rapporteur on extrajudicial, summary or arbitrary executions to carry out a preliminary investigation into allegations that victims of war crimes are to be found in certain mass graves in the former Yugoslavia.

3.3 Second special session of the UN Commission on Human Rights and the decision of the General Assembly

Based on the above-mentioned reports the UN Commission on Human Rights at its second Special Session, on 1 December 1992, adopted a resolution[12] in which it notes with alarm the three reports issued by its Special Rapporteur on the former Yugoslavia, and condemns the violations of human rights he identified, demands action to end and reverse ethnic cleansing, affirms that states are to be held accountable for violations their agents commit on the territory of another state and calls on parties to "apprehend and punish those guilty" of human rights and humanitarian law violations. Moreover, it calls for efforts to account for the missing persons. It also requests the Special Rapporteur to carry out further missions, to report to the Commission, and requests the Secretary-General to continue to make his reports available to the Security Council.

On 18 December 1992 the UN General Assembly adopted a resolution on human rights in the former Yugoslavia by consensus.[13] In the resolution the UN General Assembly condemned the "abhorrent practice of ethnic cleansing" as presented in the reports of the Special

---

[11]UN Doc. A/47/666-S/24809.

[12]Resolution 1992/S-2/1.

[13]Resolution 1992 47/147.

Rapporteur, and placed primary responsibility for such practices on the "Serbian leadership in territories under their control in Bosnia and Herzegovina, the Yugoslav Army, and the political leadership of the Republic of Serbia". The UN General Assembly furthermore condemned specific human rights violations, most of which are caused by "ethnic cleansing", and condemned the "systematic" terrorization and murder of non-combatants. It demanded steps to "apprehend and punish" guilty parties and reaffirmed the individual responsibility of perpetrators or those condoning grave breaches of international humanitarian law. It expressed the opinion that the international community "will exert every effort to bring them to justice", and called for the missing to be accounted for. The UN General Assembly considered acts under duress affecting property ownership to be invalid and recognized "rights of victims" of ethnic cleansing to reparation. It called for the closing of all improper detention centres, and the release of all those arbitrarily or illegally detained; it demanded immediate, unimpeded and continuous access to all camps and detention centres for the International Committee of the Red Cross (ICRC), the Special Rapporteur, the CSCE and other relevant humanitarian organizations. Finally, the UN General Assembly called on all UN bodies, including UNPROFOR and UN Specialized Agencies, to provide the Special Rapporteur with "all relevant and accurate information in their possession" on human rights in the former Yugoslavia and asked the Secretary-General to ensure full and effective co-ordination of the UN bodies and to provide the Special Rapporteur with staff to ensure continuous monitoring and co-ordination with other UN bodies, including UNPROFOR.

3.4 Activities of the Special Rapporteur after the second special session of the UN Commission on Human Rights

The Special Rapporteur conducted his third mission to the region in January 1993. Within his mandate a mission to investigate allegations of the widespread occurrence of rape had been organized. A team of four medical and psychiatric experts, accompanied by the Director of the United Nations Division for the Advancement of Women and staff of the Centre for Human Rights, visited Croatia, Bosnia-Herzegovina and the Federal Republic of Yugoslavia (Serbia and Montenegro) to collect and analyse the testimony of victims and witnesses as well as related statistical data and medical records.

In addition to his official missions the Special Rapporteur has conducted several other visits and discussions with political leaders which were aimed at promoting an understanding of the human rights problems in the former Yugoslavia.

His findings have been presented in his fourth report[14] submitted to the Commission on Human Rights at its forty-ninth session. In his conclusions he stated, *inter alia*:

> "To date, international action and an international presence have clearly failed to prevent ethnic cleansing from taking place. Official figures for Bosnia and Herzegovina show that the number of refugees and displaced persons in the second half of 1992 was much greater than in the early stages of conflict there. However, the deployment of UNPROFOR as well as representatives of the ICRC, UNHCR and envoys of charitable organizations has partly alleviated the consequences of the military conflicts in the former Yugoslavia."

He also addressed the unresolved problems of co-ordination of human rights activities in the area by pointing out that:

> "The Special Rapporteur acknowledges with appreciation the work undertaken by international and local actors in the field but he must emphasize that the present level of co-ordination leaves a great deal to be desired. Efficient monitoring and investigation of the human rights situation are far from being achieved."

In this context I would also like to quote his following conclusion:

> "In his first report ... the Special Rapporteur recommended 'the appointment of staff in the territory of the former

---

[14]UN Doc. E/CN.4/1993/50.

Yugoslavia'. The recommendation has been supported by the subsequent resolutions of the Commission on Human Rights and the General Assembly. Nevertheless, it has not been implemented. The effective fulfilment of the Special Rapporteur's mandate requires that all sectors of the United Nations Secretariat extend their full co-operation and assistance to him. At present, the material and human resources available to the Centre for Human Rights for this task are inadequate, both in Geneva and in the field."

The Commission on Human Rights at its ordinary forty-ninth session adopted Resolution 1993/7 - Situation of human rights in the territory of the former Yugoslavia, in which it:

"32. Decides to extend the mandate of the Special Rapporteur for one year, and requests that he continue his efforts, especially in carrying out such further missions in Serbia and other parts of the former Yugoslavia as he deems necessary, and that he continue to submit periodic reports as the situation warrants on the implementation of this and all relevant resolutions of the Commission concerning the former Yugoslavia, and requests the Secretary-General to continue to make reports of the Special Rapporteur available to the Security Council;

"33. Urges all parties to co-operate in determining the fate of thousands of missing persons in the former Yugoslavia by disclosing and exchanging information and documentation with a view to finally locating such persons and alleviating the suffering of their relatives, and requests the Special Rapporteur, in consultation with the Working Group on Enforced or Involuntary Disappearances and the International Committee of the Red Cross, to develop proposals for a mechanism to address the subject of disappearances in the former Yugoslavia;

"34. Requests the Secretary-General to take steps to ensure the full and effective co-operation of all United Nations bodies to implement the present resolution and, pursuant to paragraph 21 of General Assembly resolution 47/147 of 18 December 1992, to provide the Special Rapporteur, within the overall budgetary framework of the United Nations, with additional resources and all other necessary assistance to enable him to fulfil his mandate and, in particular, to provide for the appointment of field staff in the territory of the former Yugoslavia to provide first-hand, timely reports on observance or violations of human rights in their area of assignment."

3.5 Conclusions

When Mazowiecki accepted the mandate of Special Rapporteur he had to determine his priorities. He decided to concentrate on victims of human rights violations and to contribute to solving the existing crisis. He was less concerned with detailed documentation concerning committed crimes, including the identification of the perpetrators, but rather concentrated on organizing help for the victims. His personal background and life experience contributed to that approach. He has been criticized by various, mainly American, NGOs for neglecting the investigatory aspect of his mandate.

Thanks to the financial assistance which has recently been granted in order to conduct field operations, the Centre for Human Rights has been able to plan comprehensive, on-the-spot activity. It should enable the Special Rapporteur to prepare more detailed reports dealing with concrete human rights issues.[15]

The Special Rapporteur embarked upon very intensive activity. He managed to persuade world public opinion of the dimension of the human rights drama in the former Yugoslavia. His reports contributed to a number of resolutions adopted by various UN bodies. Neverthe-less, he has not been able to achieve his main objectives - to put an

---

[15]Within the framework of that operation, staff members of the UN Centre for Human Rights conducted an on-the-spot mission to the Tuzla region in Eastern Bosnia-Herzegovina. Their findings will be presented in the Special Rapporteur interim reports to be published in May 1993.

end to massive violations of human rights. His failure should be partly contributed to the inherent weakness of the mechanism which he represents. The mandates of Special Rapporteurs are very limited. Consequently his position vis-à-vis other actors has proved to be rather weak.

When discussing the role of the Special Rapporteur one has to bear in mind that other mechanisms within the special procedure system are also dealing with various aspects of human rights violations in the former Yugoslavia. Thematic rapporteurs (summary and arbitrary executions, torture, displaced persons, mercenaries) and working groups (arbitrary detention, disappearance) have devoted their attention to the human rights situation in Yugoslavia.

There is also another aspect to the Special Rapporteur activities - inadequate assistance offered by the UN secretariat. It seems that an in depth analysis of the question goes beyond the scope of that paper. It is, however, quite clear that without profound changes in the position of the UN Centre for Human Rights within the UN structure, the various UN human rights mechanisms will be condemned to failure.

The quality of the Special Rapporteur reports depend to a large extent on the quality of information received from various sources. Without co-operating with other agencies active in the field he is unable to verify the often contradictory information. Unfortunately, as he mentioned in the above-quoted report, he was not able to secure the co-operation of all those interested. Oddly enough, the civilian branch of UNPROFOR created various obstacles, including a refusal to share information on human rights violations.

One important lesson which may be learned from the situation in Yugoslavia is the problems involved in co-ordinating different activities and initiatives. This issue, however, will be dealt with at the end of this paper.

4. THE ROLE OF THE CSCE[16]

Within the framework of the CSCE various initiatives have been undertaken in order to stop the escalation of the crisis in Yugoslavia. A comprehensive analysis of those initiatives is beyond the scope of this paper. It must be reiterated that all relevant CSCE bodies dealt with the Yugoslav crisis. A statement on the situation in Yugoslavia was issued by the Council of Ministers in Berlin on 19 June 1991 at its first meeting. In the statement the

> "Ministers expressed their friendly concern and their support for democratic development, unity and territorial integrity of Yugoslavia, based on economic reforms, full application of human rights of minorities, and the peaceful solution of the current crisis in the country."

On 1 July 1991 the Consultative Committee of the CSCE Conflict Prevention Centre (CPC) issued an appeal stressing the importance of an immediate and complete cessation of hostilities by all parties involved.

A Declaration on the Yugoslav crisis was approved by the Heads of State and Government at the Helsinki Summit on 10 July 1992.

The Third Meeting of the CSCE Council of Foreign Ministers held in Stockholm on 14-15 December 1992 devoted much attention to the situation in Yugoslavia. The Council, *inter alia*, requested the Chairman-in-Office, assisted by the Troika,

> "to travel to Belgrade prior to the elections on December 20, 1992 to underline to Serbian Authorities the stark fate and the increased penalties with which they will be faced. She is requested also to visit as soon as possible CSCE missions in former Yugoslavia to highlight their importance and enhanced role."

---

[16]Cf., the contribution by A. Bloed in the present volume.

4.1 Decisions of the Committee of Senior Officials

On 28 June 1991 Luxembourg, on behalf of the EC countries, invoked the just adopted CSCE Mechanism on Consultation and Co-operation with regard to Emergency Situations in connection with the urgent situation in Yugoslavia. The response of 30 June 1991 by the Yugoslav Government was not considered satisfactory and as a result the first emergency meeting of the CSCE Committee of Senior Officials (CSO) was held on 3-4 July 1991 in Prague. At that meeting the CSO stated that it "offers its assistance in order to help restore peace in the area and is examining urgently relevant practical steps it can take, in particular the despatch of observers to Yugoslavia, in consultation and agreement with Yugoslav authorities". The CSO also offered a CSCE Good Offices Mission to Yugoslavia in order "to facilitate the political dialogue among the parties concerned."

At its fourth meeting on 2 October 1991 the CSO agreed to form a human rights rapporteur mission. At the same meeting the CSO issued a statement on the situation in Yugoslavia in which it, *inter alia*, "reiterates its conviction that those responsible for the acts of unprecedented violence against people in Yugoslavia and for violations of cease-fire agreements be held personally accountable under international law for their actions, including those in contravention of relevant norms of international humanitarian law".

At its seventh meeting on 27-28 February 1992 the CSO examined the need for further action concerning the human rights situation in Yugoslavia. The CSO agreed that the human rights situation, including the situation of national minorities, needed further consideration and consecutive action by the CSCE. To that end, the CSO decided to send a follow-up mission to the Human Rights Rapporteur Mission to Yugoslavia as established by the CSO decision of 22 October 1991.

At its twelfth meeting on 10 June 1992 the CSO decided to send an exploratory mission to Kosovo, Sanjak and Vojvodina.

A very important decision, based on the "consensus-minus-one" principle, was taken by the CSO on 8 July 1992 at its thirteenth meeting, according to which the participation of Yugoslavia in the CSCE was suspended. At the same meeting the Steering Group on the Yugoslav crisis was established.

At its fifteenth meeting on 14 August 1992 the CSO decided to establish a rapporteur mission to investigate allegations of human rights abuses - the so-called Sir John Thomson mission - and to establish, in co-operation with the relevant authorities, a continuous presence in Kosovo, Sanjak and Vojvodina, in the form of missions of long duration.

At its sixteenth meeting on 16-18 September 1992 the CSO decided to dispatch a CSCE Mission to Skopje to avoid any spill-over of the conflict. The CSO pointed out that CSCE participating states intend to pursue with special vigour any evidence of severe human rights abuses in several regions of the former Yugoslavia.

At its next meeting the CSO requested a follow-up to the above-mentioned Sir John Thomson mission.

4.2 Human rights fact-finding missions undertaken within the framework of the CSCE, including missions under the CSCE Moscow Human Dimension Mechanism

The first fact-finding human rights mission, in accordance with the CSO decision of 22 October 1991 to create a CSCE Human Rights Rapporteur Mission, went to Yugoslavia in December 1991 and January 1992. The mission, in accordance with its mandate, visited Bosnia-Herzegovina, Croatia, Macedonia, Montenegro, Serbia and Slovenia. It looked at the situation with respect to human rights, including the rights of minorities. The report of the mission was presented to the CSO.

The follow-up mission took place in May 1992. It was requested that particular attention should be given to the human rights situation of ethnic and national communities and minorities in Croatia, to the paralysis of public life in Kosovo and to the propaganda war in the media and its negative effects on individual freedom.

The Sir John Thomson mission took place in August 1992. Its primary task was, in close co-ordination with the ICRC and the UN Commission on Human Rights, to ensure that all alleged places of detention be inspected within the shortest possible time. The follow-up to that mission took place in January 1993.

The Moscow Human Dimension Mechanism was also used in the Yugoslavia context. The initiative to invoke the mechanism was undertaken by the UK government on behalf of the EC. The Rapporteurs were Ambassador Corell, Ambassador Türk and Mrs. Thune. Their mandate was formulated as follows: "to investigate reports of atrocities against unarmed civilians in Croatia and Bosnia, and to make recommendations as to the feasibility of attributing responsibility for such acts". The initial part of their mission to Croatia took place from 30 September to 5 October 1992. Due to the fact that the Rapporteur had been unable to visit Bosnia-Herzegovina, on 24 November 1992 they offered to make an interim report on that state, analysing the relevant penal law, and to draft a convention establishing an international *ad hoc* tribunal to deal with war crimes and crimes against humanity committed in the former Yugoslavia. In its decision on 15 December 1992 the CSCE Council welcomed that proposal. They drew up the report on 9 February 1993 in spite of the fact that they were not able to visit Bosnia-Herzegovina.

4.3 Role of the missions of long duration in Kosovo, Vojvodina and Sanjak

The CSO, based, *inter alia*, on conclusions and recommendations presented to it by the exploratory mission to Kosovo, Sanjak and Vojvodina, with reference to chapter III, paragraphs 6-11, of the Helsinki Decisions on the political management of crises, decided to establish, in co-operation with the relevant authorities, a continuous presence in Kosovo, Sanjak and Vojvodina, in the form of missions of long duration. The mandate of those missions was formulated as follows:

a) to promote dialogue between the authorities concerned and representatives of the populations and communities in the three regions;

b) to collect information on all aspects relevant to violations of human rights and fundamental freedoms and to promote solutions to such problems;

c) to establish contact points for solving problems that might be identified;

d) to assist in providing information on relevant legislation on human rights, protection of minorities, free media and democratic elections.

The missions were also to be involved in "preventive diplomacy". A Memorandum of Understanding with the Federal Republic of Yugoslavia was signed on 28 October 1992.

The missions at present have twenty members based in Belgrade, Kosovo (Pristina and a permanent presence also in Pec and Prizeren), Sanjak (Novi Pazar, with a further permanent presence in Priepolje) and Vojvodina (Subotica). At the meeting of the CSO Vienna Group on 28 January 1993 a budget for increasing the missions to a total of forty members was agreed upon.

4.4 The spill-over mission in Macedonia

An important preventive function is performed by the spill-over mission in Skopje. The mandate of that mission was formulated as follows: "to seek to monitor developments along the borders of the Host Country with Serbia and in other areas of the Host Country which may suffer from spill-over of the conflict in the former Yugoslavia in order to promote respect for territorial integrity and the maintenance of peace, stability and security; and to help prevent possible conflict in the region".

The mission has its office in Skopje. It consists of eight persons. The EC Monitoring Mission (ECMM) maintains a liaison team of two Monitors in Skopje, working under the operational control of the Head of the CSCE Mission. It co-operates closely with UNPROFOR.

4.5 Conclusions

In addition to the above-described mechanisms the CSCE observed the parliamentary elections in the Federal Republic of Yugoslavia and in Slovenia. The CSCE Office for Democratic Institutions and Human Rights (ODIHR) presented comprehensive reports concerning those elections.

The CSCE, like all other international organizations, was not able to prevent the development of hostilities in Yugoslavia. Nevertheless, it is acting positively and is playing an important preventive function in such regions as Kosovo, Vojvodina, Sanjak and the former Yugoslav Republic of Macedonia. CSCE missions of long duration are constantly improving their working methods. They also co-operate fully with other international institutions, including the Special Rapporteur. It seems that this mechanism can possibly play an important role in various conflict situations.

It is observable that there exists a certain conflict of interests between mainly preventive functions performed by the missions of long duration and fact-finding missions.

The author of the present study has serious doubts concerning the confidentiality of CSCE reports. As a rule reports of CSCE missions are confidential. The results of such CSCE fact-finding missions can be published only after the approval by the CSO, which gives these documents an internal character. The fact that these reports are not available to NGOs and the press has often seriously diminished the effects of important findings of various CSCE missions.

5. HUMAN RIGHTS DURING PEACE NEGOTIATIONS

Within the framework of the Yugoslav Conference human rights problems should - and to a certain extent do - play an important role. The Co-Chairmen of the Steering Committee of that Conference on various occasions stressed that human rights standards should be observed. Within the proposed peace agreement, the human rights provisions are very carefully elaborated and specified. According to the proposals, the future Bosnian constitution would contain a commitment that the country should ratify and apply a comprehensive list of human rights conventions. In addition, as part of the human rights machinery to be provided by the constitution, there would: first, be a constitutional court to interpret the constitution and pronounce on human rights issues; second, the constitution would provide for an interim human rights court with the majority of judges being nominated from outside by the Co-Chairmen; third the constitution would provide for the establishment of four ombudsmen, who would initially be appointed by the Co-Chairmen. After conditions had become normal, the lower house of Parliament would then make these appointments. The ombudsmen would be vested with the competence to monitor the rights of each of the country's three communities - the Croats, Muslims and Serbs - as well as of a fourth community of "others" - the Yugoslavs.

Recently, within the framework of the Conference, a discussion on the broad human rights monitoring operation in Bosnia-Herzegovina took place. Nevertheless one cannot escape the impression that human rights are treated instrumentally within that context. They have been used as an additional element of diplomatic pressure. Negotiators were unable to draw any consequences from the fact that systematic violations of human rights have been committed during the peace negotiations. In spite of verbal declarations the Co-Chairmen were very reluctant to envisage any kind of closer co-operation with the Special Rapporteur. It is characteristic that they did not even inform him about the above-mentioned plans for monitoring human rights.

It seems that the instrumental treatment of human rights standards may be very dangerous. In his last report the Special Rapporteur stated:

> "A durable solution to the conflicts in the former Yugoslavia must, above all else, guarantee protection of human rights, and particularly the rights of nationalities. The Special Rapporteur therefore recommends that human rights concerns be given priority in all peace negotiations. The good faith and credibility of the parties to the conflicts should be

measured by their proven commitment to respecting human rights."

6. OVERVIEW OF THE ROLE OF OTHER UN MECHANISMS AND BODIES

6.1 Treaty bodies

6.1.1 The Human Rights Committee

The Human Rights Committee (HRC) received reports from Croatia, Bosnia-Herzegovina and the Federal Republic of Yugoslavia at its meeting on 6 November 1992. The Committee was able to make a quick decision and requested that the reports be positively assessed. There are, however, some doubts, particularly as regards Bosnia-Herzegovina. The main perpetrators of human rights violations in that country for obvious reasons could not be asked to report to the Committee. Therefore one may ask if the HRC is adequately equipped to deal with this type of situation?

It was also very unfortunate that the UN Centre for Human Rights did not pay adequate attention to the distribution and publication of the HRC's comments.

6.1.2 The Committee on the Rights of the Child

The Committee on the Rights of the Child informed the Special Rapporteur that it took note, with interest, of its reports. It stressed its deep concerns regarding the conclusions reached by him. The Committee, being most concerned about the plight of children in the territory of the former Yugoslavia, raised its concerns during the course of a press conference held at the end of its second session on 8 January 1992. The Committee had also gravely been made aware of reports of the alleged rape of several thousand women and girls in Bosnia-Herzegovina. The Committee invited the Special Rapporteur to participate in the discussion during its session.

6.1.3 The Committee on the Elimination of Discrimination against Women

The Committee on the Elimination of Discrimination against Women expressed its deep concern about the plight of a great number of women being subjected to cruel violations of their fundamental human rights.

6.2 The United Nations High Commissioner for Refugees

The UNHCR is a leading UN agency entrusted with the task of distributing humanitarian aid and assistance to refugees and internally displaced persons. In accordance with the UN Consolidated Inter-Agency Programme of Action and Appeal for the Former Yugoslavia (adopted on 4 September 1992) it co-ordinates the actions of the United Nations Children's Fund (UNICEF), the World Health Organization (WHO), the Food and Agricultural Organization (FAO) and the World Food Programme (WFP).

In fulfilling its functions the UNHCR also collects various evidence concerning human rights violations. Therefore close co-operation between the UNHCR and the Special Rapporteur has been established.

6.3 The United Nations Protection Force

It is beyond the scope of the present report to discuss at length the role of UNPROFOR in the context of the human rights situation in Yugoslavia. Without any doubt the officers and soldiers of UNPROFOR, as well as the field officers of other organizations, belong to the heros of this tragic conflict. Moreover, one can quite easily observe their frustration, their sense of powerlessness in the light of atrocities committed too frequently in their presence. The killing of the Bosnia-Herzegovina Deputy Prime Minister or the death of several people in Konjevic Polje are just a few of many examples. Also the civilian police cannot prevent human rights violations being conducted within areas under their control. Their mandate and rules of engagement are inadequate in the existing situation. There are, however, other aspects of UNPROFOR activities which are not dependent on such rules but are conditioned by other factors. One may ask, for example, why quite so frequently UNPROFOR choose to hide rather than report evidence of known human rights violations and even war crimes?

6.4 The Commission of Experts established pursuant to the Security Council Resolution 780 (1992)

By means of Resolution 780 (1992) the Security Council requested the Secretary-General to establish a Commission of Experts with a view to providing him with its conclusions on the evidence of grave breaches of the Geneva Conventions and other violations of international humanitarian law committed in the territory of the former Yugoslavia. The Commission commenced its work early in November 1992.

The Commission differs from other bodies established by the UN to investigate human rights violations. It has received a mandate not only to examine and analyse the information provided under Security Council Resolutions 771 and 780 but also the power to obtain information by means of its own investigations or efforts. In presenting its conclusions on the evidence of grave breaches of the Geneva Conventions and other violations of international humanitarian law to the Secretary-General, the Commission has been called upon to proceed not only as a fact-finding body but also as investigators whose task it is to establish the evidence that will enable the Secretary-General to recommend further appropriate steps.

The first interim report of the Commission was presented on 10 February 1993. The Commission received a very broad mandate. It was to be expected that it will be able to investigate in depth and verify a great body of evidence regarding breaches of the provisions of international humanitarian law. After less than six months of activity it is impossible to fully assess the work of the Commission. It seems, however, that the Commission will not be able to meet those expectations, *inter alia*, due to the following reasons:

1. The conflict is still far from resolved. Parties are creating various difficulties in order to prevent objective investigations being conducted. Let us also not forget that due to the continuity of the hostilities, the security of the investigations cannot be guaranteed.

2. The structure of the Commission and the means at its disposal places limits on its activities. Only one member of the Commission - its Chairman - permanently resides in Geneva. All other members combine their functions with other obligations. A small staff, consisting of two professionals and two secretaries, assist the Commission.

3. The Commission has inadequate financial resources at its disposal. In order to conduct on-site investigations it has to rely on help offered by governments, NGOs or private donors. As a result the Commission has been forced to adopt a selective approach and to analyse only a few cases. So far, it has been able to conduct comprehensive first-hand investigations. It has managed, moreover, to create a data bank which should be of great assistance in any further legal proceedings.

Close co-operation between the Special Rapporteur and the Commission has been established. Mutual exchange of information and opinions take place on a regular basis.

In its present shape and with the resources available the Commission cannot effectively implement its mandate.

In this context the problem of the War Crimes Tribunal arises.[17] The personal accountability of the perpetrators of human rights violations plays an important role within the implementation mechanisms of human rights standards. From that point of view the establishment of such a Tribunal should be considered as a welcome step.

---

[17] See the contribution by Nicholas Howen in the present volume.

6.5 The International Court of Justice

On 20 March 1993 the Republic of Bosnia-Herzegovina went to the International Court of Justice alleging genocide on the part of the Federal Republic of Yugoslavia (Serbia and Montenegro). In an Order of Provisional Measures issued on 8 April 1993 the International Court of Justice called upon Yugoslavia to "immediately ... take all measures within its power to prevent the commission of the crime of genocide". The Court's Order states that Yugoslavia "should in particular ensure that any military, paramilitary or irregular armed units which may be directed or supported by it, as well as any organizations and persons which may be subjected to genocide, of conspiracy to commit genocide, of direct and public incitement to genocide, or of complicity in genocide, whether directed against the Muslim population of Bosnia and Herzegovina or against any other national, ethical or religious group", be prevented.

A judgment on the merits of the case will be delivered only after the Parties have fully their case.

7. THE ROLE OF NGOs

NGOs play an active role in the case of Yugoslavia. To put it briefly, their function can be described as consisting of two elements: (a) documenting the human rights situation, and (b) organizing humanitarian assistance.

Two organizations in particular are active in documenting human rights violations in that region - Helsinki Watch[18] and Amnesty

---

[18]US Helsinki Watch is a Division of Human Rights Watch (New York) and is affiliated with the International Helsinki Federation for Human Rights (Vienna).

International. Both have produced several reports covering a wide spectrum of abuses[19].

Needless to say, the leading role in performing the second above-mentioned function is carried out by the ICRC. Its tasks can be described as follows: relief for displaced persons and other vulnerable groups in combat zones and isolated emergency areas; medical assistance; supervision of protected zones; visits to and registration of prisoners; tracing missing persons; restoring contact among family members; promoting knowledge and respect of international humanitarian law and the law of war.

To other organizations active in Yugoslavia belong:

a) International Federation of Red Cross and Red Crescent Societies: It offers logistical and technical support to the national Red Cross societies assisting refugees and displaced persons, it surveys the needs among vulnerable groups, it provides infrastructure for released prisoners, and prepares for Red Cross involvement in the post-conflict rehabilitation and reconstruction phase.

b) Médecins du Monde: They distribute medical equipment, assist refugee camps in Croatia, and provide psychological aid for children and women.

c) Médecins sans Frontières: They distribute medical supplies and other basic goods.

---

[19] Helsinki Watch has published the following reports: (1) Rules of War Violations in Croatia by Croatian Forces, February 1992; (2) War Crimes in Bosnia-Herzegovina, August 1992; (3) Yugoslavia, Human Rights Abuses in Kosovo 1990-1992, October 1992; (4) report on Bosnia-Herzegovina to be published in April 1993. Amnesty International has so far published the following reports: (1) Yugoslavia, Torture and Deliberate and Arbitrary Killings in War Zones, November 1991; (2) Bosnia-Herzegovina, Gross Abuses of Basic Human Rights, October 1992; (3) Bosnia-Herzegovina, Rapes and Sexual Abuse by Armed Forces, January 1993; (4) Bosnia-Herzegovina, Rana u duši, A Wound to the Soul, January 1993.

8. SUMMARY REMARKS

Human rights mechanisms cannot stop the war in Bosnia-Herzegovina. They can only offer assistance to victims and try to influence policy making bodies. In this presented paper I have tried to describe the activities of various mechanisms and to identify reasons for their failure. It is evident that, in spite of the large presence in the region and the strong interest expressed by international public opinion, human rights organizations have failed to achieve their aims in the former Yugoslavia. They are unable to offer adequate assistance to victims, they cannot properly register the great number of violations, they are not able to help democratic oriented movements, and they cannot break the information blockade and propaganda of hatred. Why?

The conflict in the former Yugoslavia has once again proved that human rights only play a secondary role in the context of international politics. The international community has tolerated massive violations of human rights and international humanitarian law because they did not present an imminent danger to the interests of the more influential countries. Consequently, during peace negotiations the credibility of the parties has never been verified by their human rights record. One may justify the claim that the international community legitimized human rights violations by offering them the status of partners in negotiations conducted under the auspices of the UN and the EC.

The above-described attitude of the international community determines the chances of human rights mechanisms effectively fulfilling their functions. We can observe a characteristic paradox. Within the UN and the CSCE human rights mechanisms have received much attention. A number of formal steps have been undertaken. New mechanisms have been introduced, new working methods and financial assistance have been offered. It seems that these steps should serve as a substitute or excuse for political inertia. In such circumstances it is difficult to consider all these formal achievements as a success.

The case of the former Yugoslavia has also revealed other inefficiencies more directly connected with the system of international human rights protection. For the purpose of the present paper I would like to identify two types of problems.

(a) There is no single mechanism which can play the role of co-ordinator and stimulator of human rights activities. As a result we too frequently observe very harmful competition between different human rights bodies. Investigations of the alleged practice of mass rape can serve as a powerful example. Duplication of efforts and the wasting of limited resources are not the only consequences of this situation. A growing reluctance to co-operate with such missions on the part of victims is also associated with this phenomenon. Attempts to include such a co-ordinating role in the peace negotiating process has failed for political reasons.

(b) Within the UN system the country special rapporteur mechanism has acquired some elements which may be used as an effective measure to deal with cases similar to Yugoslavia. The very fact that the UN Commission on Human Rights has managed to appoint such a Rapporteur at its first special session speaks for itself. Thematic mechanisms also assist the Special Rapporteur. Close co-operation with the UNHCR, the CSCE and the ICRC has been achieved. Also some treaty bodies actively pursue their function in connection with the situation in the former Yugoslavia. The Special Rapporteur has been invited to present his report before the Security Council. Finally, for the first time in its history the Centre for Human Rights has established a permanent presence in the region. It is to be hoped that further development in the field operation will be possible. Nevertheless, it is also quite clear that the UN Centre for Human Rights, from an administrative point of view, is unprepared for more comprehensive human rights activities, in particular as regards field operations. The position of the Centre within the UN is too weak. Without any profound changes in this field we cannot expect more meaningful results as far as work of human rights mechanisms are concerned.

GENERAL RECOMMENDATIONS OF THE WORKING GROUP

The following general recommendations focus mainly on the strengthening of the inter-relationship between procedures and mechanisms for the protection of human rights rather than on improving thematic mechanisms available under the United Nations and the Inter-governmental Organizations (IGOs) engaged in human rights in Europe.

Taking Human Rights Seriously

1. The international community must view the respect for human rights and humanitarian principles as a value in itself without subordinating it to political considerations. Equal attention should be given to civil, cultural, economic, political and social rights.

2. International human rights must be based on equality and the principle of universal application to all, regardless of race, colour, sex, language, religion, political or other opinion, ethnicity, national or social origin, age, disability, sexual preference or economic status. In particular equal enjoyment of all human rights should be extended to minorities by way of non-discrimination and preferential treatment.

3. International monitoring and supervisory mechanisms must act with objectivity, impartiality and determination. Prevention of abuses, implementation of existing commitments and reaction to non-compliance are all equally important to strengthen a universal human rights culture.

4. States have a collective responsibility to ensure respect for human rights and humanitarian law. Abuses must be met by resolute action by other states, using international fora and mechanisms, the institution of inter-state complaint, the International Humanitarian Fact-finding Commission and other similar means. In case of serious violations, collective action should be taken in order to put an end to such violations. If necessary, as a last resort, recourse to coercive action should be taken decided upon by the United Nations Security Council or through binding decisions by the International Court of Justice.

A. Bloed et al. (eds.), Monitoring Human Rights in Europe, 319–324.

Focusing on Implementation

5. One should focus on the effective implementation and enforcement of existing obligations rather than on setting new standards. However, especially for situations of internal conflicts and tensions, including states of emergency, there is a need to affirm and consolidate a set of minimum humanitarian standards which cannot be derogated from under any circumstances. In this context due attention should be given to the 1991 Declaration of Minimum Humanitarian Standards.[1]

6. The elaboration and adoption of optional protocols to the International Covenant on Economic, Social and Cultural Rights, the Convention on the Elimination of All Forms of Discrimination against Women (CEDAW) and the Convention on the Rights of the Child should be stressed. In this context individual and inter-state complaint procedures should be established.

7. The respect for minority rights should be viewed as particularly important for the prevention of conflicts and restoration of peace. An implementation mechanism for the new Declaration on the Rights of Persons belonging to National or Ethnic, Religious and Linguistic Minorities should be developed either by way of a Special Rapporteur or a working group of the United Nations Commission on Human Rights.

8. Special emphasis should also be given to the issue of minority participation in implementation proceedings and policy and decision making affecting them.

---

[1]*Declaration of Minimum Humanitarian Standards* (Turku 1991), approved by a meeting of experts convened by the Institute for Human Rights, Abo Akademi University, Turku/Abo, Finland, 30 November - 2 December 1990; UN Doc. E/CN.4/Sub.2/1991/55.

9. States should be obliged to report, on a regular basis, on measures taken in order to ratify or accede to conventions. In cases of refusals to ratify or accede to conventions the reports should include an explanation for the reluctance. Furthermore there is a need for an evaluation of the great number of far-reaching reservations made by states to some conventions, in particular to the CEDAW.

10. The necessary technical assistance should be offered to states in order to help them ratify or accede to international conventions.

11. Ways should be found to streamline and simplify existing obligations to present reports. In this context the drawing up by states of "single super-reports" should be introduced covering all international conventions and agreements - universal and regional -to which they are parties. The individual IGOs and their specialized agencies should examine those parts of the report with which they are concerned.

12. As an important means to prevent human rights violations, reporting procedures should be introduced in those treaties which do not already provide for such procedures.

13. The United Nations, the CSCE, the Council of Europe and the European Community should compile and publish their recommendations, including those under thematic mechanisms concerning the monitoring and protection of human rights and the prevention of human rights violations, and they should include the extent to which these have been implemented.

14. The sharing of information is crucial, both within the United Nations and between the United Nations and other regional IGOs and their specialized bodies engaged in the protection and monitoring of human rights. To this end a comprehensive data base should be established to include all information produced by IGOs, NGOs and the academic community.

15. Means and methods should be developed to secure effective cooperation and coordination between the United Nations' mechanisms and activities and those of regional IGOs engaged in human rights. To this end, full use should be made of the existing coordinating machinery within the United Nations, such as the Administrative Coordinating Committee. Such coordination should also involve other regional and national actors which impact human rights.

16. IGOs concerned with human rights should, as a rule, invite each other to address their individual meetings in order to facilitate better understanding, coordination and cooperation.

17. Annual meetings and working groups should be established to evaluate the efficiency of the human rights machinery. The extent of coordination and cooperation between the United Nations and regional IGOs should be constantly reviewed. Each meeting should consider recommendations for improvements.

Developing the Institutional Framework

18. There is a need to streamline and make more effective the myriad of international fora and mechanisms. In the long-run the United Nations organizational structure should be revised as to include a Special Commissioner for Human Rights[2] and separate machinery for the judicial treatment of human rights and international criminal cases. To this end the establishment of a Universal Court of Human Rights and an International Criminal Court should be considered. However, in order to avoid a further proliferation of international bodies it might be more efficient and effective to create such separate machinery for judicial treatment by instituting special chambers in the framework of the International Court of Justice.

---

[2]See the proposal by Amnesty International, *World Conference on Human Rights. Facing up the Failures: Proposal for Improving the Protection of Human Rights by the United Nations*, London 1992 (AI Index IOR 41/16/92).

19. The significant lack of financial resources for human rights work on the domestic, regional and international levels is critically in contrast to the increase in human rights violations and the activities and programs rapidly required to prevent and respond to such violations. If the human rights mechanisms and initiatives are to be efficient and serve properly, adequate financing, including staff and equipment, is required. To this end, more realistic budgetary allocations are needed. In view of the limited resources a better coordination and cooperation concerning activities and information with other regional IGOs must again be stressed when setting priorities and assessing projects and their impact, including the best suitable bodies to realize them.

NGO Access to IGOs Engaged in Human Rights

20. NGOs should be involved in all human rights treaty reporting systems. As a minimum, this should include notification by the reporting states of the timing and contents of reports in advance; submitting of NGO information preferably directly to treaty monitoring bodies; and the provision of timely information about the consideration of the report to enable effective NGO follow-up.

21. The human rights treaty individual complaint procedures should be extended to permit NGOs to act in *amicus curiae*, at least those in consultative status with ECOSOC or the Council of Europe (as appropriate), to lodge complaints and not be limited to victims of the alleged violations.

22. NGO access should be provided on the largest scale possible to all human rights bodies including those making decisions with human rights implications whether within the United Nations, the CSCE, the Council of Europe or the European Community.

Protection of Human Rights Defenders

23. A strong commitment to the protection of human rights monitors must be taken. The United Nations Declaration on Human Rights Defenders should be completed and consideration given to the best means of providing legal protection for such individuals and groups.

24. The appointment of a special rapporteur concerned with harassment and attacks against human rights monitors should be established within the framework of the United Nations Declaration on Human Rights Defenders.

NOTES ON THE CONTRIBUTORS

Gudmundur Alfredsson

Lawyer from Iceland with the degree of Doctor of Juridical Science from Harvard Law School. Currently Visiting Professor at the Raoul Wallenberg Institute of Human Rights and Humanitarian Law at the University of Lund, Sweden, while on leave from his post at the United Nations Centre for Human Rights in Geneva.

Arie Bloed

PhD. Associate Professor of the law of international organizations at the Faculty of Law of the University of Utrecht; member of the Advisory Council on Peace and Security of the Netherlands Ministries of Foreign Affairs and Welfare; Secretary General of the Netherlands Helsinki Committee; Editor-in-chief of the CSCE Quarterly *Helsinki Monitor*. Delegate at various CSCE meetings.

Rachel Brett

LL.B, LL.M. with distinction, Essex, in international human rights law. Lecturer in international human rights law, University of Essex. Originator and principal researcher, CSCE Project, Human Rights Centre, University of Essex. From July 1993, associate representative (human rights), Quaker United Nations Office, Geneva.

Laurence Boisson de Chazournes

Doctor of law. Associate Professor, Faculty of Law, University of Geneva; lecturer, Graduate Institute of International Studies, Switzerland.

Vojin Dimitrijević

Doctor of law; Professor of international law and international relations, University of Belgrade. Member of the UN Human Rights Committee. President, Council of the European Movement in Serbia.

Asbjørn Eide

Doctor of law, University of Lund, Sweden. Director, Norwegian Institute of Human Rights; member of the UN Sub-Commission on Prevention of Discrimination and Protection of Minorities; Special Rapporteur responsible for various studies of the Sub-Commission; member of several missions of the CSCE and other institutions.

Nicholas Howen

Australian lawyer trained in Sydney; legal adviser with Amnesty International (International Secretariat, London).

Liselotte Leicht

Law degree, University of Copenhagen; Programme Director at the International Helsinki Federation for Human Rights.

Rein Müllerson

Law degree, University of Moscow; Visiting Centennial Professor of the London School of Economics and Political Science; member of the UN Human Rights Committee 1988 - 1992; former deputy Foreign Minister of the Republic of Estonia.

Manfred Nowak

Professor of Law at the Austrian Federal Academy of Public Administration and Director of the Ludwig Boltzmann Institute of Human Rights (BIM) in Vienna; former Director of the Netherlands Institute of Human Rights (SIM) at the University of Utrecht.

Merja Pentikäinen

Law degree, University of Helsinki; member of the Finnish League for Human Rights; board member of the Finnish Helsinki Committee.

Allan Rosas

Doctor of Law, University of Turku; Armfelt Professor of Law, Abo Akademi University; Director of the Abo Akademi Institute for Human Rights.

Martin Scheinin

Doctor of Law; lecturer in constitutional law, University of Helsinki; vice-chairman of the Finnish Advisory Board for International Human Rights Affairs; board member of the Finnish League for Human Rights; member of the Finnish Helsinki Committee.

Walter Suntinger

Law degree, University of Graz; researcher at the Ludwig Boltzmann Institute of Human Rights, Vienna.

Danilo Türk

Doctor of Law, University of Ljubljana, University of Belgrade; Professor of public international law, University of Ljubljana; 1984-1992 member of the UN Sub-Commission on Prevention of Discrimination and Protection of Minorities; Special Rapporteur on the realization of Economic, Social and Cultural Rights and on Freedom of Expression; in 1990 Chairman of the Sub-Commission; in August 1992 appointed Ambassador of Slovenia to the United Nations in New York.

Roman Wieruszewski

Associate professor of law; Director of the Poznan Human Rights Centre; currently human rights officer at the United Nations Centre for Human Rights.

INDEX

I

J

K

L

International Studies in Human Rights

1. B. G. Ramcharan (ed.): *International Law and Fact-finding in the Field of Human Rights.* 1982 ISBN 90-247-3042-2
2. B. G. Ramcharan: *Humanitarian Good Offices in International Law.* The Good Offices of the United Nations Secretary-General in the Field of Human Rights. 1983 ISBN 90-247-2805-3
3. B. G. Ramcharan (ed.): *The Right to Life in International Law.* 1985 ISBN 90-247-3074-0
4. P. Alston and K. Tomaševski (eds.): *The Right to Food.* 1984 ISBN 90-247-3087-2
5. A. Bloed and P. van Dijk (eds.): *Essays on Human Rights in the Helsinki Process.* 1985 ISBN 90-247-3211-5
6. K. Törnudd: *Finland and the International Norms of Human Rights.* 1986 ISBN 90-247-3257-3
7. H. Thoolen and B. Verstappen: *Human Rights Missions.* A Study of the Fact-finding Practice of Non-governmental Organizations. 1986 ISBN 90-247-3364-2
8. H. Hannum: *The Right to Leave and Return in International Law and Practice.* 1987 ISBN 90-247-3445-2
9. J. H. Burgers and H. Danelius: *The United Nations Convention against Torture.* A Handbook on the Convention against Torture and Other Cruel, Inhuman or Degrading Treatment or Punishment. 1988 ISBN 90-247-3609-9
10. D. A. Martin (ed.): *The New Asylum Seekers: Refugee Law in the 1980s.* The Ninth Sokol Colloquium on International Law. 1988 ISBN 90-247-3730-3
11. C. M. Quiroga: *The Battle of Human Rights.* Gross, Systematic Violations and the Inter-American System. 1988 ISBN 90-247-3687-0
12. L. A. Rehof and C. Gulmann (eds.): *Human Rights in Domestic Law and Development Assistance Policies of the Nordic Countries.* 1989 ISBN 90-247-3743-5
13. B. G. Ramcharan: *The Concept and Present Status of International Protection of Human Rights.* Forty Years After the Universal Declaration. 1989 ISBN 90-247-3759-1
14. A. D. Byre and B. Y. Byfield (eds.): *International Human Rights Law in the Commonwealth Caribbean.* 1991 ISBN 90-247-3785-0
15. N. Lerner: *Groups Rights and Discrimination in International Law.* 1991 ISBN 0-7923-0853-0
16. S. Shetreet (ed.): *Free Speech and National Security.* 1991 ISBN 0-7923-1030-6
17. G. Gilbert: *Aspects of Extradition Law.* 1991 ISBN 0-7923-1162-0
18. P.E. Veerman: *The Rights of the Child and the Changing Image of Childhood.* 1991 ISBN 0-7923-1250-3
19. M. Delmas-Marty (ed.): *The European Convention for the Protection of Human Rights.* International Protection versus National Restrictions. 1991 ISBN 0-7923-1283-X

International Studies in Human Rights

20. A. Bloed and P. van Dijk (eds.): *The Human Dimension of the Helsinki Process.* The Vienna Follow-up Meeting and its Aftermath. 1991 ISBN 0-7923-1337-2
21. L.S. Sunga: *Individual Responsibility in International Law for Serious Human Rights Violations.* 1992 ISBN 0-7923-1453-0
22. S. Frankowski and D. Shelton (eds.): *Preventive Detention.* A Comparative and International Law Perspective. 1992 ISBN 0-7923-1465-4
23. M. Freeman and P. Veerman (eds.): *The Ideologies of Children's Rights.* 1992 ISBN 0-7923-1800-5
24. S. Stavros: *The Guarantees for Accused Persons Under Article 6 of the European Convention on Human Rights.* An Analysis of the Application of the Convention and a Comparison with Other Instruments. 1993 ISBN 0-7923-1897-8
25. A. Rosas and J. Helgesen (eds.): *The Strength of Diversity.* Human Rights and Pluralist Democracy. 1992 ISBN 0-7923-1987-7
26. K. Waaldijk and A. Clapham (eds.): *Homosexuality: A European Community Issue.* Essays on Lesbian and Gay Rights in European Law and Policy. 1993 Hb: ISBN 0-7923-2038-7; Pb: ISBN 0-7923-2240-1
27. Y.K. Tyagi: *The Law and Practice of the UN Human Rights Committee.* 1993 ISBN 0-7923-2040-9
28. G. van Bueren: *The International Law on the Rights of the Child.* 1993 ISBN 0-7923-2221-5
29. L.A. Rehof: *Guide to the* Travaux Préparatoires *of the United Nations Convention on the Elimination of All Forms of Discrimination against Women.* 1993 ISBN 0-7923-2222-3
30. A. Bloed, L. Leicht, M. Novak and A. Rosas (eds.): *Monitoring Human Rights in Europe.* Comparing International Procedures and Mechanisms. 1993 ISBN 0-7923-2383-1

This series is designed to shed light on current legal and political aspects of process and organization in the field of human rights.

MARTINUS NIJHOFF PUBLISHERS – DORDRECHT / BOSTON / LONDON